❡ Between Colonialism and Diaspora ❡

# Between Colonialism and Diaspora

## Sikh Cultural Formations
## in an Imperial World

Tony Ballantyne

DUKE UNIVERSITY PRESS
DURHAM & LONDON 2006

© 2006 Duke University Press
All rights reserved
Printed in the United States of America
on acid-free paper ∞
Designed by Jennifer Hill
Typeset in Granjon by Keystone Typesetting, Inc.

Library of Congress Cataloging-in-Publication Data
appear on the last printed page of this book.

# Contents

# Preface

In April 1999, Sikhs across the world celebrated the three hundredth anniversary of the foundation of the Khalsa, the "order of the pure" that was established by the tenth Sikh guru, Guru Gobind Singh, on Baisakhi Day in 1699. By the late twentieth century, most Sikhs understood the Khalsa as embodying the "orthodox" community, a collective dedicated to protecting the teachings of the ten Sikh gurus. As such, the tercentenary of the Khalsa was an occasion of great significance. Lectures, festivals, exhibitions, sport tournaments, and gatherings for worship marked the event in places ranging from Amritsar to Dallas and Delhi to Coventry. Around the time of Baisakhi, the Sikh festival that marks the beginning of the new year, up to a million Sikhs from throughout South Asia as well as from Europe, North and South America, Australasia, Africa, and East Asia made long journeys to Anandpur, the site of the foundation of the Khalsa. These celebrations attracted considerable global media coverage, which stressed the distinctiveness of Sikhs and reaffirmed Sikhism's status as a major world religion.

In contrast, little attention was paid to an anniversary celebration, observed by relatively fewer Sikhs, that occurred approximately two weeks before Baisakhi. The date 29 March 1999 marked the one hundred and fiftieth anniversary of the annexation of Punjab by the East India Company and the formal incorporation of Sikhs into the global reach of the British Empire. The symmetry of these anniversaries, 300 years of the Khalsa and 150 years of sustained contact with Britain (with 98 of these years, between 1849 and 1947, as a colony), is not only striking in itself but reminds us that for at least half of the Khalsa's existence Sikhism has operated within the broader global contexts fashioned by British imperialism. This volume explores the interconnectedness of these histories of "religion" and colonialism by examining the reconfiguration of Sikhism and Sikh identities over the last two centuries.

Even though the chapters in this book span a wide chronological sweep (from around 1780 to World War I) and traverse many regions inhabited by Sikhs (North America, Australasia, Southeast Asia, and especially South Asia and the United Kingdom), I do not attempt here to write a total history of modern Sikhism. Further, I do not present a detailed analysis of canonical Sikh texts and, despite this work's broad temporal and spatial canvas, I do not aspire to present an exhaustive narrative or a comprehensive analysis of the institutions that have underpinned the development of the Sikh community. Rather, in this volume I explore a series of key issues relating to the pasts of Sikhism and the ways in which those pasts have been narrated, both by people belonging to the community and by those, like myself, who do not. The four chapters and the epilogue that make up this volume explore a range of issues and case studies that illuminate the diversity of the modern Sikh experience by communicating some of the richness of the cultural life of Sikhs both within Punjab and beyond it. In the course of this exploration I chart the shifting, often complex, and frequently competing visions of Sikh identity that have been produced from a range of diverse locations and contexts. In tracking Sikhs through some of the global networks fashioned by the British Empire and by offering an assessment of Sikh cultures in the postcolonial world, in this volume I suggest that we need to assess the visions of Sikhism articulated on the battlefields of Asia and Europe, on the streets of Singapore and Southall, and in the nightclubs of New Delhi and Newcastle, as well as the proclamations issued from the *gurdwara*s (places of worship) of Punjab or the *daftar*s (offices) of colonial administrators.

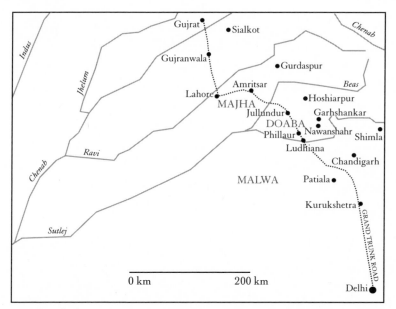

**Punjab and adjacent territories.** Drawn by David Hood

The title of this volume stresses the overlapping chronology of and strong connections between colonialism and diaspora in the transformation of Sikhism. Despite Brian Axel's observation that the "colonial rupture" is frequently identified as the genesis of South Asian diasporas, within South Asian studies and in much of the humanities scholarship the term diaspora is frequently identified as a marker of the postcolonial condition.[1] Yet, as I demonstrate herein, the end of the British Empire in South Asia did not mark the emergence of Sikhs as a mobile population, for some Sikhs had always lived outside Punjab and many more Sikhs became more mobile after the annexation of Punjab in 1849. The wealth, authority, and security of the British imperial system rested on its ability to move certain groups of people to fill crucial gaps in the empire's labor market, administration, and coercive instruments (such as the army or police force), as well as preventing "undesirable" forms of mobility (such as vagrancy, nomadism, the activities of itinerant preachers and mendicants, and "unlicensed" migration).[2] In the case of Punjab, colonialism was crucial in both intensifying and accelerating mobility as many Punjabis moved within the region (especially to the new "canal colonies" in the arid west), while others served outside of Punjab in the army or as policemen, and still others traveled to more distant lands (such as Australia or the United States) in search of work. Most of these early Sikhs on the move sit uneasily under the rubric of "diaspora" (which traditionally suggests exile, the impossibility of return, and an emotive connection to a lost "homeland"), as many returned to Punjab after laboring abroad. Further, in the case of the early Sikhs who settled overseas, very few provide evidence that suggests they thought of themselves as "exiles" from their "homeland."[3] Nevertheless, the experiences of these new forms of mobility enabled and policed by the operation of imperial power did create new social structures and thus reshaped Punjabi mentalities. Of course, these early movements of Sikhs within north India and across the borders of British India were supplemented after World War II by the subsequent waves of Punjabi migrants who began to establish large communities in Britain and North America. The building blocks of this second wave of diasporic movement were the substantial Punjabi communities that had a strong connection to their home villages, some of whom articulated an increasingly self-conscious bond to their Punjabi "homeland." In considering these historical layers that shaped the Punjabi migrant experience in connection with the experience of colonialism itself, I underscore the centrality of cross-cultural encounters in making Sikh mentalities and defining the boundaries of Sikh communities over the last two centuries.

By bringing the problematics of diaspora and colonialism together, this volume highlights the particular cultural challenges posed by the creation of colonial modernity. Punjabis were not only subject to British authority but also had to grapple with the extensive transformations that were enacted by the colonial state, including the construction of a new educational system, the dissolution of the province's army, the introduction of a complex of new communication technologies, and the reorganization of the state's revenue regime. Even when these innovations were designed to uphold "tradition," they reconfigured social relationships and mentalities in a host of often-unexpected ways. Even in the most isolated villages where important elements of continuity from the precolonial past remained, colonialism challenged and recrafted much that was familiar as it posed new questions and presented new opportunities. In this sense, the experiences of both colonialism and diaspora can be understood as what George Lipsitz has identified as "crossroads"; that is, as productive, destabilizing, and frequently dangerous sites of cross-cultural collision, contest, and change.[4]

In this volume I read these encounters by looking at an array of institutions, examining a long sequence of debates over Sikh identity, and delving into a wide variety of archives. Given my interest in colonial knowledge production and imperial archives, I offer here a critical reading of a broad cross-section of colonial source material.[5] Rather than treating British colonial knowledge as the richly textured and highly contested product of encounters in the "contact zone" of the imperial frontier, scholars working within Sikh studies have tended either to mine these colonial sources for information on particular caste groups and political organizations or to dismiss them as particularly unreliable and misleading. This volume not only breaks with this tradition by offering a closely contextualized reading of British accounts of Punjab and Sikhism but also embraces the possibilities offered by nonconventional archives that have largely been ignored within the existing historiography on Sikhism. In addition to private papers, government records, official publications, newspapers, travel narratives, and learned periodicals, I make extensive use of film, sculpture, art, fiction, and Internet sources to open up new perspectives on the Sikh past. These sources allow me to roam across a wide cultural terrain—ranging from the history of the Indian army to the "bhangramuffin" of the popular musician Apache Indian; from the workings of the colonial census to Dalip Singh's ambivalent position within the British Empire; from the place of Sikhs in rural Norfolk to the place of bhangra in postpartition Punjab—all of which would have largely been closed off to me had I restricted myself to the authoritative texts produced from within the Sikh community. Equally important, any reading of these alternative archives can serve as a reminder that the social concerns and cultural imaginations of Sikhs are not restricted to the domains of "religion" and "politics" that are the recurrent concerns of Sikh studies. Given the intense debates within the Sikh Panth (literally "path"; community) over questions of identity and the violence surrounding the struggle for an independent Sikh homeland in the form of Khalistan, this focus on religion and its intersection with high politics is entirely understandable, but it is crucial that the field enlarges its understanding of the nature of the political and engages with the full spectrum of the social and cultural history of Sikh communities in a more sustained manner. This approach is stimulated by recent cultural production from within the Sikh Panth itself. Significant Sikh periodicals (such as the *Sikh Review* and *Nishaan*) and Internet discussion groups (the "Sikh diaspora" electronic mailing list, for example) move fluidly between historiographical debate, political commentary, discussion of films and fiction, scriptural analysis, and moral prescription, thereby eschewing the rigid distinctions between "high" and "low" culture or "religion" and "politics" that are embedded in most academic approaches to Sikh history.

This book opens with a critical reading of the recent historiography on the development of Sikhism, in which points of conflict and common points of agreement are both explored. By mapping the widely divergent approaches to the Sikh past elaborated over the past three decades I underline the centrality of historical writing in the debates over Sikh identity and I establish the basic historiographical framework for the remainder of the volume. In particular I insist on the centrality of imperial structures, or what I term the "webs of empire," in producing a range of Sikh identities and in fashioning the extended political and cultural domains that underpin the emergence of the early Sikh diaspora. These webs are a key component of chapter 2, in which I examine the transformation of Sikhism from around 1780 to World War I. Rather than providing a narrow analysis of the 1875–1925 period (which marked the rise of Punjabi reform movements and is the focus of most research on colonial Punjab), in this chapter I pay close attention to the ways in which early British accounts of Punjab produced prior to the East India Company's annexation of the province in 1849 shaped British understandings of Sikhism as a "religion" and the development of company policy in the 1850s. I also examine the coterminous rise of Punjabi military service and settlement outside South Asia and how these forms of mobility within the British Empire tempered the drive to systematize Sikh practice and identity at "home."

The relationship between colonialism and the politics of the diaspora forms the core of chapter 3, in which I concentrate on the fate of the last Maharaja of Punjab, Dalip Singh. After sketching the history of Dalip Singh's exile to Britain and his efforts to recover his patrimony in Punjab, I focus on the contentious place of Dalip Singh in community memory. By unraveling the debates around the meaning of Dalip Singh's life, I highlight the varied and often competing readings of the Punjabi past produced by a range of groups both in Punjab and in Britain, placing particular emphasis on recent attempts by some Punjabi Britons to identify Dalip Singh as the founder of their community and as an emblem of the imbrication of Punjabi and British histories.

The final chapter in the volume develops this theme of cultural exchange through a history of bhangra, a cultural form that has become a key medium for projecting Punjabi identities within the global cultural economy. In addition to highlighting the role of recorded music and artists in connecting various diasporic communities to their "homeland," in this chapter I stress the pivotal role of the British encounter between Punjabi migrants and Afro-Caribbean peoples in remaking the aesthetics, social context, and style of bhangra. While the transformation of bhangra in London, Coventry, and Birmingham has elicited considerable anxiety among some Sikhs, the reworking of this "tradition" is a powerful example of the innovative cultural products produced by migrants, and it hints at the productivity and power of interracial and pan-communal engagements.

I close with a brief epilogue that returns to the central theme of the volume as a whole, the place of the interconnected histories of colonialism and the diaspora in producing a range of Sikh identities over the last two centuries. The generous length of each chapter allows for multiple contextualizations, and as such the volume is a production best imagined as a series of overlapping and interlocking essays that reexamine key events, figures, and historiographical debates over the sweep of modern Sikh history.

In light of the polemical nature of Sikh studies and the intense conflict over the ability of "Western scholarship" to sympathetically understand Sikh traditions and history, it is important to underscore the perspectives that guide the arguments elaborated in this book. Reflecting my training as a historian of British colonialism in South Asia (and elsewhere) and my commitment to transnational historical writing, my goal is to reframe the history of Sikhism in a range of broad historical contexts. These contexts include the regional history of Punjab; the history of South Asia; the history of British colonialism and the British Empire; and the history of Sikh communities in Asia, Australasia, Europe, and the Americas. While this approach diverges from the model of "Khalsacentric" history—that is, histories produced from within the Khalsa with the aim of fortifying the identity and culture of the members of the Khalsa—I recognize that histories are produced to meet various needs and come from a variety of positions, and as such I do not claim this work to be paradigmatic.

I should also emphasize that this project was not conceived as a defense or vindication of the "McLeodian" school of Sikh history, and as I make clear in a later chapter my own approach to the Sikh past is markedly different from the various "textualist" readings of Sikh tradition and history elaborated in the wake of W. H. McLeod's groundbreaking, if highly contentious, *Guru Nanak and the Sikh Religion* (1968). Instead, my chief aspiration is to explore Sikhism's encounters with imperial power, modernity, and the postcolonial world from an analytical position that recognizes both Sikhism's status as a global religion and its profound rootedness in Punjab. In positioning this volume in this way my hope is that it speaks to a range of audiences, including scholars working within the field of Sikh studies, historians of South Asia and its diasporas, historians of religion and popular culture, and Sikhs in India and abroad. Thus, while I am dependent on a huge body of literature from Sikh studies (from the precolonial to the postcolonial; from the Singh Sabhas and their rivals; from "Khalsacentric" scholars to their "Western" targets), I attempt to break down the conceptual boundaries that tend to confine Sikh studies. At the broadest level, this volume can be read as an attempt to reframe the Sikh past through close attention to the cultural traffic within, and especially across, the boundaries of the community as Punjabis have confronted both colonialism and diaspora, two agents of momentous social change. Thus, at many key points I try to reconnect Sikh pasts and Sikh studies to the larger structures that have shaped the history of Sikh communities by bringing Sikh history into a sustained engagement with South Asian historiography, British imperial history, and recent scholarship on gender, diaspora, transnationalism, and postcolonialism. By bringing these fields together, I provide an exploration of Sikh history that stands at the juncture of intellectual and cultural history and I offer an approach that highlights the importance of "knowledge production" and the performativity of identity and memory in the definition of Sikhism and Sikh pasts. I do not imagine this work as the final word on the subject but rather as part of the ongoing debates between Sikhs, other Punjabis, and scholars (non-Sikh and Sikhs) that have given Sikh studies its characteristic energy.

I assembled much of the archival base for this book during my 1995–1998 Ph.D. research, which was funded by the New Zealand Vice Chancellor's Committee; the Cambridge Commonwealth Trust; the Smuts Memorial Fund; and Wolfson College, Cambridge. More recently, a generous Otago Research Grant from the University of Otago enabled me to complete this volume. Like all historians I have been dependent on the assistance of archivists and librarians, and here I would particularly like to thank the staff at the University Library; the Royal Commonwealth Society; the Oriental Studies Library; and the Cambridge South Asian Studies Centre and Archive (all in Cambridge); the Public Record Office, the British Library, and the Oriental and India Office Library (London); the National University of Ireland, Galway (especially Geraldine and the staff at interlibrary loans); the Nehru Memorial Library (Delhi); and the University of Otago Library (again, particular thanks are due to the document delivery staff). I have been lucky to have the research assistance of Debbie Hughes and Ciara Breathnach, while Mike Bagge and Rachel Standfield provided invaluable assistance at the final stages of preparing the manuscript. David Hood again demonstrated a bewildering range of skills in creating the map at short notice.

Many of the arguments developed in this volume went through their earliest incarnations under the watchful eye of my Cambridge Ph.D. supervisor, Chris Bayly. It is hard to imagine a finer supervisor than Chris, and his guidance was central in building my research trajectory over the last decade. I have learned much from Chris's work on the intellectual and cultural history of north India, as well as his pioneering explorations of the history of communication within the British Empire and his insistence on the crucial elements of continuity between precolonial and colonial social orders in South Asia. While in Cambridge, I also learned a great deal about Punjabi history from Anil Sethi and about the interfaces between British and South Asian history from Robert Travers. In Britain, India, and the United States I benefited from the assistance of many Sikhs, especially those who welcomed me into gurdwaras or were happy to talk about the history of their own families.

Some of the material discussed in the volume has been tested and refined through presentations at the University of Michigan's "Sikhism in Light of History" conference; the Program for South Asian and Middle Eastern Studies seminar at the University of Illinois at Urbana-Champaign; the Cultural Studies Group at Urbana; the history department at the University of Otago; and most recently at the "New Directions in Sikh and Punjab Studies" conference held in Dunedin in December 2003. In Urbana, Ania Loomba, Nils Jacobsen, Simona Sawhney, Antoinette Burton, Clare Crowston, Kristin Hoganson, Marilyn Booth, Ken Cuno, and Hans Hoch offered thoughtful (and occasionally dissenting) responses to early versions of chapters 1 and 3. I have also benefited from the support and expertise of many of the Sikh studies "crowd," especially Van Dusenbery, Jerry Barrier, Pashaura Singh, Lou Fenech, and Hew McLeod. More recently I have drawn much from my discussions with the participants at the Dunedin conference, particularly Shinder Thandi, Ian Kerr, Amrit Kaur Singh, Rabindra Kaur Singh, and Ian Catanach. At Otago, I have gained a great deal from discussions with my good friends John Stenhouse and Brian Moloughney. John offered an insightful reading of chapter 2 while Brian carefully read the entire manuscript. Antoinette Burton also read the manuscript in its entirety. My ongoing conversations with Antoinette about history and colonialism—carried out over e-mail communications and phone calls—remain fundamental to my work. I greatly value her intelligence, collegiality, and friendship.

Sally Henderson, my wife, has lived with this project. We traveled through Punjab together, she has read many different versions of the chapters that follow, and she has engaged enthusiastically with South Asian culture. She has also tolerated my attempts to reproduce the alu gobhi and rajma she loved in Punjab and, most important, she has listened to a lot of bhangra. So too has our young daughter, Evie, who at the age of eight months found great delight in Bally Sagoo's "Mera Laung Gawacha" and Panjabi MC's "Mundian To Bach Ke," thereby confirming the universal appeal of the dhol. Together, Sally and Evie enrich my life greatly and keep my work in perspective.

As I note above, the chapters that make up this volume have had a long gestation. In some ways they reflect the analytical concerns I explored in two essays that I wrote over a decade ago as a new postgraduate student. One essay, on Ranjit Singh's kingdom, not only examined the innovative state practices fashioned by that warrior king but also explored the powerful pull of European markets and imperial systems. The other essay, on the janam-sakhis (traditional stories that recount the life of the first Sikh guru, Guru Nanak), challenged me to think about the relationship between community memory, "traditional texts," and history as a discipline. Those essays were written for a class that I took with Hew McLeod on Sikh history; a class that helped set my life on a path that I never imagined. I owe Hew a great debt: he is a wonderful teacher, mentor, and friend; one who has encouraged me but has also allowed me to follow my own interests and approaches, even when they take me a long way from the texts that he knows and loves. Together with his wife Margaret, who has been an enthusiastic supporter and dispenser of sage advice, Hew has been very important to both Sally and myself over the past decade. In recognition of that debt, I dedicate this volume to Hew and Margaret.

# 1

# Framing/Reframing
# Sikh Histories

Sikhs and Sikhism confound many of the stereotypes that are used to make sense of South Asian society, especially now at the start of the twenty-first century. The Sikh community is frequently defined in masculine terms, whereas India and Indian culture continue to be imagined as feminine. The stereotype of a caste-bound India is punctured by any visit to the *langar* (kitchen and dining hall) of a Sikh place of worship (*gurdwara*) where free food is distributed to worshippers and visitors alike who sit together without distinction or hierarchy. Where Indian thought is known for its elusive abstraction and the nation is renowned for its philosophers and poets, Sikhs are famous for their pragmatism, earthiness, and work ethic. And although generations of Western observers have suggested that "history" is fundamentally foreign to Indian mentalities and that India is commonly packaged to tourists as a "timeless" land, Sikhs have a profound interest in history and historical writing.

Certainly many Sikhs are skeptical of the ability of non-Sikhs to interpret "their" past, but it is very hard to imagine many Sikhs endorsing the line of argument forwarded in *Hinduism Today,* a popular journal with a large subscription base both in India and in South Asian diasporic communities. The December 1994 issue of the journal suggested that "India and Hinduism live beyond history. . . . Other faiths, excluding some tribal and pagan paths, are rooted in events. They began on such and such a day, were born with the birth of a prophet or the pronouncements of a founder. Thus they are defined, circumscribed by history. Not Hinduism. She has no founder, no birthday to celebrate. Like Truth, she is eternal and unhistorical." Conversely, history, in fact, is at the forefront of Sikh politics and in discussions within the Panth over identity. In an important 1987 essay, Robin Jeffrey noted that Sikh politicians seemed to experience a "constant pressure to invoke history," a concern that characterized the language of Sikh politics and separated Sikhs from other South Asian communities.[1] Although Jeffrey's essay is pessimistic in tone given that it was written in the midst of the fallout from Operation Bluestar (when the Indian army was sent into the sacred Golden Temple in Amritsar) and subsequent to the assassination of Indira Gandhi by her Sikh bodyguards, it did focus attention on many Sikhs' preoccupation with history. In fact, Jeffrey's argument might have been pushed further had he looked beyond high politics to other domains where this interest was manifest, most especially in the historical images of the gurus and Sikh heroes that have been a staple of popular bazaar prints since the nineteenth century.[2]

The emergence of e-mail and the Internet have fed the Sikh communities' ongoing engagement with the historical debate over the last decade or so. The recent launch of the Sikh cybermuseum is an excellent example of the ways in which new technologies allow the preservation and dissemination of historical material, thereby allowing Sikhs throughout the world to access an impressive range of documents and images.[3] Various Sikh individuals and groups also use the Internet to provide a bewildering array of historical material. On the Web, Punjabis frequently and fiercely debate history on various discussion lists, Web sites, and news groups. The "Sikh diaspora" Internet discussion list, for example, is one important forum that allows Sikhs throughout the world to engage with the leading historians of Sikhism as well as exchanging information and interpretations. On this list, a vast range of issues are discussed and debated, including the promotion of the Punjabi language within the diaspora; the teachings of the gurus; court cases relating to Sikhs such as those that deal with the legal status of wearing turbans and ceremonial daggers outside of India; and the contentious question of who is a Sikh.[4]

Such debates are of great intellectual and cultural significance for Sikhs, especially when they focus on the origins of Sikhism, the composition and provenance of sacred texts, and the "five Ks"—the outward signifiers of Sikh identity (so named because each begins with a "k"): *kes* (uncut hair), *kangha* (comb), *kara* (steel bracelet), *kirpan* (ceremonial dagger), and *kachh* (short breeches). While these discussions frequently take on a polemical tone—reflecting the very real political stakes attached to representations of Sikhism in the wake of the Indian government's campaign against the Sikh activists who sought to create an independent Sikh homeland—they are borne out of ongoing encounters between scholars of the Sikh past and Sikh communities, both within South Asia and abroad. By and large, scholars of Sikhism have focused their attention on historical issues that are close to the heart of many Sikhs, and this effort has meant that the field has been nourished by a profoundly important and mutually sustaining engagement between Sikh studies as an academic discipline and the Sikhs themselves.[5] Unfortunately, however, there have been relatively few attempts to explore the fundamental assumptions that shape Sikh studies. Those that do exist, typically present either a narrative of the subdiscipline's development or explore the supposedly fundamental rifts between Western critical scholarship and understandings of the Sikh past produced from within Sikh communities.[6] Here I adopt a more schematic approach that charts the shape of the field by identifying a variety of analytical positions that are differentiated by their divergent visions of the shape of Sikh history, their various epistemological frameworks, and the conflicting methodologies they deploy.

Thus, what follows is an attempt to map the major analytical positions that dominate the historical work produced within the subdiscipline of Sikh studies in the hope that both common ground and points of conflict within the field can be brought into stark relief. In other words, in this chapter I identify the most important ways in which scholars have narrated and framed Sikh history. I identify five "framings" that dominate the study of the Sikh past and I briefly examine key works that represent the methodologies and assumptions that shape the historical vision of each framing. In so doing I explore a series of epistemological and methodological problems in order to clarify the assumptions that currently govern the field and to push Sikh studies toward a more sustained engagement with a broader set of questions that are central to contemporary humanities scholarship. After setting out this heuristic typology, I map an alternative vision of the Sikh past, an approach that underscores the importance of cross-cultural encounters, the power of colonialism, and the important forms of cultural traffic that have cut across the borders of the Punjab region and the Indian nation-state.

## A Map of the Field

Here at the start it is useful to identify five divergent approaches to the Sikh past: the "internalist," the "Khalsacentric," the "regional," the "externalist," and the "diasporic." Even though the boundaries between these approaches are not always absolute or rigid, as a group they provide a useful heuristic device that allows us to "map," or set out schematically, the dominant framings of the Sikh past that have been elaborated over the past century or so.[7] The following discussion of this fivefold typology, which also highlights important variations within each position, undercuts the easy oppositions and binary logic that shapes the opposition between "Khalsacentric" and "Eurocentric" approaches to the Sikh past that have been drawn recently by opponents of Western critical scholarship. Such a typology also marks a significant refinement of the simple opposition between "internalist" and "externalist" approaches to Sikh history that I have highlighted elsewhere.[8]

### "Internalist" Approaches

The first of these five analytical traditions is what I have termed the "internalist" approach, the way of framing the Sikh past that has dominated Sikh historiography over the last century. Despite the significant methodological, epistemological, and political differences that can be identified as marking four distinct versions of the internalist scholarship—normative, textualist, political, and cultural—those working within the internalist

tradition are united by a common analytical orientation. Internalist scholars prioritize the internal development of Sikh "tradition," the authority
of its sacred texts, the social composition of the Panth, and political struggles within Sikh communities rather than the broader regional, political,
and cultural forces that shape the community from the outside.

The oldest of these traditions is what might be termed the "normative
tradition," or what Harjot Oberoi has identified as the "Tat Khalsa"
tradition.[9] This vision of the Sikh past, which I discuss at some length
in chapter 2, emerged out of the intense struggles over forms of devotion,
community identity, and political power that dominated colonial Punjab's
public sphere during the last quarter of the nineteenth century. Just as
colonial officials, Christian missionaries, Hindu reformers, and Muslim
leaders forwarded conflicting visions of Punjabi history and culture, Sikh
pamphleteers, editorialists, and social reformers debated the boundaries of
their community and the nature of the Panth's development. Within the
context of colonialism, history writing became a crucial tool for community leaders who crafted epic poems, polemic pamphlets, and commentaries on "scripture" in the hope that by clearly defining the community's
past they would be able to cement their own vision of the community's
present and future.[10]

In particular, history writing was a crucial tool for the rival factions of
the Singh Sabha reform movement, which flourished throughout Punjab
after it was initially established in Amritsar (1873) and Lahore (1879). The
so-called Sanatan faction of the Singh Sabha insisted that their practices
were in keeping both with Sikh custom and with what they imagined as
the ancient, even eternal, devotional practices of north Indian Hindus.
Sanatanis frequently saw the gurus as avatars (incarnations) of the Hindu
gods Ram and Krishna, worshipped images and idols, and accepted the
*varnasramadharma,* the paradigmatic Brahmanical view of the centrality
of the fourfold divisions of *varna* (caste) and *asrama* (stage of life) in
shaping an individual's identity and obligations.

On the other hand, the modernist Tat Khalsa faction of the Singh
Sabha advocated a clearly delineated Sikh identity and used historical
writing to argue that Sikhism was a religious tradition entirely independent of Hinduism. Most famously, the great Sikh intellectual Bhai Kahn

Singh Nabha proclaimed, in a 1898 pamphlet, "Ham hindu nahim" ("We are not Hindus"). Nabha's pamphlet, like other texts produced by Tat Khalsa ideologues, was simultaneously an attack on the power of the Hindu reformers of the Arya Samaj in Punjab and a response to the Sanatan tradition that remained popular with Punjabi aristocrats and the rural masses. These Tat Khalsa reformers rejected Urdu as a medium for education and administration, proclaiming that the Punjabi language written in the Gurmukhi script, the very script used in the sacred *Adi Granth,* was the primary language of Punjab. While they battled the threat of Islamicization they saw embodied in Urdu's dominance, they also crafted a complex series of life-cycle rituals that set them apart from Punjabi Hindus. The Tat Khalsa leaders insisted that Sikhs were a distinct and self-sufficient community, and this belief was articulated most clearly when Sikh leaders informed the governor-general in 1888 that Sikhs should not be "confounded with Hindus but treated in all respects as a separate community."[11]

To inscribe a firm boundary between Sikhs and Hindus, historical texts produced by Tat Khalsa historians have rested on two narrative strategies. First, they evoke ideal types—that is, historical role models who embody the ideals of the Khalsa. Suspicious of Maharaja Ranjit Singh's piety and morality and unsettled by Dalip Singh's conversion to Christianity, these works look back to a more distant Sikh past, untainted by colonialism, for heroes who were proper Sikhs. The heroic martyrdom of the ninth guru (Tegh Bahadur) and the martial spirit of the tenth, Gobind Singh, served as exemplary models, as did the great protector of the fledgling Khalsa in the early eighteenth century, Banda Singh Bahadur. These heroes and martyrs devoted their lives to faith in, and the promulgation of, a distinctive Sikh identity in the face of Mughal oppression, and Tat Khalsa historians enjoined their contemporaries to be equally resolute in the proclamation of the distinctiveness of their Sikh identity.[12]

Following from this, the second key element of Tat Khalsa historical narratives is an insistence on the dangers posed by "Hinduism."[13] Like many British administrators, Tat Khalsa reformers conceived of Hinduism, especially in its popular forms, as an all-consuming jungle or as a boa constrictor capable of crushing and consuming religious innovation through its supposedly stifling weight and incessant expansion. The efforts of Hindu reformers and the laxity of uneducated Sikhs not only blurred the boundaries of the community but also threatened the very future of Sikhism. Only a return to the teachings of the *Adi Granth* and the strict maintenance of the rahit (code of conduct) would prevent Hinduism from engulfing Sikhism altogether.[14]

This normative tradition of historical writing was consolidated in the early twentieth century by the likes of Bhai Vir Singh, and after partition it was increasingly professionalized by a new generation of scholars, most notably Ganda Singh and Harbans Singh. Both of these authors wrote what we might term "corrective histories"—that is, works that challenged interpretations of Sikhism popular outside the community (such as the belief that Nanak's teachings were essentially syncretistic) and disputed evidence within the historical record that indicated diversity in Sikh identity and practice. This corrective approach is most obvious in Ganda Singh's edited collection of European accounts of Sikhism, where his glosses and footnotes not only correct European misapprehensions, but also rebut European claims that Sikhs engaged in practices that contravened the injunctions of the Rahit.[15] In short, this framing of the Sikh past became the dominant vision within the Panth, or at least within the Khalsa, and was increasingly regarded by informed non-Punjabi South Asians and British commentators as the authoritative vision of Sikh history.

In the late 1960s this normative tradition faced its first serious challenge with the publication of W. H. McLeod's *Guru Nanak and the Sikh Religion*. McLeod, who quickly established himself as the most influential modern historian of Sikhism, introduced rigorous professionalism into the study of the Sikh past at the same time that he proffered the new interpretive strategy of textual criticism. Published in 1968, one year before the quincentennial of Nanak's birth, McLeod's *Guru Nanak and the Sikh Religion* was at odds with the reverential and even hagiographical tone of the numerous volumes that marked this important celebration. Indeed, McLeod's book was not a celebration of the Nanak of faith who was cherished by Sikhs as the founder of their religious tradition; instead it was a critical assessment of what we know about "the man Guru

Nanak."[16] As his sources McLeod used the *janam-sakhis*, the life stories of Nanak that circulated among his followers, and from this material he set about evaluating the reliability of each *sakhi* or *gost* (chapter). On the basis of the material's miraculous content; the existence of corroborating external sources, including the *Adi Granth*; the agreement between different janam-sakhis; and the genealogical and geographical evidence, McLeod placed each narrative into one of five categories: the established, the probable, the possible, the improbable, and the impossible.[17]

According to this typology many treasured narratives were discounted entirely (such as that of the young Nanak's restoration of a field of wheat ruined by buffalos), others were dismissed as improbable, while still others were identified as merely possible. McLeod placed 87 out of 124 sakhis in these three categories. The remaining thirty-seven McLeod accepted as either probable or as established on the basis of corroborating evidence, and from these sources he reconstructed the life of Nanak. After his meticulous reading of each sakhi and careful weighing of evidence, McLeod produced an account of Nanak's life—"everything of any importance which can be affirmed concerning the events of Guru Nanak's life"—in just three short paragraphs. He insisted that in "the janam-sakhis what we find is the Guru Nanak of legend and of faith, the image of the Guru seen through the eyes of popular piety seventy-five or a hundred years after his death." The janam-sakhis, McLeod insisted, "provide only glimpses" of the historical Nanak.[18]

Not surprisingly, McLeod's critical reappraisal of the historical Nanak in *Guru Nanak and the Sikh Religion* proved to be highly controversial. Earlier works by both Sikh and non-Sikh scholars were less critical of "traditional" Punjabi sources, and McLeod's relentless and systematic empiricism stimulated a defensive reaction from within the Sikh community that bears many analogies to debates triggered by the approach of "Higher Criticism" to the Gospels. Despite the desire of many Sikhs to shore up "tradition" in the face of this methodology, the close philological and historical examination of Sikh texts practiced by McLeod has over the last three decades formed the backbone of much of the work of professional Sikh studies scholars, especially those based in Europe, North America, and Australasia. It is therefore worth underlining here four of the key features of this analytical strategy. First, McLeod's fundamental approach is grounded in a close empirical reading of texts. This form of textual analysis exhibits a deep concern with the teachings of the gurus and the development of the community as revealed by prescriptive tracts and other authoritative historical sources. Second, this method is underpinned by careful source criticism that pays close attention to the provenance of particular texts and the relationships between texts. Third, philology is central in McLeod's analysis, as he assiduously attends to questions of meaning, translation, and linguistic history. Fourth, in light of McLeod's substantial oeuvre as a whole (and recognizing his significant pioneering contributions in the study of popular art, gender, and diaspora), it can be noted that the real focus of his work is the period prior to Western intrusion and the rise of Ranjit Singh, and he is primarily interested in the development of textual traditions and the internal dynamics of the "traditional" community that developed up to the close of the eighteenth century.

McLeod's textualist approach transformed understandings of Sikh history and established a new analytical framework that has been extended in the last fifteen years by a younger generation of scholars. Where McLeod has focused largely on the janam-sakhis and rahit-namas (codes of conduct), two recent works have focused on the core "scripture" of the Sikhs, the *Adi Granth*. Pashaura Singh's meticulous yet controversial *The Guru Granth Sahib: Canon, Meaning and Authority* scrutinized the production of the *Adi Granth* and its canonization as "scripture," as well as explored the ways in which the relationship between Sikhs and the *Adi Granth* have changed over time. Gurinder Singh Mann's *The Making of Sikh Scripture* drew on recently discovered manuscripts in order to offer a brief yet broad vision of the development of Sikh scripture, thereby extending and modifying McLeod's explorations of the making of the core Sikh textual tradition.

Lou Fenech's monograph *Martyrdom in the Sikh Tradition*, published in 2000, works within the textualist approach pioneered by McLeod; at the same time, however, he moves in an important new direction by using textual analysis to explore the development of a distinctive Sikh cultural tradition focused on the figure of the *shahid* (martyr). By reading culture through textual analysis, Fenech's work, to a greater extent than that of McLeod, Gurinder Singh Mann, or Pashaura Singh, marks a sustained engagement with neglected cultural questions, popular culture, and the workings of community memory over the broad sweep of Sikh history. Fenech has also extended this approach in an important article on the place in Sikh memory and political discourse of Udham Singh, the shahid who in London in March 1940 assassinated Sir Michael O'Dwyer, the governor of Punjab at the time of the Amritsar massacre in 1919.[19] Jeevan Deol's work shares Fenech's concern with literary expression, and his essays to date fruitfully explore a number of theoretical issues related to narrative and discourse while returning Sikh texts and history to a wider Punjabi cultural field.[20]

Another variant of the internalist approach is firmly rooted in the study of Sikh politics. Most notable here is the work of N. G. Barrier. As one of the leading specialists on Sikh history in the colonial era, Barrier's work in the 1970s explored broader aspects of Punjabi administration and politics before the rise of Gandhi, and his work on Sikh politics remains highly cognizant of both this regional context and the power of the colonial state. Unlike the textualist approach, Barrier's work foregrounds community mobilization and access to political power, providing valuable insights into the institutions, power structures, and internal struggles that have shaped Sikh politics in the last 150 years, both in Punjab and beyond.[21] His current work on institutional and textual authority within a global Sikh community promises to create a paradigmatic and nuanced analysis of recent Sikh politics, thereby filling a gaping hole in the scholarly literature on Sikhism.

While Barrier's work has been central in shaping our understanding of Sikh politics in the colonial era, Harjot Oberoi has produced the most sophisticated cultural analysis of social change in the late nineteenth century and the early twentieth. Oberoi's critics have frequently identified him as a member of the "McLeodian school," thereby failing to recognize the fundamental epistemological and methodological break that Oberoi's cultural framing of Sikh history makes from the textualist tradition and McLeod's strict empiricism. Although Oberoi's *The Construction of Religious Boundaries: Culture, Identity and Diversity in the Sikh Tradition* notes that "the field of modern Sikh studies has for long been nurtured by the writings of Professor W. H. McLeod" and acknowledges an "enormous debt" to McLeod, his analytical framework is an entirely original one, at least within the context of Sikh studies.[22] The very title of the work, which foregrounds the construction of Sikh identity, signals an important shift away from empiricism toward a social constructivist approach. This rupture is also confirmed by Oberoi's epigraph extracted from Tzvetan Todorov's discussion in *The Conquest of America* of the openness and multiplicity of historical narratives, which underlines Oberoi's keen interest in the production of narratives and their cultural power. Oberoi's monograph casts a wide theoretical net that draws from the classical sociology of religion (Durkheim, Weber, and Evans-Pritchard) and runs through to Foucault's work on the shifting epistemological foundations of knowledge construction. If these theoretical interests set *The Construction of Religious Boundaries* apart from the tradition pioneered by McLeod, so too does Oberoi's interest in the centrality of colonialism. Although McLeod's work covers a huge geographical and temporal terrain, his most detailed research explores the period up to the middle of the eighteenth century and resolutely focuses on transformations that were driven from within the community. Oberoi, on the other hand, focuses on the period between 1849 and 1920, recounting the birth of a new Sikh episteme under colonialism. It is important to note that for Oberoi this crucial shift was not the direct result of British rule; rather, it was the social, economic, and cultural reconfigurations of colonialism that created the conditions for the momentous reshaping of Sikh intellectual and cultural life. It is against this colonial background that Oberoi reconstructs the role of indigenous elites and propagandists in the reordering of indigenous identity along communal lines.

Moreover, in *The Construction of Religious Boundaries* Oberoi details the clash between the Sanatan tradition and the systematized religious vision of the Tat Khalsa, a modernist vision that inscribed clear boundaries between Sikhs and other communities by insisting on the maintenance of a cluster of new rituals and social practices as markers of community. In short, in his work Oberoi documents the undermining of an "enchanted universe" of popular religious syncretism in the villages of the Punjab by a highly ordered pattern of practice and clearly delineated Sikh (i.e., Tat Khalsa) identity formulated in the province's urban centers and disseminated through print culture, community organizations, and sustained proselytization. Doris Jakobsh's *Relocating Gender in Sikh History*, published in 2003, compliments nicely the general thrust of Oberoi's argument as it examines the gendering of Sikhism under colonialism. Although Jakobsh surveys the broad sweep of Sikh history, the core of the volume (chapters 3–6) explores the gender ideologies of both the colonial state and Punjabi reformers, highlighting the reorganization of ritual practices, the cultural impact of the new educational programs developed under colonial rule, and the innovative prescriptive forms that increasingly circumscribed the social position and identity of Sikh women between 1849 and 1925.

*Khalsacentrism*

In embracing an approach to Sikh history that emphasizes the essentially constructed nature of Sikh identities and rituals, Jakobsh's work, like Oberoi's, challenges both those Sikh studies scholars whose work remains purely empirical as well as the important group of Sikhs who have contested the authority of any Western or critical approaches to Sikhism. In this regard, Oberoi's *The Construction of Religious Boundaries* pushed Sikh studies in a new direction, thereby stimulating an analytical reorientation that was strongly resisted by many Sikhs. Indeed, the book and its author were targeted by fierce polemics. For example, in the introduction to *The Invasion of Religious Boundaries,* a sustained rebuttal of *The Construction of Religious Boundaries,* Jasbir Singh Mann, Surinder Singh Sodhi, and Gurbakhsh Singh Gill characterize Oberoi's work as being shaped by "clumsy distortions, mindless anthropological constructions and assumptions, producing ignominious forged postures, sacrilegious statements about mystic Gurus . . . [the] bland, blunted, unattached, constricted, shallow, pathetic Oberoi has produced a disjointed cynical, conscienceless and unscrupulous book . . . to attack the independent Sikh Identity . . . In writing this book, he has shown his pathological identification with Eurocentric paradigms, and has attempted to bring nihilistic depersonalisation by biting the hands that fed him."[23] In addition, elsewhere in the *Invasion of Religious Boundaries* Sodhi and Mann argue that "Oberoi has become prisoner of [the] McLeodian Eurocentric research paradigm."[24]

To counter to Western critical scholarship, the writings of Mann, Sodhi, and Gill advocate the adoption of a Khalsacentric approach to the Sikh past, which requires the complete rejection of Western analytical models and scholarly traditions. Sodhi, for example, insists that Khalsacentric research eschews "the use of European social science methods" and instead grounds scholarship in a belief that is in essence holistic and introspective. As a result, it describes "Sikh realities from a subjective faith point of view of the Khalsa values and ideals."[25] While this approach exhibits the same deep concern with the maintenance of a prescriptive normative order that typified the older Tat Khalsa tradition, because Khalsacentric scholarship is characterized by its thorough rejection of Western critical scholarship it is not simply a superficial repackaging of a long-established intellectual tradition. Whereas the Tat Khalsa tradition developed out of an urbanized late-nineteenth-century Punjabi elite that was receptive to colonial education and Western disciplines, the Khalsacentric tradition repudiates the authority claims of disciplines like history, sociology, anthropology, women's studies, and religious studies. Gurdarshan Singh Dhillon, for example, has asserted that "a proper study of religion . . . is beyond the domain of Sociology, Anthropology and History," while Sukhmander Singh has argued that "methodologies relevant to Christian ideology where scriptures developed as a result of history and culture, [are] inapplicable to Sikhism where scripture is revelatory and authenticated by the prophet himself."[26] It follows from this that Sikhism can only be understood from a "scriptural" basis, and Mann, Sodhi, and Gill state that the application of Judeo-Christian principles in Sikh studies "will bring about the wrong results. . . . The Sikh thought is its cause, and the historical events that followed, represent the unfolding of the philosophy preached by the Gurus, and enshrined in Sri Guru Granth Sahib.[27]

This rejection of Western disciplines is energized by the social concerns of a conservative section of a transnational Sikh elite. Many members of this group are professionals based in North America who are anxious about the maintenance of tradition in a diasporic age. "Khalsacentrism" is thus largely the product of the gurdwaras and community organizations of the west coast of North America where many highly educated Sikh migrants grew very anxious in the 1980s and 1990s about Indian politics and the future of Sikhism. Their anxieties were, of course, well founded in the wake of the political turbulence that engulfed Punjab in the 1980s as the Indian state attempted to crush the Khalistan movement and Sikhs became the objects of suspicion within the Indian national imaginary as well as the victims of very real violence. In light of these pressures, diasporic Sikhs turned to historical writing (if not the discipline of history) both to legitimate their claims to distinctiveness and to shore up the boundaries of the community against attacks by "outsiders," including the Indian state, the Hindu Right, or historians who critically examined key aspects of the Sikh textual corpus or "traditional" understandings of Sikh history. By mobilizing the gurdwaras and community organizations; organizing conferences and publishing books and periodicals; enthusiastically embracing the Internet; and protesting against the work of Western scholars, notably the nature of research on Sikhs undertaken in North American universities, Khalsacentric scholars have created a large body of historical literature that has reached many Sikhs, both within the diaspora and at home in Punjab itself.

What is striking about the discourse of Khalsacentrism is its transnational underpinnings and the ways in which it has mobilized elements of American multiculturalism and ethnic politics against both the Indian state and Western scholarship. Not only does the very name "Khalsacentrism" invoke the "Afrocentrism" that Sikhs encountered within fiercely contested public debates in the United States, but its American-based advocates are finely sensitized to the politics of representation that mold the American public sphere and educational institutions. While Khalsacentric critiques of Western scholarship are motivated by a legitimate concern about the colonial origins and the Eurocentric freight of many academic disciplines, they rework American discourses on the representation of minorities to insist that Sikhism cannot be understood through the lens of Western disciplines. The Khalsacentric refutation of Western knowledge rests on the supposed materialism of all Western scholarship (an assertion that seems dubious in the wake of poststructuralism, postmodernism, gender studies, and the linguistic turn), along with an engagement, albeit a scant and seemingly haphazard one, with the work of Edward Said, Talal Asad, and other critics of orientalism.[28] Given this view, however, it is ironic that the Khalsacentric critique of Western knowledge replicates the binary logic that structured the most pernicious forms of colonial discourse, thereby merely reversing the moral and political value attached to spirituality as opposed to science, tradition as opposed to modernity, faith as opposed to scholarship.[29] Despite its invocation of the language of multiculturalism, as well as the support it has drawn from non-Sikh scholars (most notably Noel King), Khalsacentrism is enabled by a nativist politics that simply rejects the authority of non-Sikh scholars and dismisses many professional Sikh historians in *ad hominem* attacks as "brain-washed," "role-dancing" or "fallen."[30]

Khalsacentrism is thus fundamentally an "occidentalizing" discourse that caricatures Western culture and academic disciplines in an effort to insulate the community from the "invasive" effects of professional scholarship and to enable the construction of an autonomous, self-contained, and privileged interpretative tradition within the community. Not surprisingly, Khalsacentric discourse replicates many of the arguments made by its enemies on the Hindu Right against Western scholarship and the "historical religions" of the West, while simultaneously closing down debates about history and identity with "outsiders."[31] At a fundamental level, such arguments merely reinforce the long-established orientalist stereotypes of South Asia as a land of unchanging and eternal spirituality, the very tradition that much recent post-orientalist scholarship on South Asia has been working against.[32]

So while there is much to admire in Sodhi's insistence that Khalsacentrism is grounded in "humanistic and emancipatory anti-racist awareness" and that it will "screen out oppressive assumptions," the work produced by Khalsacentric scholars to date suggests that this model may itself create and enforce "oppressive assumptions."[33] This likelihood seems very real in light of the polemics against the personality and morals of Harjot Oberoi, Hew McLeod, Pashaura Singh, and others. Moreover, by insisting that scholarship should be produced from within the Khalsa and should affirm its values and program, this approach to the Sikh past calls

into question the faith and identity of those Sikhs who do not accept all of
the practices and identity markers of the Khalsa. This is clear, for example, in the work of Manjeet Singh Sidhu, who dubs Oberoi a "mendacious
gleaner" and dismisses the Sanatan faction of the Singh Sabha as "Hindu
saboteurs" and "conspiratorial and peripheral Sanatan Sikhs."[34] Used in
this way, Khalsacentrism can only reify community boundaries, disem-
power non-Khalsa Sikhs, and prevent the possibility of any positive dialogue with other South Asian religious communities or with non-Sikh
scholars.

*Regional Approaches*

While the internalist models often recognize that the Sikh community
has been molded by the broader structures, institutions, and cultural
patterns of Punjabi life (even in the diasporic context), they share a tendency to abstract Sikhism from its crucial regional context.[35] At a fundamental level, of course, this is a product of the Tat Khalsa insistence on the
originality, internal coherence, and incomparability of Sikh tradition. As a
result, internal scholarship tends to privilege religious identity over social
and commercial affiliations or regional identity, and Sikhism is extracted
from the dense webs of economics, social relations, and political traditions
that have conditioned its development in Punjab and beyond.

In contrast, several historians have made a break with the internalist
tradition through their explicit emphasis on the importance of Sikhism,
regional context. Indu Banga, whose writings cover the late eighteenth
century through to the early twentieth, has consistently foregrounded the
importance of Punjab as a context. Banga's effort in part seems to be a
product of her groundbreaking work on Ranjit Singh's kingdom, a state
that is frequently imagined as being explicitly Sikh yet also dependent on
the maharaja's skillful balancing of different faiths and ethnicities in both
his administration and military establishment. Banga's emphasis on the
importance of the regional context also reflects her strong interest in the
economic and agrarian history of the region, the crucial milieu within
which Sikhism emerged and developed.[36]

J. S. Grewal has also consistently grounded his explorations of Sikhism
in the regional context of Punjabi history. Of all the historians working on

Sikhism, Grewal has published the most widely on Punjabi history more generally, and his research consistently foregrounds the importance of the region's geography, its institutions and political structures, its economic fortunes, and its cultural ethos. In light of this insistence, Grewal's work typically uses a wider range of sources and deploys a range of approaches—from literary analysis to discussions of political economy—in teasing out the multifaceted nature of Sikh history. For Grewal, Sikh history is a dynamic story of the shifting relationship between this community and its regional environment. It is telling that a recent festschrift for Grewal was titled *Five Punjabi Centuries: Policy, Economy, Society, and Culture.*[37]

For the colonial period, the work of Kenneth Jones in *Socio-Religious Reform Movements in British India* and *Religious Controversy in British India* firmly located Sikh debates over identity and Sikh socioreligious reform movements within a wider regional and national context. His landmark 1973 *Journal of Asian Studies* essay on Arya Samaji–Singh Sabha relations located the articulation of an increasingly clearly defined Sikh identity within the broader dynamics of educational change, urbanization, and class formation in Punjab.[38] For Jones, it was clear that the religious reform and the definition of clear-cut boundaries between Hindus and Sikhs was not only the product of encounters between the communities but also the result of struggles within the communities between newly powerful urban elites and the older "orthodox worlds" of rural life. Although Jones's exploration of these struggles within the Sikh community have been elaborated and refined by Oberoi, there has been limited effort to extend his pioneering work on the relationship between Arya Samajis and Singh Sabha reformers. Anil Sethi's work provides some insight into this process within his analysis of the changing operation of community boundaries in key spheres of Punjabi popular culture and daily life, including commensality, festivals, and popular entertainment.[39]

## "Externalist" Approaches

Relative to the advocates of the approaches described above, a smaller group of historians have privileged imperial power relations over regional structures as they emphasize the centrality of colonialism in the making of

Sikhism. This approach is most obvious in Richard Fox's *Lions of the Punjab,* which argues that the British played a central role in constituting the orthodox "Singh" (i.e., Khalsa) identity when they hoped that a distinctive and loyal Sikh soldiery would form a bulwark to British authority.[40] In short, Fox suggests that the British pursued a project of "domestication" when they used military recruitment "to turn the Singhs into guardians of the Raj" while using "Sikhism's religious institutions to discipline them [Sikh soldiers] to obedience."[41] Through the mechanism of the "martial races" policy, the British were thus instrumental in the constitution of a new "orthodoxy," a religious identity that fulfilled the needs of the British, not the Punjabis themselves. Although Fox suggests that "antecedent conditions of class relations and religious identities set the material and cultural limits for the making . . . of the Punjab's culture," his monograph foregrounds the instrumentality of the colonial state and fails to acknowledge the significance of precolonial structures, practices, and identities.[42] Thus, in contrast to the long-dominant internalist historiographical tradition, Fox's work was characterized by an "externalist" approach. In stressing the pivotal role of British cultural assumptions and the mechanisms of the colonial state in the creation of modern Sikh identity, Fox effectively relocated the drive-wheel of historical change from within the Sikh community to British offices, libraries and drill halls. Fox's work, however, did challenge the tendency to treat the Sikh community as self-contained, thereby underlining the transformative power of colonialism and identifying colonial rule as the major rupture in Punjabi history.

Fox's Chicago colleague Bernard Cohn developed similar arguments in his important essay on the symbolic and political importance of clothing, including the Sikh turban, in South Asian society. Cohn argues that the "British rulers in nineteenth-century India played a major part in making the turban into a salient feature of Sikh identity." While Cohn briefly reviews Sikh history, beginning with the age-old (and erroneous) assertion that Sikhism "grew out of syncretic tendencies in theology and worship among Hindu and Muslims in north India," his discussion of the *dastar* or *pagri* (turban) fails to note its significance in eighteenth-century texts such as the *Chaupa Singh Rahit-nama*; its status in the ranks of Ranjit

Singh's army; and its prominence in Indian representations of Sikhs before the Anglo-Sikh wars (such as the Rajasthani painters who were based in Patiala, or Imam Bakhsh's representations of Punjab around 1840).[43] Such evidence suggests that the turban had already become an important marker of identity for some Sikhs (at least some Sikh men) long before the extension of the East India Company's authority over Punjab in 1849. Certainly, Cohn is correct in suggesting that during the colonial period the turban increasingly became a standard marker of Sikh identity within the colonial state's knowledge regime, but his neglect of the precolonial period and the turban's place within a long-established prescriptive tradition allows him to overplay the extent of this transformation. By privileging the power of the colonial state in such a way, Cohn also effaces the role of indigenous reformers, especially the members of the Tat Khalsa, who also strove to establish the turban as a distinctive marker of Sikh identity in the late nineteenth century and early twentieth century.

Thus both Cohn's and Fox's externalist interpretations of the genesis of modern Sikh identity are enabled by truncated chronological frameworks that effectively erase the precolonial period. Ironically, by defining the rise of a distinct Sikh identity as the direct product of the initiatives of the colonial state, these visions of Sikh history actually make it difficult to gauge the exact nature, extent, and legacy of the colonial moment in Sikh history. Indeed, this story would be recast if the question of modern Sikh identity were reimagined within a broader exploration of the problem of identity under imperial regimes in general rather than under British colonialism in particular, for then we might have a fuller understanding of how the imperial systems of the Mughals and of Ranjit Singh dealt with the heterogeneous nature of Punjabi society. We await a study that will place the reformist zeal of the final three decades of the nineteenth century in a broad chronological context, allowing us to assess the true extent of British power and the cultural program of the Tat Khalsa.

## Diasporic Approaches

The most recent approach to emerge regarding the Sikh past frames the study of the Sikh community as a transnational and diasporic social formation. At one level, this approach grew out of an older tradition of work on Sikh (and Punjabi) migration, such as Arthur Helweg's *Sikhs in England*, which is comprised of sociological studies of the British Sikh community, and W. H. McLeod's pioneering work *Punjabis in New Zealand*. These early studies dealt largely with basic issues in immigration history as it developed in the 1970s and 1980s, such as the decision to immigrate, the nature and organization of the community in its "host country," and the questions of "assimilation" and "acculturation" in the development of the new community.

This immigration history paradigm has been called into question recently as some scholars have adopted a range of approaches that have emerged out of the analytical problematic of the diaspora. As Verne Dusenbery has argued in "A Sikh Diaspora?" the shift toward a diasporic model marked a significant reconceptualization of the position of the Sikh community and the project of Sikh studies. Where histories of Sikh mobility in the vein of immigration history took the "host nation" as their analytical unit, imagining a Sikh diaspora invoked a very different model. The term "diaspora," which originally was used to describe the Jewish experience and thus is well established as an analytical category in Jewish studies, suggested that diasporic Sikhs were a people unified by a common culture yet also were a people dispersed, either temporarily or permanently, from their "homeland." At an analytical level, the concept of a Sikh diaspora was both promising and troubling. In conceiving of the diaspora itself as the analytical focus (rather than the Sikh community in a particular nation), the possibility of a genuinely transnational approach to Sikh studies is opened up. In so doing, a strategy is produced through which we might recover not only the social networks, institutional structures, and cultural traffic that have linked Sikhs living overseas with the Punjab, but also the ties that directly connect different diasporic communities (for example, in Britain and Canada).

Darshan Singh Tatla's *The Sikh Diaspora: The Search for Statehood* provided the first monographic study of the Sikh diasporic experience.[44] Tatla's text focuses on the post-1947 period, notably on the 1980s and 1990s, by tracing the development of Sikh political institutions in the United Kingdom, Canada, and the United States. It is particularly valuable because it documents crucial debates within the community as well as the rise of community organizations that actively linked various Sikh communities into a shared space of debate and exchange. Further, Tatla's exploration of the development of a vigorous diasporic Punjabi print culture is particularly important as it underscores the importance of technology and communications in shaping the social patterns and political aspirations of an increasingly dispersed and diverse global Sikh community.[45] In mapping the global context of the demand for Khalistan, Tatla has fashioned an important window onto recent Sikh politics, but his political focus pushes to the margins other cultural issues—for example, the dynamics of marriage within the diaspora, the position of Sikh women, and Sikh relationships with non-Sikh communities in Britain and North America.

More recently still, Brian Keith Axel's *The Nation's Tortured Body* rereads the last 150 years of Sikh history through the lens of the contemporary global Sikh community. In keeping with much of the recent work on the politics of diasporic communities, Axel suggests that the notion of Punjab as the "Sikh homeland" was not something created in India and carried out into the world by migrants. Rather, it was the diasporic experience of displacement that actually created the notion of the homeland. Although this formulation erases the ways in which Sikhism was territorialized under colonialism and during partition, Axel's transnational approach does allow him to produce and juxtapose ethnographies and histories for a number of important sites for various Sikh communities, ranging from Harmindar Sahib (the Golden Temple) in Amritsar to Southall's Glassy Junction pub. Not only does Axel return these "local" sites to the broader field of the diaspora, he also examines the ways in which these various sites and communities are connected. He makes a convincing case that it is the circulation of images of the male Sikh body—with Maharaja Dalip Singh serving as the exemplary case—that mediates between far-flung Sikh communities.

Most importantly, Axel argues that since 1983 it has been the images of the tortured bodies of Sikh "militants" and Khalistanis, which are widely disseminated through the Internet, that have played a central role in creating the social relations that constitute the diaspora. Axel shows that these images remind diasporic Sikhs of the constant threat of violence they face, and thus foreground the dislocation, longing for home, and struggle for power that are implicit in the diasporic condition. Unlike Tatla, Axel is sensitive to gender and representation, and his work underlines the crucial but often overlooked place of masculinity in representations of Sikh politics and identity. Nevertheless, in focusing on the cultural politics of the drive for Khalistan *The Nation's Tortured Body* once again privileges the political concerns of a certain sector of the diaspora. In so doing it effaces what we might term the politics of the everyday—that is, how Sikhs relate to each other and to non-Sikhs; the reproduction of Sikh identities through gurdwaras, community groups, and the family; and the engagement of Sikhs with local, national, and global forms of popular culture.

But Tatla's and Axel's foundational category of diaspora remains a contested term in the Sikh case. The significance of Khalistan, for example, must be carefully contextualized within the history of Sikh mobility and thought. Axel himself acknowledges that the struggle for a "Sikh homeland . . . remained within India between 1947 and 1971 and was not a concern for Sikhs living in other parts of the world," and that the "fight for Khalistan . . . remained somewhat obscure until 1984."[46] But when Axel continues on to assert that Khalistan has "become a generalized trope of social practice and representation central to the post-1984 (re)constitution of the Sikh diaspora" he presents an overdetermined reading of recent Sikh history. The boldness of this claim has to be viewed with considerable caution given that many Sikhs contested the aspiration for Khalistan, as well as the methods of attaining it, during the 1980s and 1990s. Moreover, any broad survey of diasporic cultural production reveals that Khalistan did not monopolize Sikh imaginations or social concerns. Access to education, the status of the Punjabi language, the maintenance of the five Ks, the "human rights" of Sikhs in the West and the centrality of marriage in cultural reproduction as well as the teachings of the gurus were crucial concerns for most diasporic Sikh communities regardless of their commitment (or lack of commitment) to Khalistan. In a similar vein, Dusenbery has convincingly argued that diasporic Sikhs are not simply motivated by projecting a publicly recognizable Sikh identity, but rather manifest concern with maintaining a range of what he terms "ancestral genera," that is, the linguistic usages, occupational traditions, marriage patterns, and village connections that shape Punjabi culture as a whole.[47] Such valued elements of culture and of social relationships are often lost in the recent work on migrant Sikhs, which tends to place undue emphasis on the quest for territorial sovereignty or, as in the case of Cynthia Mahmood's work, focuses narrowly on groups whose religious and political commitments put them at the margins of "diasporic" communities.[48]

More generally still, Dusenbery, McLeod, and Karen Leonard have pointed out that the notion of a "Sikh diaspora" may in itself be misleading because it privileges religious identity at the expense of other social markers, economic ties, and kinship networks.[49] Not only do we have to guard against the fetishization of religious identity that is implicit within the notion of a "Sikh diaspora," but we also have to be cautious in the changing analytical purchase of the concept across time. While Axel's work demonstrates the very real strengths of a diasporic interpretation of Sikh identity formation in the post–World War II period, both McLeod and Leonard have suggested that the concept may be of limited use for work on migration and community formation among Punjabi migrants in the early twentieth century because early Punjabi settlers in Britain, Canada, the United States, and Australasia, like many rural Punjabis, did not necessarily define themselves in terms of their religious community. These complex analytical problems again underscore the ways in which both regional context and historical contingency disrupt the easy creation of new paradigms, thereby reminding us that while concepts such as a "Sikh diaspora" are useful heuristic tools, they should be deployed with care and self-reflection.

## The Question of "Tradition"

Thus far I have presented a schematic "map" of Sikh historiography by highlighting some of the major epistemological and methodological difficulties that face each of the positions identified above. In what follows, I will elaborate on this critical commentary and sketch the foundations of an alternative vision of Sikh history, one that sees the precolonial past, colonialism, and the diaspora within a common analytical field. This vision provides the framework for the three chapters that follow, and it raises a set of questions that I hope will open up important avenues of new research.

As my discussion of the notion of a Sikh diaspora suggests, an important starting point for reimagining Sikh history is the assessment of the subdiscipline's existing conceptual vocabulary and the exploration of new analytical concepts. Given the contentious status of "history" as an interpretative discipline for some Sikhs as well as the centrality of hermeneutic debates over the interpretation of sacred texts, historians of Sikhism have paid considerable attention to the question of translation. This has been a particular hallmark of the textualist approach pioneered by McLeod, and much of his work proceeds from the close analysis and discussion of a particular key term or concept. McLeod firmly respects linguistic and cultural difference by highlighting the problem of translation, and he has frequently argued that, where possible, Sikhism should be understood on its own terms rather than according to a Judeo-Christian framework. He has, for example, been a firm advocate of the use of the term "Panth" to describe the Sikh community, preferring it to other terms such as "sect" or "denomination."[50] McLeod has, moreover, been even-handed in his attentiveness to questions of translation: he is just as concerned with the way in which English terms are mapped onto Punjabi concepts as he is with the accurate renderings of Punjabi words into English. Harjot Oberoi has also paid close attention to this issue, particularly with regard to the origins and use of the term "Sikhism." In drawing on the work of other historians of South Asian religions, most notably Romila Thapar, Oberoi has highlighted the difficulties in translating the very notion of "religion" into the South Asian context (especially before 1900), and he notes the centrality of the colonial state in fashioning and consolidating "religion" as a concept in South Asia.[51]

The term "tradition" is one that is in wide currency among Sikh historians, and as such it requires careful scrutiny. Historians of Sikhism use "tradition" as a catchall phrase that describes the textual corpus, practices, and discourses produced by Sikhs. Yet this term is problematic for two reasons. First, it frequently stands in contradistinction to modernity by representing the authentic essence of a premodern community. While historians generally see the notion of tradition as being disrupted, undermined, and frequently supplanted by modernity, in Sikh studies the term is frequently used in discussions of the contemporary moment and diasporic communities.[52] This is not surprising given the strength of the internalist approach and the tendency to insulate the Sikh past from both the transformative power of colonialism and from migration. The category of "tradition" itself has not been subject to sustained analysis, even though the work of both Lou Fenech and Harjot Oberoi seems to suggest that the very notion of tradition was itself the product of the Singh Sabha movement. But are there limits to this interpretation? What elements of "tradition" are actually the product of precolonial times? In other words, what elements of precolonial culture were either accepted or left untouched by the colonial state and urban reformers? Equally important, how did precolonial texts, institutions, and ideologies influence the "constructions" of Tat Khalsa reformers?

The second problem with the use of "tradition" as a concept is that it tends to imagine a homogeneous and strictly unified community, thereby evacuating the Sikh past of struggle and contestation. This tendency is particularly marked in the scholarship for the precolonial era, in part because of the predominance of textualist readings of the pre-1849 period. A more sophisticated social and cultural history that attended to precolonial social differentiation and political struggle would fundamentally transform our understandings of the precolonial past in the way that Oberoi has revised the visions of the 1870 to 1930 period.

In the next chapter I help to initiate this project by paying close attention to the transition to colonialism, especially the development of British visions of the Sikh past and how these visions shaped the program of the colonial state in the 1850s. A close consideration of this transition enables a critical interrogation of the ways in which concepts such as tradition have been produced. The research of Fenech on martyrdom and of Oberoi on the Tat Khalsa episteme mark important starting points for this project, but despite their pioneering work there are fundamental aspects of the colonial period that require careful reexamination. The cultural values and political pressures that shaped the "Punjab school" of colonial admin-

istration remain largely unquestioned and thus reflect a central uneven-
ness in the scholarship on the colonial period. Thanks to Oberoi, we have a
rich anthropological understanding of Punjabi culture under colonialism,
and although there is a substantial literature on colonial policy, especially
relating to land, the values and motivations of the British in Punjab remain
inadequately studied.[53] As it stands, Sikh historiography is in danger of
replicating the long-established and pernicious assertion that "natives"
have culture while Europeans have history. A two-sided rereading of the
colonial period, as my discussion of Fox and Cohn above suggests, must
also attend carefully to questions of both power asymmetries and agency,
thereby recognizing the importance of long-established community dynamics and the important reformist and prescriptive literature produced
by Sikhs themselves (both in the precolonial and colonial periods).

One way that we might avoid privileging the instrumentality of the colonial state is to delineate what can be termed the "points of recognition"
that shaped the cultural terrain of colonial Punjab—that is, those values, ideals, and practices that Britons and Sikhs believed that they have
shared.[54] These points of recognition, especially notions of masculinity
and martiality, were produced by the ability of Punjabis and Britons to
translate each other's culture in such a way that they found values or traditions that seemed roughly equivalent to important elements of their own
worldview. Through these points of recognition, Sikh leaders could secure
their cultural authority and win economic benefits (especially through
military service) from the colonial state. At the same time, these perceived
commensurabilities between colonizer and a particular colonized community provided discourses and practices where colonial policy could gain
purchase, creating new institutions and reshaping cultural patterns with
the aim of shoring up imperial authority. As I argue in chapter 2, these
processes that constructed and affirmed cross-cultural commensurability rested on the identification and marginalization of other groups that
lacked those qualities that Sikhs and Britons supposedly shared. In other
words, the production of sameness also required the production of difference.[55] The British celebration of the "manliness" and "warrior ethos" of
Khalsa Sikhs depended on a complex series of comparisons made between

monotheistic Sikhs and polytheistic Hindus—the sturdy Punjabi and the effeminate Bengali; the manly meat-eater of the north and the physically weak vegetarians of the Gangetic plains and the south—as well as the almost complete erasure of Sikh women from colonial discourse. The most crucial shared discursive formation articulated by Tat Khalsa reformers and British scholar-administrators was that of "Sikhism in danger," and from the 1850s the colonial state worked hard to protect the distinctiveness of Sikhism. In short, the British saw their role as the policemen of tradition, installing *granthis* (readers of the Granth) for Sikh regiments, supplying *jhatka* meat (from animals killed with a single blow and thus approved for consumption by Khalsa initiates) for Sikh soldiers, and collecting a dense archive of ethnographic information about patterns of popular practice. They had to protect Sikhism from the "all-consuming jungle" of popular Hinduism.

## The Polylogics of Identity

One useful model for making sense of the debates over cultural boundaries comes not from Punjabi historiography but from recent work on colonial South India. Eugene Irschick, in his excellent book *Dialogue and History,* insists that the colonial social order was "a negotiated, heteroglot construction shaped by both weak and strong, the colonized and colonizer, from the present to the past." Irschick's study of land tenure in the Madras hinterland traces the interplay between the demands of colonial administrators and the authority of indigenous knowledge traditions, stressing the "dialogic" nature of British colonial knowledge.[56] In so doing he warns that "we can no longer presume" that British understandings of India were the "product of an 'imposition' by the hegemonic colonial power onto a mindless and subordinate society."[57] Local aspirations and colonial agendas were in a constant dialogue and hence formed a dynamic process of exchange where claim and counterclaim led each interest group to modify its position almost constantly. It is crucial to reshape Irschick's formulation to place more emphasis on the divergent positions of the groups engaged in these interactions, to underscore that these dialogic exchanges took place within the highly uneven power relations of developing colonialism and that the ultimate outcome of these processes was to empower one group at the expense of the other.

In the Punjabi case it is perhaps most useful to think of the construction of knowledge and identity as being polylogic rather than dialogic. Where Irschick's case study explored the encounter between peasant cultivators and a small cadre of British officials in one part of Tamil Nadu, the negotiation of Sikh identity was a more diffuse and open process. Not simply the product of an encounter between colonizer and colonized, the renegotiation of Sikhism was produced by contestations within Sikh communities as well as encounters with various Hindu reformers, Christian missionaries, and colonial officials. Pamphleteers and preachers were aware of the multiplicity of arguments that they were responding to and the divergent audiences they were addressing: their texts are deeply imprinted by these multiple engagements and the necessity to construct multifaceted arguments suited to the heteroglot population of the region.

This argument for an approach that explores the complex and polylogic negotiation of identity under the uneven power relations of colonialism reflects an insistence on the heterogeneity of Punjabi society. The region's inherently diverse and hybridized population reflects the reality that Punjab has long stood at the confluence of the Islamic and Indic worlds and the cultures of Central and South Asia. As a result, the British encountered a heterogeneous society in Punjab, a society where numerous social groups were differentiated by a range of socioeconomic, cultural, and political factors. Given this, any search for a representative Sikh voice, yet alone a representative Punjabi voice, in the colonial archive is futile in the face of the multiplicity of local actors whose pamphlets, speeches, and testimonies survive in British and Punjabi archives. Efforts to trace the interrelationships between these various Punjabis; establish points of recognition as well as points of conflict between the colonized groups and various British interests; and fight against the limits of the colonial archive to recover the experiences of underrepresented groups (especially tribals, Dalits, and women) will allow us to locate the negotiation of Sikh identity within the deep structures and complex dynamics of Punjabi life.

More broadly still, this polylogic model of the construction of culture and identity also recognizes that Sikhs were incorporated into the British Empire and that this imperial system worked as a system of mobility, which both enabled and controlled the circulation of certain ideas, commodities, and people. Sikhs, especially Sikh soldiers, were conspicuous in this imperial world, and the turbaned Sikh soldier became one of the most potent imperial symbols. Unfortunately, most scholarship to date on the Sikh diaspora focuses on Sikh "settlers"—those migrants who left Punjab and established permanent homes in North America, Britain, Europe, Africa, Asia, or Australasia. We know much less about "sojourners," those Sikhs who lived outside Punjab for a short period of time or who traveled backward and forward from Punjab. In part, this lacuna is the product of our limited knowledge of the early decades of the diaspora and, in particular, the absence of work that explores the important connections between British imperialism and the very genesis of the diaspora in the second half of the nineteenth century. To a large extent, these blind spots of historiography are the product of the tendency to separate colonialism and mobility (whether understood as "migration" or "diaspora") and to imagine them as entirely distinct heuristic tools or analytical fields.

## Sikhism and the Webs of Empire

One way out of this division between histories of colonialism and mobility is to reexamine the imperial framework of the Sikh past. To my mind, recent work in the "new imperial history" has opened up some fertile avenues of analysis for historians of Sikhism. Mrinalini Sinha's *Colonial Masculinity* (1995) highlighted the intersections between, and the growing enmeshment of, British and Indian ideas about gender at the end of the nineteenth century. In making sense of these engagements, Sinha elaborated the notion of an "imperial social formation"—the integrative but uneven social order fashioned by British colonialism—as a valuable heuristic tool for reconceptualizing the empire. Antoinette Burton's *At the Heart of the Empire* (1998) built on Sinha's work, as her examination of Indian women travelers in Victorian England stressed that the metropole itself was a "contact zone" and that important aspects of British culture were fashioned out of the imperial experience. By highlighting the inter-dependence and mutually constitutive nature of metropolitan and colo-nial histories, the work of Sinha and Burton is very suggestive for future work on the interweaving of British and Punjabi histories, and their insights shape many of the arguments that follow. Elsewhere, I have argued that we can extend the notion of an "imperial social formation" by paying close attention to the "horizontal" connections that linked colonies directly together as well as the "vertical connections" between metropole and colony, and by reconstructing the various "webs" that gave the empire its shape and power.[58]

In the remainder of this volume I locate the development of Sikhism within these "webs of empire." Societies that were colonized by the East India Company (or other agents of British imperialism) did not simply "encounter" the British but were drawn into the institutions, markets, communication systems, and cultural networks that made up the empire. Important flows between colonies of capital, personnel, and ideas ener-gized colonial development and the function of the larger imperial sys-tem. Such exchanges have received only limited attention in the historiog-raphy of the British empire in general and of Punjabi history in particular, because they transgress the analytical boundaries of both metropolitan-focused imperial history (where the empire is viewed from London out-ward) or histories of individual colonies (where the view is from the colony toward London). The web metaphor has several advantages for thinking about the relationship between Sikhism and colonialism. At a general level, it underscores that the empire was a structure, a complex fabrication fashioned out of a great number of disparate parts that were brought together into a variety of new relationships. The web captures the integrative nature of this cultural traffic, recovering how imperial institu-tions and structures connected disparate points in space into a complex mesh of networks.

The inherently relational nature of the empire is also underlined by the image of the web. Where so much writing on imperial/colonial history reduces the empire to a series of metropole-periphery binaries, the web reinforces the multiple positions that any given colony, city, community, or archive might occupy. Lahore, for example, might be seen as being in a subaltern position in relation to London or even Calcutta, but in turn it might be a sub-imperial center from which colonial authority flowed into the countryside and where the pull of its bazaars drew in commodities, products, and money from within Punjab and elsewhere in South Asia and beyond.

These arguments are central to my earlier work on the production of colonial knowledge in India and the working of larger imperial knowledge systems.[59] But where my *Orientalism and Race* largely focused on the imperial institutions, intellectual networks, and British discourses that integrated the empire, this volume focuses on two interwoven, overlapping, but occasionally independent sets of webs. The first set is composed of the imperial structures largely produced to meet the needs of British merchants, missionaries, and administrators. These political, commercial, communication, and cultural networks connected Punjab to the rest of British India and reached out to distant parts of the empire, whether to Britain itself or to Southeast Asia, Australasia, Canada, or Africa. The second set of webs was largely constructed by the Punjabis themselves, who fashioned them to meet their needs within a world that was being remade by colonialism and migration. The key elements of these Punjabi "webs of empire" were the migrant networks. Although these were laced into imperial labor markets and communication systems, they were actually shaped by Punjabi kinship structures and underpinned by Punjabi religious institutions and religious networks, and were at a fundamental level a crucial Punjabi response to the economic and cultural pressures of colonialism. The emergence of these Punjab-focused networks meant that even as cities like Lahore and Amritsar were key seats of authority at the margins of the imperial system, they simultaneously emerged as important centers of spiritual and cultural authority for a global community of Sikhs. At the same time that these cities contained key institutions and sacred sites, certain large villages and particular *tahsils* (subdistrict) also emerged as centers from where Punjabis migrated and found their brides; through which they made financial and correspondence transactions; and around which crucial migratory networks were built. The significance of these villages was frequently given material expression in the *pakka* houses (literally, "cooked" or "finished"; made from sun-dried bricks) and enlarged holdings that were the product of the remittances, military pay, and pensions that came as the economic fruit of mobility. As Sikh communities overseas became well established, they themselves could emerge as crucial nodes that gave shape to and anchored particular webs within the Punjabi world. In chapter 3 I demonstrate this clearly through an analysis of the reformulation of bhangra in London and Birmingham— centers that stand at the heart of a complex series of networks that connect Britain to Punjab, to other Punjabi diasporic communities, and outward to non-Punjabi audiences in Europe, North America, and the Caribbean.

Thus, the new vision of modern Sikh historiography here that I gesture toward calls into question the rigid divisions commonly drawn between the colonial period and the age of the diaspora, and it highlights the various forms of mobility that have shaped Sikh experiences. It also underlines the importance of encounters, both within and outside South Asia, in shaping Sikh identity. Although Kenneth Jones and Himadri Banerjee have explored some of the important intellectual connections between Bengal and Punjab, we still know relatively little about the experiences of Sikhs living in other parts of South Asia. This leaves significant gaps in our understanding of the relationship between Sikhs and the project of building a national Indian culture, and it means that some crucial processes, such as the Punjabization of Delhi, remain largely unexplored.[60] Similar questions can be raised about the scholarship on the diaspora, where much work has focused on the development of community institutions and relations with the "host" state rather than assessing the ways in which Sikh identities have been shaped by daily encounters with non-Sikhs. Thus much work on the diaspora continues to treat Sikhs as a self-sufficient community insulated from other individuals and collectivities. As a result, relations between Sikhs and other prominent South Asian diasporic communities, such as Gujaratis and Sylhetis, go unexplored; the encounters between diasporic Sikhs and Asian, Afro-Caribbean, and European migrant communities remain uncharted; and the broader social contexts that have shaped modern Sikh life continue to be inadequately studied.

## Conclusion

By urging a move toward a mobile and transnational history of Sikhism, this essay encourages historians of Sikhism to engage with broader debates in history, anthropology, sociology, and gender studies. This is not to suggest that Sikh studies should shift its focus from addressing the Panth. Rather, in this chapter in particular and the volume as a whole I argue for what might be termed "Janus-faced" scholarship—an approach that is attentive both to the historical questions that interest Sikhs and the epistemological, methodological, and theoretical debates that animate humanities scholarship more generally. By recovering the various forms of cultural traffic and diverse encounters that have molded the Panth, such an approach is not only more in keeping with recent directions in historiography that are sensitive to cross-cultural contact, but also recognizes that although the Panth is united by its devotion to the gurus and the Guru Granth Sahib, Sikhs occupy diverse cultural locations and articulate a multiplicity of identities. The recognition of the cultural exchanges and hybridized social patterns borne out of the inequalities of colonialism and the upheavals of migration necessitates the creation of new historiographical visions and forms of practice.

# 2

# Entangled Pasts: Colonialism, Mobility, and the Systematization of Sikhism

One of the central debates in the study of South Asian history is about the nature of social change under colonialism and the degree to which the British colonial project reshaped, consolidated, or even invented key aspects of South Asian social structures and cultural life. To date, these debates have mainly focused on the changing status of caste in the nineteenth century and the extent to which communal identities were the product of colonialism. Much of this literature focuses on Bengal, the Hindi-speaking belt, and those portions of India with a settled Hindu majority, and as a result it makes scant reference to Punjab, a region where many of the understandings of "Indian" society that were formulated in port cities or on the Gangetic plains foundered. Nineteenth-century Punjab's distinctly mixed population, with its sizable Hindu and Sikh minorities coexisting with a Muslim majority community, destabilized many of the stock images of "Hindu" India. This was a region where British administrators found a mobile population reshaped by trade, migration and war rather than a "timeless" social order, where key social groups valorized martial values instead of the supposedly effeminate tendencies that the British were quick to identify in most South Asians (especially Bengalis), and where colonial officials found many "stout" meat eaters rather than the "weak" vegetarians they believed to be the norm in South India, in temple towns, and in large urban centers.[1] Punjab's relatively "flat" social structure, the dominance of the Jat agriculturalists and Sikhism's explicit repudiation of caste (at least in theory) were also at odds with the classical varna model of caste, which supposedly divided society into a four-tiered hierarchy, that many colonial officials believed ordered Indian society.

Although Punjab has not figured significantly in the historiography on British orientalism in India, there have been parallel discussions of the "production" of tradition within Punjabi history. This historiography focuses on the redefinition of Sikh identity between 1870 and 1925 when new reform movements were established (especially the Singh Sabha); community leaders pushed for the recognition of Sikhism's status as a separate religion; and many Sikhs argued for a greater stake in the management of holy sites (especially Darbar Sahib). Rather than being the product of recent debates within Indian historiography over the history of communalism or reflecting the Foucauldian turn within Subaltern Studies, this scholarship on religion in colonial Punjab has emerged out of the efforts of several generations of Sikhs and historians (both Sikh and non-Sikh) to make sense of the feverish late-nineteenth-century exchanges between pamphleteers, preachers, and politicians over cultural boundaries within the region. Since the pioneering work of Kenneth Jones and N. G. Barrier reconstructed the basic contours of Punjabi politics in the colonial period, most scholars have agreed that Sikh identities were significantly redefined under British rule.[2]

But the processes through which these colonial transformations were enacted remain fiercely contested. As noted in chapter 1, Richard Fox has argued that the British played a central role in constituting the orthodox "Singh" (i.e., Khalsa) identity with the aim of forming a much-needed bulwark to British authority. Fox suggests that the British promoted "Sikhism as a separate religion and [the] Singh as a separate social identity," thereby effectively creating a new Sikh "culture" and consequently solidifying the boundaries between religious communities.[3] By framing his approach to Sikh history within such a reductive view of cultural change under colonialism, Fox's history of Sikh identity is historically thin as it neglects the importance of martial symbols associated with the "Singh" identity under colonialism (for example, the five weapons or the symbolic weight attached to swords in the doctrine of *miri-piri*) in the precolonial Panth, as well as entirely overlooks the importance of the prescriptive *rahit-nama* tradition that predated the onset of colonialism by more than a century.[4]

Harjot Oberoi's *The Construction of Religious Boundaries* was a welcome corrective to Fox's truncated vision of Sikh history. While Oberoi located the rise of the Singh Sabha movement against the backdrop of colonialism, he placed primary stress on the ability of Punjabi elites and propagandists to reorder identity along communal lines. Oberoi's sophisticated "internalist" approach to the Sikh past focused on developments within the Panth, detailing the clash between two factions of the Singh Sabha movement that emerged in the 1870s. In so doing he highlighted the clash between the latitudinarian spirit of Sanatan Sikhs (who were sympathetic to idol worship, pilgrimage, the authority of "Hindu" scripture, and many rural traditions) and the systematized religious vision of the Tat Khalsa. In his work Oberoi suggested that this faction of the Singh Sabha was able to inscribe clear lines between *kes-dharis* (Sikhs who kept their hair uncut) and other Sikhs by insisting on the maintenance of a cluster of new rituals and social practices as markers of a distinctive and self-contained community.

In this chapter I offer a rereading of cultural change under colonialism with the aim of making three interventions in Punjabi historiography. First, I relocate the transformation of Sikh identity within a larger temporal and spatial frame than is typically used for the discussion of the transformation of Sikhism under colonialism. The overwhelming weight of research on colonial Punjab focuses on the period between the 1870s (which were marked by the rise of the Singh Sabha and the Arya Samaj) and the 1925 Gurdwara Reform Act. Here I recontextualize this period of what might be called "mature colonialism" by framing the development of the colonial state from 1849 against the precolonial period and the understandings of Punjab and Sikhism generated by the East India Company prior to the annexation of the province. Particular emphasis is placed on the ways in which this "precolonial knowledge" formed the basis for colonial policy toward Sikhism in the 1850s, a neglected period that saw the elaboration of the colonial state's understanding of Sikhism and the creation of the key interfaces between the colonial state and the various communities that were brought under its umbrella. In this chapter I also reframe the colonial encounter within an enlarged spatial frame. Rather than treating the history of colonialism and the "diaspora" as separate concerns, I see these histories as heavily entwined. While I do not produce a comprehensive overview of the early development of overseas Sikh communities, I do highlight the divergent economic contexts and social formations that were navigated by Sikhs on the move.

Given these concerns, the second contribution that I make toward an understanding of colonialism in Punjab is that of rematerializing the diverse sites and methods through which Punjabis and the colonial state engaged with each other. If we accept that important changes were enacted or at least unleashed by the colonial state, any history of the Khalsa and the Sikh identity must take seriously the role of the British. Unfortunately, although Oberoi makes effective use of a range of colonial sources, *The Construction of Religious Boundaries* provides limited insight into the cultural assumptions and values of the British. Therefore, an important aim here is to recover the intellectual world of the British; that is, to understand the function of, and tensions within, their cultural values and to approach the British side of the colonial encounter with the same sensitivity to differentiation and conflict that characterizes the rich historiography on the interaction between Arya Samajis, Sanatanis, and Tat Khalsa reformers and the various Muslim groups of the Punjab. To date, the weight of the work done on colonialism in Punjab focuses on agrarian policy and the place of the Punjabi peasant in the "official mind." While much of this work is suggestive, its rather narrow focus sheds little light on the broad contours of the cultural projects of colonialism, and thus it tends to mark off the history of the colonizer and colonized as separate domains.

In attempting to recover the shifting points of contact and contention between Britons and Punjabis, my third overarching argument focuses on the centrality of "religion" as a heuristic tool in this imperial contact zone. Following P. J. Marshall's and Romila Thapar's examination of the production of the category of "Hinduism," Oberoi noted that Europeans tended to construct images of Indian religions in the mold of Christianity, stressing that the "isms"—Hinduism and Sikhism—were largely the product of the European intellectual frameworks of the late Enlightenment.[5] However, Oberoi does not delineate these frameworks in sufficient detail: in *The Construction of Religious Boundaries,* Punjabi values and traditions are anthropologized more consistently and rigorously than British mentalities. In tracing the growing purchase of "religion" as a lens for making sense of cultural difference; highlighting how "religion" was produced as a category in various colonial texts (district gazetteers, the census, recruitment manuals); and identifying the various mechanisms (such as military recruitment) through which the colonial state reproduced religious identities, in this chapter I reveal the growing investment of a range of Punjabi groups in a very particular vision of "religion." However, I conclude by revealing the limits of these attempts to textualize and systematize Sikhism as I explore the early history of Punjabi migration outside of India as well as the emergence of a range of heterodox identities within this emerging diaspora as Sikhs quickly adapted to the varying positions they found themselves occupying in Southeast Asia, Australasia, and North America. By highlighting this tension between cultural adaptation and systematization, I locate "religion" at the heart of the colonial encounter in Punjab and in the emergence of a global Panth at the turn of the twentieth century.

## Precolonial Encounters and the "Discovery" of Sikhism

Considerable scholarly attention has been devoted to early European accounts of Sikhs and Sikhism, especially those produced by British diplomats and travelers between the 1780s and the annexation of Punjab in 1849. Much of this scholarship has been "corrective" in orientation, motivated by an understandable desire to rectify some of the earlier misapprehensions that continue to mold the understanding of Sikhism by outsiders (for example, the common assertion that Nanak was essentially a syncretist who blended Hinduism and Islam). This tradition reached its apogee in Ganda Singh's important edited collection *Early European Ac-*

*counts of Sikhism,* a work whose footnotes provide a critical running commentary on the shortcomings of European representations of Sikhism. The corrective tradition has, however, two limitations. First, there is a danger that such works become an exercise in anachronism, as contemporary views on Sikh mores, social practices, and history are used unquestioningly as a framework for the assessment of European texts, thereby dehistoricizing Sikhism. Second, the tradition fails to explain why Europeans represented Sikhism in the ways in which they did, and as such it offers limited insight into the cultural influence and political weight of these texts.

From the early 1780s, the East India Company built an increasingly dense archive of information on both Punjab itself and on Sikhism. This material was significant because it not only shaped the diplomatic relationships between the Company and Ranjit Singh (and his heirs) but also provided a substantial knowledge base on which the colonial state could draw as it formed its vision of Punjabi history and formulated its policies on a range of issues. Most importantly, it is in these early texts that the British formulated a vision of Sikhism as a self-contained, independent, and coherent religious system. According to Oberoi, this way of seeing Punjabi society abstracted "religion" and "religious communities" from the "complex idiom[s] of kinship, patron-client relationships and [the forms of] asymmetrical reciprocity" that he has identified as mediating and determining "religious traditions" in nineteenth-century Punjab.[6]

The earliest British account of Sikhism, *The History of the Origin and Progress of the Sikhs,* was produced by Major James Browne who served as the East India Company's personal agent at the court of Shah Alam in Delhi between 1782 and 1785.[7] This text, which ultimately was published in 1788 by the company, was born out of British anxieties about Sikh resistance to Mughal imperial hegemony. Browne garnered what information he could about "the people called Sicks" through the intelligence he was able to access at the Mughal court as well as through "other channels" he acquired.[8] The most significant of these alternative resources was a Persian text produced for him by Buddh Singh Arora of Lahore.[9] On the basis of Buddh Singh's text, Browne surmised that Nanak's religion appeared "to bear that kind of relation to the Hindoo religion, which the Protestant does to the Romish."[10] Browne's description of Sikhism as a reformed Hinduism established an interpretative framework that dominated Sikh studies until the early twentieth century. Sikhism was consistently seen as an improvement on the Hindu tradition, as it seemed to break away from the polytheism, idolatry, and caste sensitivities that British observers believed retarded the development of India's Hindu population.

Other British observers quickly confirmed the outlines of Browne's argument, most notably Charles Wilkins, whose sketch of Sikhism was also published in 1788. For Wilkins, Nanak's reforming vision created a new religion grounded in a belief in "one God, omnipotent and omnipresent." Nanak's monotheistic teachings had a strong moral component, as "there will be a day of retribution, when virtue will be rewarded and vice punished."[11] What is striking about these earliest British accounts of Sikhism is the deployment of Protestant terminology and explicitly European points of reference to make sense of Sikhism. When Browne and Wilkins saw Sikhs in the late eighteenth century, they recognized elements of themselves. At a moment when Protestantism was becoming fundamental to both regional and national identities within the United Kingdom, these East India Company men were delighted to find that the spirit of Protestantism existed in India too.[12]

In the early nineteenth century, the leading administrator and historian John Malcolm placed greater emphasis on Nanak's debt to the Hindu tradition, but once again Nanak was represented as a "reformer" who sought to rid the Hindu tradition of the accretions of polytheism, superstition, and idolatry.[13] Once established by these three influential early texts, the "Sikhism as Reformation" metaphor was one of the great stock passages in British analyses of Indian religion. Most importantly, J. D. Cunningham reiterated this argument in his sympathetic and controversial 1849 account of Sikhism. He identified Nanak as an heir to a tradition of medieval Hindu reform in north India, but noted that Nanak's reform was more comprehensive, compelling, and effective. While "Ramanand and Gorakh had repeated that faith leveled caste, [and] Kabir had denounced images and appealed to the people in their own tongue," these earlier reformers were, in Cunningham's view, "so impressed with the nothingness of this life, that they deemed the amelioration of man's social condition to be unworthy of a thought."[14] Of all the Hindu reformers, Nanak alone was able to "perceive the true principles of reform," and the resulting reformed creed of Sikhism continued to be, in Cunningham's time, "an active and living principle."[15] This recurrent emphasis on the energy of Sikhism, on its rejection of hierarchies and its simplicity, meant that the British vision of Sikhism was highly gendered. While British observers did identify the treatment of women as an important index of civilization, they offered only limited accounts and shallow analysis of the position of Sikh women. In part, this marginalization of women reflected the greater prominence of men in the domains of Punjabi life that British observers had access to (especially those relating to war and diplomacy), as well as the particular codings attached to gender by the early British travelers in Punjab. These British writers were drawn to Sikhism's monotheism, its rejection of idols and priests, and its repudiation of caste, and they read these elements of Sikh practice as underpinning the masculine restraint that they saw as characteristic of Sikhism. As a result, colonial texts typically framed Sikhism as a simple masculine faith, defined by its martial sensibility and the visibility of the turbaned kes-dhari male, within a religious landscape dominated by the supposed effeminacy of Hinduism and Islam's despotic patriarchy.

## Contextualizing Sikhism as a "Religion"

While these nineteenth-century interpretations were always influenced by British access to reservoirs of indigenous knowledge,[16] they were also molded by a complex set of assumptions about the nature of religion, the structure of religious communities, and the pattern of Christian history. Within the existing historiography, there has been a strong tendency to view British discourses on Sikh tradition and identity within a self-contained analytical field, reflecting the emergence of both "Punjab studies" and "Sikh studies" as areas of scholarly specialty within the modern academy. However, this dangerous abstraction dislocates British discussions of Sikhism from the broader contexts of British colonial knowledge, European understandings of Hindu tradition, and the religious and social values of the British colonizers. In particular, it is essential to locate British understandings of Sikhism within a broader set of imperial discourses on "religion."

In light of this, we need to begin by briefly examining what Britons understood by the term "religion." Most importantly, we must recognize that the notions of "religion" deployed by British observers in Punjab were the relatively recent product of debates within European culture and its encounters with traditions beyond Europe's borders.[17] As Talal Asad has emphasized, although religion is commonly understood as a "trans-historical and transcultural phenomenon," "its constituent elements and relationships are historically specific" and its very definition is "the historical product of discursive processes."[18] Indeed, these discursive processes have been at work over the *longue durée* of Christian history. The modern concept of "religion" emerged slowly and unevenly out of debates within Christian communities and European encounters with non-European cultural forms, ritual practices, and textual traditions. For making sense of British understandings of Punjabi culture, it is important to appreciate the ways in which the Enlightenment systematized and "enlightened" Christianity. Recent work within British history, especially by David Bebbington, Roy Porter, and Alun David, has stressed both the Protestant framework of the British Enlightenment and the influence of Enlightenment thought on British Protestantism. Rather than seeing the Enlightenment as marking the onset of Christianity's demise in the wake of the emergence of new secular knowledge and moral systems, this revisionist work has stressed the centrality of "enlightened" Christianity in shaping British understandings of cultural variation, religious difference, and the human condition.[19]

Most importantly, however, Peter Harrison's work on religion in the English Enlightenment has made it clear that the shift in meaning of "religion" from "faith" or "piety" to "religion" as a "system of beliefs" during the seventeenth and eighteenth centuries should be seen as the outcome of heated post-Reformation doctrinal debates within the Protestant tradition. In an Enlightenment age of classification and taxonomies, Protestants increasingly imagined "religion" as a series of propositions or beliefs that could be simply summarized and even conveyed in the form of a chart or diagram.[20] In this form, religion could be identified as distinct and self-contained, something that could be separated from economics or politics, a definition that has recently been identified as an important move toward the essentialized and increasingly privatized vision of the cultural practices we denote as "religion."[21] The textualization of European culture underpinned this important cultural shift. Protestantism's drive to vernacularize Christianity not only placed greater emphasis on what we might term "scriptural literacy," but also stimulated a proliferation of religious almanacs, devotional texts, household guides, and pamphlets ascribing new models of Christian behavior targeted specifically at women and children.[22] If this process of textualization was central in propagating models of piety and social discipline, print and literacy also played a central role in setting apart the Protestant tradition from magic, paganism, and Catholicism, with its "idols," sacramental "magic," and "priestly ritual."[23]

If this new understanding of "religion" as a system of beliefs, practices, and institutions was molded by Protestant practice and propaganda, encounters with non-Christian communities were another crucial context for delineating the nature of religion. Questions of religious belief and practice were prominent in traveler's accounts, the letters and journals of explorers, missionaries, and merchants, and the correspondence of political envoys. These encounters in the "contact zone" of the imperial frontier provided opportunities for the analysis of new and unfamiliar belief systems, thus creating analytical spaces both for the reevaluation of Christianity and for the discussion of the nature of religion at a general or theoretical level.[24] "Religion" itself was frequently elusive in these encounters, as Europeans attempted to map this concept onto the cultures they encountered. But these attempts to universalize religion as a category of analysis were frequently problematic, as cultural forms such as *tapu* (in conjuncture with the supernatural, inviolate) in the Pacific or *dharma* (duty, obligation, virtue) in South Asia were not exact synonyms for "religion."[25] The incommensurability of these cultural key words forcibly remind us that "religion" was never a self-evident and trans-cultural category awaiting discovery. Rather, it was the product of complex acts of translation, codification, and social reform that outlined core beliefs, stipulated normative forms of practice, and delineated the boundaries of the believing community.

Within Punjab, there was considerable debate among early European observers over the relationship between Sikhism and Hinduism, but there was no doubt that Sikhism was a "religion" (even if it was closely related to Hinduism). Given the prominence of gurdwaras, Guru Granth Sahib, granthis, and the sangat in Sikh practice, British observers had no problem in viewing Sikhism as a "religion" because these structures could be translated as places of worship, as scripture, as priests, and as a congregation—that is, as key elements of any "religious system." Yet this approach tended to abstract "religion" from the complex set of kinship, economic, and political relationships that were central to Punjabi life. As such, this is a striking feature of the British texts when they are read against Ganesh Das's early-nineteenth-century text *Char Bagh-i-Panjab,* a work that embedded Sikhism firmly within the geographic frameworks of Punjabi life and in the political history of the region, or when they are seen as a counterpoint to Pandit Debi Prasad's *Gulshan-i-Punjab,* a history of Punjab from the birth of Nanak that foregrounded Sikhism's enmeshment with the developing Punjabi polity.[26]

## Sikhism, Hinduism, and the "Indian Reformation"

Britons also framed their understandings of Sikhism within a more particular series of imperial debates about the relationship between religion and rationality, the nature of Hinduism, and the history of Protestantism itself. Most obviously, the "Sikhism as a Reformation" trope set Sikhism against the religious traditions of North India that Europeans came to know as "Hinduism," even though Islam was a powerful force in shaping the cultural terrain of the Punjab. In deploying this narrative, British commentators framed Sikhism as an improvement of the increasingly degenerate forms of belief and ritual that they believed to characterize popular Hinduism. While late-eighteenth-century orientalists praised the beauty of Sanskrit, the sophistication of the Vedas, and the ancient wisdom of the Brahmans, they expressed doubts over the faith of the masses. The influential East India Company publicist and historian Luke Scrafton, for

example, suggested that Brahmans believed in a single Supreme God and
their monotheistic creed was pure and admirable. However, these high
truths were beyond the reaches of the simple folk who struggled to understand the subtle sophistication of monotheism. Thus, the Brahmans relied
heavily on images and idols, believing that "sensible objects were neces-
sary" for teaching "the vulgar" masses.[27] In a similar vein, the leading
Sankritist Charles Wilkins argued that although there was an elite Hindu
belief in "the unity of the Godhead," popular Hinduism was a crude and
ignorant code based on "idolatrous sacrifices."[28]

The dichotomy between "high" and "popular" forms of religion that
ordered British interpretations of Hinduism drew on the Brahmanic opposition between *vaidik* (Vedic, or high) and *laukik* (popular, or low)
practice and reflected the degenerationist nature of Brahmanic understandings of history.[29] But as Evangelicalism and Utilitarianism emerged
as powerful forces in British culture, both at home and overseas, the value
attached to Brahmanic traditions was undercut. Although the British
Evangelical revival had its origins in the late 1730s and early 1740s, it was
only in the 1790s that its vision consistently turned beyond the shores of
Britain. William Carey's *An Enquiry into the Obligations of Christians, to
Use Means for the Conversion of the Heathens* (1792) provided a strong theo-
logical justification for targeting missionary activity at non-Europeans,
and thus functioned as a rallying cry for the globalization of Evangelical
Protestantism through voluntary missionary societies that would carry
the "good news" to Africa, Asia, and the Pacific.[30] Evangelical printing
presses produced numerous pamphlets and essays identifying social and
religious evils in distant lands—cannibalism in New Zealand, marriage by
capture in Australia, slavery in Africa, foot binding in China, polygamy in
the Muslim world, and *sati* in India. Within this literature, the elements of
polytheism, superstition, and idolatry were now depicted as the core of
Hinduism and thus overshadowed the vigor of the high textual tradition
of Sanskrit.[31] Hinduism, like all other heathen creeds, was perceived as a
stronghold for Satan. Charles Grant's "Observations on the State of Society among the *Asiatic* Subjects of *Great Britain*" (1796) signaled this shift
in understanding; after returning from India, Grant wrote "Observations" as an attack on British orientalism, and he advocated an aggressive

program of company-sponsored Christianization.[32] Hinduism was thus
marked as a polytheistic creed whose gods were given to sexual profligacy;
where worship was tainted by signs of sexual corruption (as seen in temple
prostitutes or the adoration of Shiva *lingam*); and where Brahmans ("a
crafty and imperious priesthood") enslaved the masses and underwrote
the despotic rule of Indian tyrants.[33] By the 1830s, many British officials,
travelers, and missionaries routinely dismissed Hinduism as an assem-
blage of "horrid rites" and a "fabric of superstitions," and it was against
this backdrop that nineteenth-century Europeans understood Sikhism.[34]
For British observers, Nanak's attacks on idolatry, pilgrimage, and slavish
devotion to religious authorities echoed powerful strands in Protestant
tradition, while the gurus' rejection of caste embodied in the brotherhood
of the Khalsa freed its members from an inherently conservative socio-
religious institution that crushed innovation.

As noted earlier in the case of Browne and Wilkins, the continued
centrality of Protestantism in British identity and the importance of anti-
Catholicism in the British imagination molded British accounts of Sikhism. Over the past fifteen years, historians have paid closer attention to the
role of religion in British history, and numerous studies have documented
the pivotal role of Protestantism as an idiom for articulating an emergent
and contested "British" identity after the union with Scotland (1707) and
Ireland (1800). Raymond Tumbleston, for example, has argued that after
the break with Rome in the sixteenth century, "England had to conquer
its Catholic heritage to reinvent itself as a Protestant nation."[35] By the
early nineteenth century British Protestants felt that this need had become
urgent as the gradual expansion of the Catholic (both Irish and "native")
population within Britain and the Bourbon restoration in France suggested a Catholic resurgence was at hand.[36] The war against Catholicism
was seen as a global battle that was fought in the South Pacific, in Asia, in
Ireland, and in the cities of industrial Britain: the power of the Pope had
to be combated, the influence of the priesthood thwarted, and the spread
of idolatry prevented.[37]

These concerns shaped British reactions to Indian culture. Just as
British Protestants attacked the Catholic veneration of the Virgin Mary
and argued that the Catholic belief in the intercession of the saints was

idolatrous, they dismissed Hinduism as superstitious idolatry. Arguments condemning priestly power, the debauched sexuality of monasteries, and Catholic ritual were easily turned against popular Hinduism.[38] British Evangelical missionaries, who were often in competition with Catholic rivals, believed their brand of Christianity would bring about moral and religious regeneration in India, in the same manner that it was the perfect antidote to Catholic superstition and corruption. Evangelicalism would create an egalitarian, moral, and religious society, and as such it was to be a vehicle for global reform and religious renewal. Claudius Buchanan, a company chaplain and a strong advocate of the evangelization of India, argued that missionary activity was central to India's future: Christianity had to replace the abominable practices of Hinduism. Buchanan believed that Hinduism was characterized by "horrid rites" that were even more offensive than the "inhuman practices" to be found among the "savages" of New Zealand.[39]

Of course, as noted above, many British writers perceived Sikhism as a vast improvement on the excesses of popular Hinduism and even on the superstitions of Catholicism. The influential evangelical essayist and judicial commissioner of Punjab, Robert Needham Cust, produced the first biography of Guru Nanak in English (a work that has been curiously neglected by historians). This text, *The Life of Baba Nanak*, argued that Nanak's teachings established that he "must be considered truly Good as well as truly Great." Nanak, in fact, was an instrument of God: "We cannot but admit, that he was one of those, on whom the Almighty has vouched safe special blessings . . . he laboured unceasingly . . . to reform the lives and religion of his countrymen, to break through the tyranny of Priestcraft, outward Ritual, and Caste. He taught that purity of thought, word and deed, abstinence from Lust, Anger, and Avarice, were better than feeding Brahmins, or making offerings at Temples."[40] Although Cust believed that Nanak's followers failed to establish Sikhism as a fully independent religious tradition, he stressed that Nanak, like Luther and Calvin, attempted to break free from the excesses of idolatry and priestly power of the established tradition. Cust hoped that the colonial state could aid Sikhism in achieving its potential by promoting a clear and systematized vision of the "religion" and endorsing only correct forms of

social practice. Most importantly, rational scholarship (such as his own biography) and the production of new editions of Sikhism's "sacred books"
would allow Sikhs to realize the "precepts of their great Teacher."

Cust's text clearly demonstrates the ways in which British visions of
Punjabi society were produced out of a complex array of comparisons and
inflected by understandings of the British past itself. This underscores not
only the intersections between British and Punjabi histories but also the
ways in which the construction of cross-cultural affinities (between Sikhs
and Britons, for example) actually rested on the "othering" of other communities. Following the thrust of David Cannadine's *Ornamentalism*, we
might seize on this praise of Nanak and the identification of Sikhism as
the most rational of Indian faiths to demonstrate that colonialism did not
rest upon "othering."[41] But such a reading would be possible only if we
ignored the ways in which this celebration of Sikhs and Sikhism depended on the depiction of popular Hinduism as an all-consuming jungle
and the constant use of the "effeminate" Bengali and caste-bound Brahman as crucial points of contrast to the Sikh. The construction of cross-
cultural affinities was a power-saturated strategy, one that produced a
host of "others" in the drive to delineate the common ground between the
colonizer and a particular colonized group.

## The Colonial State and Sikhism

Cust's account of the life of Nanak was part of a series of biographies
designed for use in Punjabi schools. Other volumes in the series focused
on Saint Paul and on Rama, while volumes on Muhammad, Buddha, and
Krishna followed Cust's *Baba Nanuk*. As part of the colonial state's support of "useful knowledge" as an important tool that would both en-
lighten and discipline Indians, this text is a clear example of the colonial
state's support for Sikhism. Although the outlook of key company administrators in Punjab was shaped by evangelicalism and the emergence
of "muscular Christianity" (which one might suppose would produce a
strong commitment to Christianizing Punjabi society), these administrators were consistently concerned with the state of Sikhism and Sikh
communities, and were especially so after the company annexed the king-

dom in 1849.[42] Much of the work on colonialism in Punjab has focused on the period between 1875 and 1925, with narratives that view social change under colonialism through the emergence of the Singh Sabhas and the Arya Samaj. In reality, the 1850s were crucial in securing Sikhism a privileged place in the British "official mind" and in establishing state practices in relationship to religion.

Company concerns over the future of Sikhism were a strong feature of the series of general reports produced by the province's administration in the 1850s. John Lawrence, the chief commissioner for the Punjab, suggested that the

> Seikh faith and ecclesiastical polity is rapidly going where the Seikh political ascendancy has already gone. Of the two elements in the Old Khalsa, namely, the followers of Nanuck, the first prophet, and the followers of Gooroo Govind, the second great religious leader, the former will hold their ground and the latter will lose it. The Seikhs of Nanuck, a comparatively small body of peaceful habits and old family, will perhaps cling to the faith of their fathers; but the Seikhs of Govind, who are of more recent origin, who are more specially styled the *Singhs* or "Lions," and who embraced the faith as being the religion of warfare and conquest, no longer regard the Khalsa, not that the *prestige* has departed from it. These men joined in thousands, and now they desert in equal numbers. They rejoin the ranks of Hindooism whence they originally came, and they bring up their children as Hindoos.[43]

The fate of Sikhism concerned administrators like Lawrence for two reasons. First, they accepted the arguments that identified Sikhism as the product of an "Indian Reformation" and hoped to foster a faith that they saw as embodying the most progressive and rational spirit of Indian civilization. Second, they also believed that they needed to protect Sikhism to secure their rule. David Gilmartin has traced the relationship between the colonial state and Sufism in colonial Punjab by highlighting the attempts of the colonial state to use Sufi *pir*s (renowned teachers), who exercised considerable power in rural Punjab, to help project and protect British authority.[44] In a similar vein, the company's "Punjab Commission" moved quickly to stabilize relationships with the Darbar Sahib, initially appointing Extra-Assistant Commissioner Sardar Jodh Singh to oversee the management of the Golden Temple. Although, as Ian Kerr has noted, administrators occasionally questioned the connection between the government and holy sites, this relationship was integral to the British search for a stable relationship with the Sikh community.[45] In fact, the British administration also devoted considerable financial resources to supporting the Golden Temple (and its attendant institutions) and other key religious centers, thereby in effect maintaining many of the practices of Ranjit Singh.[46] Although the company suspended the *jagirs* (rent-free grants of land) of "rebel" Sikh leaders such as Jawahar Singh and banished others like Raja Sher Singh in the wake of their annexation of Punjab, they continued to dispense jagirs and pensions to large numbers of the Sikh elite that had prospered under Ranjit Singh.[47]

The colonial state in Punjab also cautiously adopted courtly practices such as the dispensing of *khilat* (gifts of incorporation) and the holding of *darbars* (ceremonial gatherings) that had long been established in north Indian kingdoms such as that of Ranjit Singh. Reinvented under British rule, these symbolic displays were integral to the representation of colonial authority in the region.[48] At the same time, under the lieutenant-governorships of Robert Montgomery and Donald McLeod, the colonial state also opened up new channels for Sikhs to participate in the lower levels of government, thus allowing Punjabis to take a "goodly part in the management of their own affairs."[49] These policies reflected both the state's conviction that Sikhism occupied a special position in Punjabi society and an awareness that this was a community that had to be both monitored and mollified, given its independent spirit and military prowess.

## Imperial Fault Lines: Critiques of the Colonial State and Sikhism

Even in the Punjab, where of all regions in British India it appeared that the administration was unified by a common set of policy objectives and an ethos molded by "muscular Christianity," there was debate over the nature of the indigenous communities as well as considerable criticism of the state's policies—including its support of Sikhism. It is through these debates over religious responsibilities of the colonial state that we can explore what Jeffrey Cox has termed "imperial fault lines"—that is, the points of conflict over religion that dramatize the contradictions of the colonizing culture.[50] Even though leading members of the "Punjab school," such as Herbert Edwardes, argued that the East India Company was an agent of providence in India and thus appealed to Christianity to justify British rule in Punjab, these administrators remained committed to preserving the central social structures that underpinned Punjabi society, including its long-established religious traditions. Many missionaries and evangelicals in Britain were frustrated by this reluctance to support the Christianization of Punjabi society. At the heart of the resulting exchanges over the colonial state's policies relating to religion and culture was the very nature of Punjabi religious traditions themselves. We have already seen that Robert Needham Cust, the leading evangelical essayist and colonial administrator, suggested that Nanak's teachings contained glimmerings of the revelation, and this argument was also articulated by some of the missionaries stationed in Punjab. One female missionary from the Church of Scotland, for example, argued that the Sikhs were "surely a chosen people, meant to inherit the gift of eternal life, with many other nations who shall at that day be found saved, and walking in the Light of the Lamb."[51]

But even though some British observers praised Nanak as a reformer of medieval Hinduism, most evangelical observers believed that Sikhism was still too close to Hindu tradition to merit any praise. In July 1851, soon after the annexation of Punjab and the publication of Cunningham's sympathetic account of Sikhism, the leading evangelical periodical, the *Church Missionary Intelligencer*, offered a rather caustic assessment of the newly annexed region. This article was a battle cry for Christian proselytization, and its starting point was an attack on the desiccating effects of Sikhism: "The inhabitants of the Punjab are like the lands around them, which are laying waste for want of irrigation. The Sikh religion cannot benefit them. It has been tried and found worthless." Punjab's future without "the fertilizing stream of the gospel" was bleak. Further, Nanak's vision was "crude and unconnected" and he was too "latitudinarian" to wrench Punjabis free of "the polytheistic tendencies of the Hindu."[52] Sikhs were rapidly being absorbed back into Hinduism and the minimal progress made by Nanak was lost. Even though Sikhism might exhibit some external affinities with Protestantism, the colonial state's support of Sikh tradition was misplaced and stood in the path of Britain's responsibility to Christianize India. The only hope lay in the Gospel, which promised great spiritual rejuvenation and renewal.

Ernest Trumpp, the most powerful nineteenth-century critic of Sikhism, extended the evangelical attacks on Sikh belief. In 1869 the secretary of state for India approached Trumpp, a skilled Tubingen-trained linguist, to begin work on translations of the Kartarpur Granth manuscript of the *Adi Granth* and the *Dasam Granth*.[53] Trumpp's initial enthusiasm for the project soon evaporated, however, when he discovered that he was unable to decipher "a considerable residuum of words and grammatical forms to which I could get no clue," concluding that "native assistance" would be required if his project was to advance.[54] Trumpp thus returned to India in late 1870, where he immediately encountered further problems. The two Sikh granthis he had enlisted to aid him in Lahore warned that the *Granth* could not be translated "in the literal grammatical way" that Trumpp desired, and they were unable to help him with many of the difficult constructions and idioms.[55]

Trumpp decided that his slow progress was entirely the product of the decay of Sikhism: that is, he believed that the Sikhs had "lost all learning," and he felt that he was "frequently . . . misled" by the granthis.[56] But these difficulties were as much a product of Trumpp's own arrogance and insensitivity as they were a product of a decline in the Sikh intelligentsia. Indeed, Trumpp alienated the granthis at Amritsar by blowing cigar smoke over the pages of the *Granth,* which they considered to be the embodiment of the Guru.[57] In the end, after working for eight years, largely independently with limited lexicographical support, Trumpp concluded that the language of the *Granth* was "incoherent and shallow in the extreme, and couched at the same time in dark and perplexing language, in order to cover these defects. It is for us Occidentals a most painful and almost stupefying task, to read only a single Rag."[58]

This disappointment, combined with Trumpp's tense relations with the granthis, the difficulties he faced in translating a heterogeneous text of various dialects into his nonnative English, and his financial squabbles with the Indian government, did not incline Trumpp to create a positive image of Sikhism.[59] He believed that Sikhism was a "reformatory movement" in spirit, but it had completely failed to achieve anything of real religious significance. Trumpp argued that his translation would attract very few readers, as "Sikhism is a waning religion that will soon belong to history."[60] Moreover, he suggested that the *Adi Granth* did not actually represent or shape "the popular notions of the masses." While the Sikh intelligentsia only had a partial understanding of the *Granth,* the "vulgar" Sikhs were not interested in its "lofty metaphysical speculations" as their religion was "concrete and adapted to their every-day wants."[61] He noted that the "vulgar" did not observe many of the injunctions of the *rahit-namas* (codes of conduct): for example, to recite the formal prayer of *ardas* before starting work and recite the hymns of *rahiras* when eating the evening meal.[62] Moreover, for Trumpp, the injunctions of the rahit-namas regarding relations with Muslims revealed "a narrow-minded bigotry and a deep fanatical hatred."[63] In fact, Trumpp argued, the Sikh "reformation" was short-lived and "soon ended up in a new bondage, which was quite as tiresome as that which they had thrown off." This bondage was the "martial spirit" inculcated by Guru Gobind Singh's Khalsa, a military brotherhood largely composed of "rude and ignorant Jats." Further, the Khalsa was not the brotherhood of the "pure," as its members "surpassed their fellow-countrymen in all sorts of vices and debauchery, to which they added a rapacious and overbearing conduct."[64]

Thus, Trumpp struck at the heart of Sikh history and identity. He minimalized the impact of Nanak's teaching, ridiculed the Jats who increasingly dominated the Panth, questioned Sikh morality, and dismissed the *Adi Granth* as an obtuse and juvenile work. Early in his project, he rejected the possibility of working on the *Dasam Granth*. According to Lepel Griffin, the officiating secretary of the Punjab government, Trumpp left Lahore in early 1872 "unwilling to undertake the translation of the Granth of Guru Gobind Singh, which he considers a work which would not repay translation, and which would be, from its puerility and difficulties of style, so distasteful to him as to make it impossible for him to complete the translation."[65]

## Intersecting Interests: Macauliffe and the Tat Khalsa

As N. G. Barrier has pointed out, Trumpp's unapologetic dismissal of Nanak and Sikhism had an influential effect on Sikh mentalities. The publication of Trumpp's text provided a powerful call to arms for a newly emerging Sikh intelligentsia, who were striving to clearly delineate Sikh identity and to represent Nanak's "Reformation" as a clean break from the Hindu tradition.[66] In addition, of course, it was Trumpp's harsh assessment of Sikhism that was an all-important catalyst for M. A. Macauliffe's account of the Khalsa tradition in his volume *The Sikh Religion*. Macauliffe was posted to the Punjab as an Indian Civil Service (ics) officer in 1862 at the age of twenty-five. In 1893 he resigned from the ics after a distinguished career in the Punjab administration, where he served as a deputy commissioner between 1882 and 1884 and as a divisional judge from 1884. Around the mid-1870s, Macauliffe became interested in the ethnography and religious history of the Punjab, and in 1875 his article on the shrine to Sakhi Sarvar in the Suliman Mountains was published in the *Calcutta Review*, which established him as an important interpreter of Sikh tradition and marked the beginning of a distinguished career as an orientalist.[67] Macauliffe's *The Sikh Religion* (six volumes, 1909) created a vision of Sikh scripture and history that has remained tremendously influential within the Sikh Panth.

Macauliffe began the first volume of *The Sikh Religion* by asserting that "the fifteenth century was a period of singular mental and political activity. Both in Europe and India men shook off the torpor of ages, and their minds awoke to the consciousness of intellectual responsibility."[68] This passage echoed his earlier observation that a "great succession of men, the Sikh Gurus" had transformed and purified the Hindu tradition, and that "in them the East shook off the torpor of ages, and unburdened itself of the heavy weight of ultra-conservatism which has paralysed the genius and intelligence of its people. Only those who know India by actual

experience can adequately appreciate the difficulties the Gurus encountered in their efforts to reform and awaken the sleeping nation."[69] The
rhetoric of these passages is extremely revealing. Macauliffe manipulated
stock orientalist images (of India's timelessness, sloth, and cultural decay)
to emphasize the strength and significance of Sikhism. Nanak and his
followers were thus represented as a group animated by a newly discovered religious enthusiasm that allowed them to break out of the spiritual lethargy of medieval Hinduism. British texts produced both before
and after 1849 used these stock devices to construct oppositions within
South Asian cultures, in this case between Hinduism and Sikhism, as well
as between India and Europe. Nineteenth-century European understandings of non-European societies were rarely the product of a simple self
versus other opposition; rather, both contemporary narratives of "universal history" and complex multipoint comparisons were central to the
production of "Sikhism" in the European mind.

These debates surrounding Sikhism as an "Indian Reformation" not
only reflected the continued influence of Christianity on British historical
consciousness in the post-Darwinian age but also the widespread belief
among colonial administrators that there was a "cultural congruence"
between the Sikhs and the British. Simeran Man Singh Gell has suggested
that this was largely underpinned by a belief in the shared Aryan origins of
Punjabis and Britons and, in a similar vein, David Omissi has stressed the
centrality of colonial racial ideologies in shaping the recruitment of Sikhs.
While I agree that race was a crucial idiom of British rule in colonial South
Asia, the perceived similarities between Sikhism and the Protestant tradition were even more influential than racial ideas in shaping British constructions of Punjabi culture.[70] For British observers Nanak's attack on
priestly authority and the promulgation of a monotheistic faith that to
some degree resembled Protestantism, the Khalsa's repudiation of caste
and its war against the "oriental despotism" of the Moguls exhibited beliefs valued by the British. In comparison to the weak, pliant Hindu and
the treacherous, tyrannical Muslim of the popular British imagination,
Sikhs appeared rational, proud, and independent—values that were often
evoked in nineteenth-century discussions of British history and identity.
Of course, one must recognize that there were profound dissimilarities be-

tween Nanak's vision of God and that of Luther, and that Sikh and Protestant visions of religious authority diverge at important points, but the reality of cultural congruence was not as important as the perception of it.

In colonial Punjab there was one very important vision shared by Tat Khalsa reformers and British administrators: their understanding of "popular Hinduism" as corrupt and degenerate. As demonstrated above, the British believed that popular Hinduism was an all-consuming jungle that threatened to stifle the reforming impulses evident in more "rationalistic" movements such as Sikhism. British scholar-administrators and Tat Khalsa leaders alike feared the decay of Sikhism. The leaders of the Tat Khalsa were fighting battles on several fronts simultaneously; they hoped to popularize their understanding of Sikhism among both Hindus and Sikhs, and as such they championed the use of Punjabi and the "words of the Gurus." When Sanatan Sikhs were sympathetic to the hierarchies and folk traditions of rural Punjab, Tat Khalsa reformers railed against vestiges of caste, popular "superstition," and the pretenses of modern "gurus" and launched educational campaigns to fortify Sikh understandings of their sacred texts and past.[71] Through their *diwans* (meetings), *prachar* (preaching), and numerous pamphlets the Tat Khalsa were desperately trying to have their vision of Sikhism recognized as legitimate by the colonial state and to use the state's practices—especially its emphasis on enumeration and its valorization of history—to cement their authority. In fierce exchanges with Arya Samajis, they struggled to delineate the elements of both orthodoxy and orthopraxy that delineated Sikhs from Hindus, placing particular emphasis on the taking as markers of "true" Sikh identity the *amrit,* the "five Ks," and the turban.[72] The resultant flood of periodical literature, newsletters, substantial works of scholarship, and edited texts produced out of these campaigns enabled members of a literate, urban elite to produce an increasingly refined vision of Sikh history and identity.

This massive body of literature was generated by an eruption of cultural energy and was marked by a sense of crisis. Sikh leaders were concerned about the large number of Christian missionaries who had become active in the province in the wake of annexation and about the perceived cultural and political dominance of Punjab's majority Muslim population. In addition, there were worries about the great power that folk religious practice continued to exert over many Sikhs in the Punjabi countryside. Gyani Ditt Singh, for example, remained deeply concerned about the ways in which many Sikhs, especially the uneducated and the agriculturalists, remained attached to both the mother goddess and the *pir* (renowned Sufi saint) Sakhi Sarvar.[73] Even after the establishment of the Singh Sabhas, these anxieties about the maintenance of "orthodox" Sikhism were voiced by British officials as well. In the wake of the 1881 census, the leading colonial ethnographer Denzil Ibbetson suggested that key elements of traditional Sikh practice were perishing: "The daily reading and recital of the Granth is discontinued. . . . The precepts which forbid the Sikh to venerate Brahmans or to associate himself with Hindu worship are entirely neglected . . . while in current superstitions and superstitious practices there is no difference between the Sikh villager and his Hindu brother."[74] In the mid-1880s, an officer from Ambala District reported with concern that the Sikhs in his area were "given to eating large quantities of opium, drinking *bhang,* and smoking *charas.*"[75] In a similar vein, the missionary Henry Martyn Clark noted in *Panjab Notes and Queries* that he had encountered a group of seasonal workers who observed the injunctions of the rahit at home, but would cut their hair and openly smoke when they were working away from their villages. Surely this was evidence of the decay of Sikhism?[76] Many Sikhs shared these anxieties and hoped that the colonial state would foster the regeneration of Sikhism and shore up the position of their community within the political landscape of colonial Punjab. Within this context, Macauliffe's work was extremely important as it produced a coherent vision of Sikhism, one that European orientalists and the colonial state quickly recognized as an authoritative work. Some leading Sikh intellectuals hoped that Macauliffe's *Sikh Religion* would act as a buttress to their community. The *Khalsa,* a leading Sikh periodical, proclaimed that as a result of Macauliffe's translation "the promiscuousness in Sikh ideas will vanish, and Tat (pure) Khalsa will begin to start on a new career."[77]

This brings us back to Macauliffe and his relationship with the Sikh elite. Macauliffe insisted that Sikhism was a distinctive religion and that its history was characterized by a constant battle against Hinduism. Popular Hinduism, he argued, was like a "boa constrictor of the Indian forests. . . . it winds round its opponents, crushes it in its fold, and finally causes it to disappear in its capacious interior." Sikhism was threatened with this same fate: "The still comparatively young religion is making a vigorous struggle for life, but its ultimate destruction is . . . inevitable without state support."[78] In a lecture titled "The Sikh Religion and Its Advantages to the State," which he delivered to the United Services Institution of India, Macauliffe argued that the interests of the colonial state were served by fostering the Khalsa and the distinctiveness of the kes-dhari Sikh. To the large audience of Sikh notables, colonial administrators, and military officers assembled in Simla, Macauliffe again stressed that Sikhism was borne out of the same historical forces that produced the Protestant tradition, that "great cyclic wave of reformation [that] overspread both continents."[79] Sikhism's monotheism, rationality, and rejection of caste set it apart from Hinduism, and Sikh religious teaching itself was crucial in producing strong, manly, and trustworthy soldiers. Sikhism's rejection of caste encouraged self-reliance, the "fraternity" of the Khalsa inculcated fellow feeling, and Guru Gobind Singh's prohibition of certain practices common among other communities, such as smoking, produced "the stalwart physique of the Sikhs."[80] Macauliffe insisted that the state needed to protect these distinctive physical, moral, and religious attributes, an argument that was not lost on his audience.[81] Sir C. M. Rivaz, the lieutenant governor of Punjab, endorsed Macauliffe's argument, agreeing that the "Sikh Jat, taking him all round, is the best agriculturalist and the finest type of manliness in the Punjab."[82] Macauliffe's audience agreed that the various forces—environmental, economic, ethnic, and religious—that produced this unique form of Indian masculinity, which was of obvious use to the colonial state, needed to be protected.

This argument dovetailed nicely with the agenda of Tat Khalsa Sikh reformers who were proclaiming "Ham hindu nahim" ("We are not Hindus"). Bhai Kahn Singh Nabha's 1898 *Ham Hindu Nahim,* which was originally published in Hindi, stressed to a Hindu audience that Sikhism was distinct from Hinduism and that a clearly defined Sikh identity had been promulgated from the time of Nanak. Written in a dialogue form, Kahn Singh's text asserted that even though Sikhs might share food with

Hindus (in keeping with the injunctions to reject caste practices relating to commensality) and marry Hindus, Sikhs were as distinct from Hindus as Muslims were from Christians. This distinctiveness, Kahn Singh stated, was grounded in the Guru Granth Sahib and the universality of the gurus' teachings (in comparison to some Hindu texts that valorized the special position of the Brahmans). Moreover, Kahn Singh also cited the *Adi Granth,* the *Bachittar Natak,* and other texts to stress the superiority of the *Granth* over the Vedas, the Puranas, and the *Bhagavad Gita.* Kahn Singh soon produced English and Punjabi versions of *Ham Hindu Nahim* (with the Punjabi text being reprinted several times), and his arguments were endorsed by the joint secretary of the Chief Khalsa Diwan, as well as drawing strong support from the Sikhs of Amritsar. Kahn Singh told the Sikhs that realizing Sikhism's distinctiveness and rejecting the position of being a subordinate branch of the Hindu *qaum* (people, nation) would restore the power of the Panth. This independence was to be achieved by rejecting old patterns that saw the wealth of the Sikhs (and former Sikhs) flowing to the Brahmans, and by shunning Hindu forms of devotion (such as mantras or fasting) and reasserting the distinctive Sikh symbols associated with the Khalsa (such as kes). This text was crucial in voicing the claims of the Tat Khalsa to those Arya Samajis who were asserting that Sikhism was simply a form of Hinduism; to those Punjabis who practiced forms of Sikhism that did not fit with the goals of the Tat Khalsa; and to a colonial state that ordered its administration around the enumeration of communities and their understandings of the history of those communities.

Harjot Oberoi has highlighted the importance of the Tat Khalsa's creation of a distinctive set of life-cycle rituals in its attempt to realize the arguments of *Ham Hindu Nahim.* Through a range of manuals as well as polemical literature, Tat Khalsa members set out a series of rites to mark the crucial transitions in life. As close as possible to birth, a set of five verses from the *Adi Granth* were to be recited to mark the occasion, and the Sikh mother was to be free of the polluted status that many rural communities and "orthodox" Hindus ascribed to new mothers. Rather than approaching a Brahman for assistance in the naming of the child, Sikh parents were to consult a granthi who would select a name for the child after consulting

the *Adi Granth*. Singh Sabha reformers also sought to differentiate themselves from Hindus through the promulgation of a new death ritual.
"Traditional" Hindu practices surrounding death were to be rejected, and
Sikhs were to take great care to carefully wash the corpse and ensure that
the "five Ks" were carefully maintained. Prior to the cremation of the
body, the Ardas and Kirtan Sohila were to be recited. After cremation,
under no circumstances were Sikhs to inter the ashes and the bones of the
dead in the Ganges or to observe Hindu ceremony. Instead, the only
observance that pious Sikh were to observe was the continuous forty-eight
hour recitation of the *Adi Granth*.[83]

Most importantly, Tat Khalsa reformers sought to reform the rites
surrounding marriage by reflecting the centrality of marriage and con-
jugality in the production and reproduction of "custom" and identities
within South Asia. Sikhs, Tat Khalsa publicists argued, should reject
many of the rituals that surrounded marriage in nineteenth-century rural
Punjab. *Nais* (barbers) were not to be used as intermediaries in the ar-
rangement of marriages; astrologers were not to be used to fix an aus-
picious time for the ceremony; and there was to be no indulgence in the
ribald fun-making and earthy celebrations that had typically accompanied weddings. The ritual itself was to be simple and conducted not in
Sanskrit but in Punjabi, and instead of circumambulating a fire seven
times, the bride and groom would circle the *Adi Granth* four times to the
accompaniment of verses therefrom. The Anand Marriage Bill was pro-
posed by Yuvraj Ripudaman Singh (who was tutored by Bhai Kahn
Singh) in 1908, and when it passed into legislation in October 1909 a Sikh
ritual was for the first time recognized and protected by the state.[84] This
legislative protection was extended in 1925 when the Punjab state government passed the Sikh Gurdwaras Act that "freed" the gurdwaras from
the control from their Udasi *mahants* (custodians). This law contained a
declaration that offered clear definition of Sikhism as a distinctive, independent, and exclusive religious tradition: "I solemnly affirm that I am
a Sikh, that I believe in the Guru Granth Sahib, that I believe in the Ten
Gurus, and that I have no other religion."[85]

This systematizing drive, which aimed to set apart Sikhs from their
Hindu neighbors through a sequence of rituals and a regime of bodily

discipline (most notably through the maintenance of the "five Ks" and the turban), was also extended through the reworking of the rahit-nama tradition. This can be clearly seen in Kahn Singh's *Guramat Sudhakar* (1899), which presented a range of carefully selected and edited rahit-nama texts in its exploration of the times of Guru Gobind Singh. W. H. McLeod documented the dynamics of this process in his work from 2003, *Sikhs of the Khalsa,* where he reconstructs Kahn Singh's reordering of the *Tanakhah-nama* in *Guramat Sudhakar,* especially the elision of anti-Muslim material and "superstitious" passages (such as injunctions relating to fire), and the ways in which Kahn Singh's footnotes elaborated or refined earlier prescriptions.[86] Although there is no doubt that Kahn Singh believed that he was freeing the "pure" rahit from corrupting accretions and Hindu influence, he reworked, repackaged, and rationalized "tradition" to forward the particular vision of the Tat Khalsa, authorizing their social vision through a meticulously constructed re-presentation of earlier prescriptive texts. Extending this project, a committee established by the Chief Khalsa Diwan produced a new text that both synthesized key elements of previous rahit-namas and codified these new rituals.[87] The *Gurmat Prakash Bhag Sanskar* (1915) embodied this systematizing impulse by prescribing long and precise instructions for the rites surrounding birth, marriage, initiation, and death. The complexity of these instructions proved unpopular, however, and the failure of this volume to gain wide support resulted in the Shiromani Gurdwara Parbandhak Committee's decision in 1931 to fashion a new rahit-nama, which culminated in the publication of the authoritative *Sikh Rahit Maryada* in 1950, a work that firmly equated Sikhism with the Khalsa and consolidated the range of new rituals and bodily regimens fashioned by the Tat Khalsa around the end of the nineteenth century and beginning of the twentieth.[88]

## Reproducing Masculinity and Martiality

Running through these discussions of the relationship between the colonial state and the Sikh community was a series of assumptions, assertions, and arguments about the masculine and martial qualities of Sikhs. Even though the early British visitors to Ranjit Singh's kingdom were divided over the quality of the Punjabi army (especially the Akalis), they generally agreed that Punjabis, particularly the Sikhs, were marked by their sturdy physique and masculine values.[89] Charles Masson, for example, asserted that "as men, physically speaking, the natives of the Panjab are superior to those of Hindustan Proper. Their limbs are muscular and well proportioned, and they have a stoutness of leg and calf, seldom seen in the Hindustani . . . the Sikhs are certainly a fine race of men, particularly the better classes."[90] It is important to note that these arguments were replicated by non-Punjabi Indians as well—most notably by Shahamat Ali, who was schooled in the East India Company's college in Delhi and who accompanied Captain C. M. Wade's mission to the court of Ranjit Singh. Indeed, Ali argued that "in enduring fatigue, absences from the prejudices of caste, and patience of discipline, the Sikh is not easily surpassed."[91]

These assessments were confirmed during the Anglo-Sikh wars, when the kingdom of Punjab's army stretched the company's military resources in a way that no Indian kingdom had done since the age of Tipu Sultan. After the annexation of Punjab in 1849, many British commentators saw immense value in Sikh martiality and in the former soldiers of the Punjab army. In June 1850, the *Lahore Chronicle* argued that defending the recently annexed Punjab raised pressing issues for the company. Not only did Punjab's proximity to the ancient invasion route of the Khyber Pass pose new geopolitical problems, but the company's intrusion into the northwest region of South Asia had brought it into contact with a host of martial peoples. In light of this, noted the *Chronicle*, the company's army had to be reorganized: "The same force which conquered and kept in subjection Hindostanees" was insufficient for "the subjugation . . . of Affghans" or to defend India against "the warlike Asiatics of the northwest" and "the great bugbear of [a] Russian invasion." No degree of training, drill, or "civilization" would ultimately overcome the deficient stature and masculinity of "Hindostanee" or Bengali troops, because they would not "add a cubit to man's stature." Given this view, the *Chronicle* recommended that the company "recruit their native army in the Punjab . . . rather than in the exhausted plains of Oude or Behar, with no-half-frightened limitation of 'ten Sikhs a Company.' "[92] On the very same day, the *Delhi Gazette* made an almost identical argument about the superiority of the Sikhs and the central role that they should play in the defense of the empire. It reported that the European officers of the 13th Native Infantry, which had absorbed some seventy Sikh soldiers from the old Punjab army, "would gladly fill the ranks of the entire corps with the sons of the Khalsa, who transcend the Hindostanees by far in all the essential qualities of soldiership. For prompt and cheerful obedience, no less than for superiority in bone and sinew, they are unmatched except by British troops." What is important to note here is the way in which ideas about physique, moral character, and religion were interwoven in this discourse on Sikh martiality. The *Gazette* suggested that Sikh soldiers will "be hated and feared, for their contempt for caste, their disdain of idolators will always render them disliked by their Hindoo and Muslim comrades, whilst their superior courage and higher military virtues are sure to win for them the favour of their officers."[93]

Although there were some anxieties about the loyalty of Sikh soldiers before the "Mutiny" of 1857, senior colonial administrators were also convinced of the physical prowess, discipline, and reliability of Punjabi and especially Sikh soldiers. John Lawrence, in his official report on the administration of Punjab for the period from 1851 to 1853, suggested that "the infantry regiments of the Punjab force probably contain as fine a body of native soldiers as ever have been brought together in India. The average height of the five regiments is 5 feet 8 3/4 inches. In breadth of shoulder, muscular appearance, and soldier-like demeanour they vie with any troops in the world."[94] The rebellion that shook British authority in India during 1857–1858 soon tested these assertions. The comparative stability of Punjab during the "Mutiny" and the pivotal role played by Sikh and Punjabi troops in the "pacification" of the "rebels" confirmed British faith in the soldiers they had raised in the newly annexed province. Within a week of the rebellion of the Bengal Army at Meerut on 10 May 1857, Arthur Moffat Laing, who was stationed in the Mian Mir cantonment in Lahore, stated, "If we survive this, never will a Hindustani be enlisted again. Our army should be entirely European, Afghan, Gurkha and Sikh." When news of the rebellion in Gwalior reached Laing he suggested that "Punjab seems to be our saving. Here alone we stand fast, and from here we send regiment after regiment to win back Hindustan proper for us."[95]

By June 1858, the new units raised by John Lawrence, which amounted to some 80,000 soldiers and 50,000 paramilitary police of whom 75,000 were Punjabis and 23,000 Sikhs, had played a pivotal role central in shoring up British authority.[96] In the aftermath of the rebellion, in an article in the *Lahore Chronicle*, Lawrence reflected: "I am lost in astonishment that any of us are alive. But for the mercy of God we must have been ruined. Had the Sikhs joined against us, nothing, humanly speaking could have saved us." In the same issue the *Lahore Chronicle* confirmed the centrality of Sikh loyalty and military prowess in protecting British authority: "English skill and English valor succumbed, and but for the fidelity of the Sikhs every vestige of European civilization, would in all probability, have been eradicated."[97]

In the wake of the rebellion, as the reformed colonial state attempted to build the three presidency's armies around blocks of soldiers recruited from rival communities to protect British power, recruitment for the Bengal army shifted noticeably to Punjab as recruiting officers attempted to enlist enough Punjabis to balance the soldiers recruited from the Gangetic plains. By 1875, Punjabis made up 44 percent of the Bengal Army, a proportion that increased markedly over the following decades.[98] The Eden Commission's 1879 report to Parliament anticipated this shift, as it suggested that recruitment should be concentrated even more closely on Punjab because "the Punjab is the home of the most martial races of India and is the nursery of our best soldiers."[99] Lord Roberts, who presided over India's military from 1876 to 1893, suggested that the shift to recruitment in Punjab reflected the divergence between the Sikhs and the "sepoys of Lower India" in terms "of courage and physique."[100] The Punjabization of the Indian Army was effected both by increasing the number of battalions being raised in the region (with the number of battalions doubling between 1862 and 1914) and by an actual increase in the number of Punjabi soldiers serving throughout the Indian Army (in the early twentieth century, significant numbers of Sikhs served in regiments that were previously restricted to Mappilas and other groups from South India).[101]

For the Sikhs, this reshaping of recruitment policy was of great significance. It drew large numbers of Sikh agriculturalists into military service, thus providing an important and lucrative source of employment that may have helped alleviate (at least temporarily) the pressure on land and other resources that resulted from population growth.[102] Equally important, Sikh reformers identified military service as a domain that could produce, reproduce, and police their vision of a coherent Sikh identity. The British shared this hope as they strove to preserve the martial qualities of Sikhism, qualities that had become integral to the very stability not only of the British Empire in India but also to the security of the empire as a whole, thanks to the distinguished service of Sikh regiments outside of India. This anxiety over the "decay of Sikhism" was at the heart of British recruiting efforts. Indeed, British recruiting officer R. W. Falcon noted the "great slackness there is at the present time in taking the *pahul* (Khalsa initiation rite), very many who call themselves Singhs . . . omit to take the pahul though adopting the surname and keeping some of the observances."[103] Falcon's 1896 officer's handbook suggested that recruitment should be aimed only at those "Sikh tribes which supplied converts to Sikhism in the time of Guru Gobind Singh, who in fact formed the Singh people"; more recent converts were to be avoided as they could not be considered "true Sikh tribes."[104] The ultimate test of "Sikhness" was whether an individual maintained the external symbols of the Khalsa: "Singhs, the members of the Khalsa; these are the only Sikhs who are reckoned as true Sikhs. . . . the best practical test of a true Sikh is to ascertain whether [in] calling himself a Sikh he wears uncut hair and abstains from smoking tobacco."[105] Non–kes-dharis (that is, the sahaj-dharis, shaven *mona*s, and *patit* Sikhs)—groups who might have identified themselves with (elements of) the Sikh tradition—were to be avoided. Only Khalsa Sikhs were "true" Sikhs, and it was they who would exhibit the true values of a warrior. Falcon mapped these martial qualities across the different regions of Punjab, warning officers away from the eastern and southern regions where the "Hindustani type" was prevalent as well as from regions where Sikh identity was "very diluted by Hinduism."[106] Once recruited, Sikh troops were placed in Sikh regiments; kes-dhari Sikhs who were not amrit-dhari were required to undergo the Khalsa's *khande di pahul* initiation rite; and all Sikh troops were to maintain the external symbols of their Sikh identity and were expected to accept the authority of the granthis appointed by the army to perform Sikh rituals.[107] To help ensure the maintenance of regimens, Falcon provided translated excerpts from various rahit-namas to guide British military men and recruiters. Commanding officers were not only to inculcate military discipline into their troops but also police religious discipline as well.[108] Thus, leading figures in the colonial state identified the fastidious maintenance of religious identity as central to the esprit de corps and general effectiveness of the Indian Army, a force that was increasingly reliant on the ability and loyalty of its Sikh soldiers.

## The Limits of Systematization: The Persistence of Diversity

Thus far in this chapter I have placed particular emphasis on British ways of seeing Punjabi culture and the interfaces between Sikhs and the colonial state—forces that were crucial in the reorganization and systematization of Sikhism between 1849 and the middle of the twentieth century. In the remaining sections of the chapter, I will complicate this narrative in two ways. First, I will briefly suggest that although the Tat Khalsa was remarkably successful in cultivating its reformed vision of Sikh history and religion, there is strong evidence that there were important limitations to the extent of this systematization, especially in rural Punjab. Second, by paying close attention to the coterminous histories of systematization within Punjab and the rise of the diaspora, the discussion that follows underscores the argument that the entry of Sikhs into imperial institutions, military service, and new labor networks produced a novel range of identities that coexisted, competed, and even destabilized the authority that was increasingly attached to the turbaned kes-dhari as the embodiment of Sikhism.

Despite the productivity of Singh Sabha pens and presses and the devoted efforts of the reformers to regularize religious practice in the villages of Punjab, long-established cultural patterns were not immediately displaced nor were heterodox identities entirely erased. As described above, the intricate instructions set out for the new Sikh rituals in *Guramat Prakash Bhag Sanskar* proved unpopular, a telling reminder that there frequently was a considerable gap between prescription and reality and that the innovations endorsed by urban Sikh elites did not always gain purchase in the countryside.[109] Despite the authority attached to the Anand marriage ritual, for example, it is clear that until World War II Brahman continued to officiate at some "Sikh" weddings in the countryside and that such occasions continued to be accompanied by the music, performances by *mirasis* (folk entertainers), and energetic celebrations that worried educated urban Sikhs. There is also evidence that suggests that military service bolstered the number of Sikhs, as some Punjabis, especially those from celebrated recruitment grounds, adopted the outward symbols of Sikhism in order to enter into military service. It seems that this pragmatic embrace of Sikhism often expired after discharge from the army.[110]

Most importantly, while the data recorded in the region's census was ordered around the categories that shaped British ways of imagining Punjabi society, it also hints at both the successes and limits of the attempts to demarcate a clearly defined and differentiated Sikh identity. While the 1901 census suggests that the drive of the colonial state and the Singh Sabhas to arrest the "decline" of Sikhism was very successful,[111] it also records the persistence of a wide range of Sikh groups and identities.[112] In fact, the census records that Punjabis offered over 130 different designations that were then placed into the category "Sikh" within the census. Many of these designations are unsurprising: such as simply "Sikh" (40 percent of returns), "Nanak-panthis" (21.9 percent), and "Sikhs of Guru Govind Singh" (30.9 percent). However, the census records a host of other ways that Punjabis designated themselves. Some mediated their Sikh identity through the lens of caste, identifying themselves as "Mazhabi Sikhs" or "Ramgarhia Sikhs," or most strikingly by the saints ("Sakhi Sarwar") and gods they devoted themselves to ("Durga Opasak," "Devi-Dharm," "Vaishno," "Sewak Shiv," or "Baba Mahesh"). Over 1,100 defined themselves as "Arya Sikhs," testifying to the ability of some Punjabis to reconcile competing traditions and rival reform movements.[113] Even though the colonial officials who gathered census data operated with a clear definition of a Sikh—"one who wears the hair long, (*kes*), and refrains from smoking"[114]—defining religious boundaries remained extremely difficult, especially since the "line between Sikhs and Hindus is vague in the extreme." The census takers were well aware they were probably underreporting the number of "Nanak-panthis" because they did not necessarily maintain these external markers of Sikh identity.[115]

By the time of the 1921 census this diversity had begun to erode, but the existence of a range of devotional practices and affiliations within the Panth remained an important element of Punjabi culture. In their census report, L. Middleton and S. M. Jacobs commented on the rapid growth of the Sikh population in Punjab over the previous four decades and the divergent rates of growth between the Sikh community (a 7.8 percent increase from 1911) and the Hindus (4 percent increase) and Muslims (5.4 percent increase). They suggested that this rate of growth reflected the ability of Sikh organizations to "reclaim" Sikhs from the Hindu "depressed classes" in addition to the growing number of Mazhabis who embraced Sikhism. They also recognized the ability of the Singh Sabhas to embed the categories "kes-dhari" and "sahaj-dhari" within the Punjabi imagination, as well as the marked growth in the "kes-dhari" category during the second decade of the twentieth century. But once again they also stressed that it remained "very difficult to define Sikhism because it is not sharply divided from Hinduism as regards religious beliefs," and they recorded a number of divergent identities within the community.[116] Increasing numbers of Sikhs did define themselves within the categories endorsed by both the Tat Khalsa and the colonial state, but these identities were constantly being remade, reasserted, and frequently contested, especially within a social order that was beginning to take on a new shape because of new opportunities presented by the empire and migration.

## The "Webs of Empire" and the Emergence of a Global Panth

The crucial contests and intellectual shifts delineated above are frequently treated as being both unrelated to and unaffected by the beginnings of significant Sikh migration outside South Asia. Too often, the history of

Sikhs in Punjab and that of Sikhs outside Punjab are framed as separate narratives. But this ordering of Sikh history around two divergent narratives—the Sikhs "at home" and Sikhs "abroad"—tends to mask the concomitant histories of the drive to delineate a coherent Sikh identity and the emergence of new forms of mobility. In other words, the program of the Tat Khalsa was articulated against the backdrop of the exile of important precolonial leaders, the mobility of large numbers of Punjabi soldiers, the first significant flows of labor migration to destinations outside South Asia, and the emergence of fledgling Punjabi communities in Europe, America, Asia, and the Pacific.

As I demonstrate in the following discussion, most of these forms of mobility were enabled by the incorporation of the Punjab into the British Empire. In a very real way, the empire functioned as a system of exchange and mobility where key institutions (such as the military and the police force), communication networks (steamship routes, telegraph cables, and the circulation of newspapers), and markets constructed crucial "horizontal" connections between colonies as well as linking individual colonies to the metropole. As I suggested in chapter 1 (and have argued elsewhere), the web metaphor is a useful heuristic tool for conceptualizing these networks and the various forms of cultural traffic that they enabled within the empire. Whereas so much of the writing on Sikh history focuses narrowly on the relationship between Britons and Sikhs within Punjab, and, in a similar vein, most imperial historiography reduces the empire to a series of metropole-periphery binaries, the web reinforces the multiple positions that any given colony, city, or community might occupy. In the case of Punjab, the region certainly occupied a position at the periphery of the imperial economy as it functioned as an important producer of raw materials, but as I make clear in the remainder of this chapter, the region simultaneously began to function as a hub in its own right, as a series of extensive and culturally significant networks reached out across the Bay of Bengal and the Indian Ocean from a cluster of Punjabi villages.

Thus the annexation of Punjab in 1849 did not just mark the onset of colonialism but also initiated the rapid integration of the region into the interregional and global structures that gave the empire its shape. As Punjabis were drawn into the complex international webs of the British imperial system and tentatively explored distant lands beyond the empire, the spatial boundaries of the Punjabi world were suddenly stretched, elongated, and reconfigured. Just as the merchants and laborers from Hyderabad, in Sindh, followed the paths of steamship routes and telegraph networks to establish a set of complex global networks in the late nineteenth century, Punjabis also traveled many of these imperial communication structures and sought employment in labor markets far from India.[117] Within the global world of empire, Punjabis suddenly had to make sense of new landscapes, grapple with new forms of cultural difference, adjust to new state systems, and negotiate a path through complex and frequently exclusionary regimes. The political and cultural terrains traversed by Sikh soldiers in British service, by the pioneering migrants in Australasia and North America, and by the leaders exiled in Britain or Singapore encouraged the production of an almost bewildering array of new visions of personal and collective identity. In what follows I explore some of these innovative cultural formations, examining the strategies that these mobile individual and communities adopted in the face of profound legal, economic, and religious pressures, and I map some of the new political allegiances and visions that were produced by these early Punjabis on the move.

It is important to note here that reconstructing the motivations, experiences, and identities of most Sikh travelers and migrants before the late twentieth century is extremely difficult because of the limited sources and fragmentary archives that record their lives. Given the limited extent of literacy in colonial Punjab, the vast majority of the migrants who left the area before independence did not produce written records—letters, diaries, or published accounts of their travels—that might allow the historian to explore their subjectivities. While certain groups of mobile Punjabis did leave substantial records, as I describe in the next chapter in the case of Dalip Singh, massive gaps remain in the archival record. Some of these pioneering migrants, of course, appear in the archives created by the states in which they made their new homes, but collating a full picture of their life histories, yet alone making sense of their subjectivities, is extremely difficult. While the very mobility of these Punjabis ensured that their lives might be fleetingly recorded in immigration files and passenger logs, they were less likely to produce substantial bodies of written texts or to publish accounts of their lives. Moreover, their movement across borders, their desire to limit their interface with the machinery of the state, and their cultural difference meant that they were not the kind of subjects or citizens that were easily legible for state bureaucracies outside of South Asia.

These archival limits pose real problems, and the picture we have of the history of Sikh migration and the relationship between Sikhs on the move and communities in Punjab remains partial. What is clear, however, is that significant Sikh communities were long established in parts of Central and South Asia outside Punjab well before the onset of colonialism and that other intrepid Sikhs embraced the possibilities posed by the rise of European and American trade with India. We know, for example, that Captain Stephen Phillips, a leading Massachusetts trader, recruited "a tall black-bearded Sikh" in the late eighteenth century and that this pioneering Sikh traveler "stalked around town [Salem] in the turban and white woollen coat and red sash of his sect."[118] The first significant international movement of Sikhs was toward states on the fringes of South Asia (Burma) and in Southeast Asia, especially Malaya.

While these regions had been long linked with India, the connections that facilitated the movement of large numbers of Sikhs were essentially a product of the new labor and economic networks created by colonialism.[119] In British Malaya, for example, Sikhs came to play a crucial role in the colonial state's regimes of coercion and surveillance, structures that were organized along ethnic lines. Malaya's mixed and mobile population—where Tamils, Punjabis, Siamese, Sinhalese, Eurasians, Europeans, Bugis, Javanese, Filipinos, and various Chinese groups met, and where Islam, Christianity, Sikhism, Hinduism, Buddhism, Confucianism, and Taoism coexisted—posed significant problems for a colonial regime that sought to arbitrate between the distinct interests of these various confessional groups and communities of descent. Political concerns, including fear of the power of dispossessed Malay chiefs and anxieties about the operations of Chinese secret societies, meant that the Colonial Office (which in 1867 took over from the India Office the administration of the Straits Settlements) was reluctant to rely heavily on either the Chinese or Malay populations in policing the colony. At the same time, doubts over the physical and moral aptitude for police work of candidates from South Indian and Jawi Pekan (children of Indian and Malay intermarriage) groups were widespread among the colonial bureaucracy and were a recurrent concern of the Straits Settlements Police Commission, which was appointed in 1879 to oversee the reform of the colony's police force.[120] These constructions of cultural difference not only reflected the real difficulties facing a colonial state that hoped to meld a multifaith, multiethnic, polyglot population into a harmonious and productive polity, but also reflected a common set of racial theories that doubted the industry of Malays, questioned the masculinity and morality of Dravidians, viewed intermarriage as debasing "racial stocks," and commonly associated Chinese populations with intrigue and crime.[121]

These racialized concerns over how the colonial state would project and enforce its authority were the crucial backdrop to the beginnings of Sikh migration to Malaya.[122] As noted earlier, Punjabis were widely valued within the empire for their martial prowess. Sikhs were thus identified as significantly more moral and reliable than Hindus, partly because of the relative "loyalty" of Sikh troops during the rebellion of 1857–1858 and also because colonial officials in Malaya accepted the vision of Sikhism as a rational and monotheistic tradition that shunned the lasciviousness, idolatry, and polytheism that supposedly characterized Hinduism. In short, Sikhs were reliable, "fairly uncorruptible," hard working, and frugal—qualities that made them ideally suited to police work and more culturally akin to Malaya's colonial masters than were the local populations they ruled over.[123] Moreover, the successful introduction of Sikh policemen into Hong Kong in 1867 (where the Sikh rejection of tobacco saw them guarding key ammunition stores in addition to their regular duties), served as an important precedent that was carefully noted by the administration of Malaya, which appreciated the particular respect the Sikhs received among the Chinese.[124]

In fact, the military prowess of Punjabis was also widely known within the elites of Malaya from the early 1870s when the Malay chief Ngah Ibrahim authorized the recruitment of north Indian troops to defend his tin mines in Perak from his Chinese rivals and to quell conflict between competing Chinese clans. In September 1873, a mixed force of ninety-five

Pathans, Sikhs, and Punjabi Muslims arrived and quickly asserted their authority: when Perak was subsequently absorbed into Britain's colonial holdings in Malaya, Punjabis formed the nucleus of the newly formed Armed Perak Police.[125] However, it was from 1881, when the first Sikhs arrived to serve as policemen in Malaya, that a steady stream of Punjabis entered into of the colonial state and in the police forces of various Malay states. The prominence of these Sikhs in the machinery of states throughout Southeast Asia, together with the slow growth of Sikh communities that had local roots in Burma, Malaya, Singapore, and Hong Kong, meant that the turbaned kes-dhari Sikh became a potent signifier of imperial power throughout Asia. Encounters with Sikh policemen, soldiers, and doormen became a typical set piece in imperial travel accounts of Singapore, Penang, Hong Kong, and Shanghai, while the turbaned kes-dhari "Sikh policeman" became a popular staple in imperial ephemera, especially on postcards and, ironically given the rahit-namas' injunctions against smoking, cigarette cards.[126]

While in Southeast Asia, these Sikhs established some significant relationships with other mobile South Asian groups. Of particular importance were the close relationships established between Punjabi Sikhs and Sindhi migrants. A significant number of these mobile Sindhis were Nanak-panthis, and many other Sindhi Hindus had long-standing relationships with Sikhism. They were accustomed to worshipping at the *tikhanas* (temples) that were common in the vicinity of Hyderabad, which were typically managed by Nanak-panthis. Claude Markovits has argued that hybrid nature of these sacred sites, which contained the *Adi Granth* in addition to Hindu idols, underscores the fluidity of the Hindu/Sikh boundary outside Punjab. In effect, the failure of the Singh Sabha to gain purchase in Sindh allowed blurred religious boundaries to persist in that region well into the twentieth century. These interconnections were reestablished in Southeast Asia, where Sindhis and Sikhs often shared places of worship in the early stages of community building and where Sindhi merchants played a key role in sponsoring and financing the erection of gurdwaras (such as the gurdwara erected in Manila in 1933 with funds donated by the Sindwork firm Wassiamall Assomull).[127]

Although the evidence is fragmentary, it seems that it was through the imperial and diasporic networks in Southeast Asia that Sikhs gleaned important information about other potential destinations for migration. The first of these "new" lands was Telia (Australia) and as the nineteenth century drew to a close Punjabis in Southeast Asia and in Punjab itself became aware that Telia "was open."[128] Early migrants, who arrived in the mid 1880s, carried out agricultural work in the Clarence District of northern New South Wales and in the Atherton Tablelands of northern Queensland. Labor in sugar cane fields and banana plantations as well as work as hawkers allowed these men to remit significant sums of money home, which was used to buy land and build *pakka* (made of bricks and mortar) houses in Punjab.[129] Some of these migrants were very mobile: Waryam Singh of Masoolpur village arrived in Australia in 1898, where he worked for six years in New South Wales before returning home to India. He stayed in India, however, only for a year before returning to Australia for a further fifteen years.[130]

While some of these migrants trimmed their kes, dispensed with their turbans, and were clean shaven, they all clung to old traditions as best they could, and some were scrupulous in the maintenance of customs relating to commensality.[131] Even though some male children of these pioneering migrants journeyed to Australia to join their male elders, the effort to reproduce Punjabi culture and Sikh practices was difficult given the context of itinerant or semi-itinerant labor and, most importantly, the absence of Punjabi women in Australia until just before World War II.

A similar pattern is discernible in New Zealand, to which small numbers of Punjabis migrated from Australia, and the pattern also was repeated for the sugar plantations of Fiji, which is logical given the heavy flow of information and the relative affordability of transport within the southern Pacific region. McLeod's study of migrants to New Zealand documents the history of pioneering Punjabis and their ability to maintain some key customs and adapt to the new environment, housing, foodstuffs, and ethnic dynamics that they found in their new home. While some individuals were punctilious in the maintenance of the rahit, in other cases the pressure of the new environment saw them trimming their kes and abandoning the turban, accommodations that were entirely understandable for a small community living in a context where maintaining all of the rahit-nama injunctions was extremely difficult. Some descendants of the early migrants to New Zealand described their ancestors and predecessors as "Hindu-Sikh," an ambiguous religious identity that early colonial officials had grappled with in Punjab itself.[132] It is also striking to note the ways in which McLeod's New Zealand informants layer the identities of these early Punjabis (in terms of caste, religion, "sect," subregion and village), which is not surprising in light of the discussions of "religion" and identity offered above.[133] Of these multiple identities, it seems that migrants from Punjab before World War II were most confident in defining themselves through caste and subregion (e.g., Malwa, Majha, Doaba) rather than through either religion or even region (Punjab). Although the structural position of certain castes was open to debate and underwent change in Punjab, there was little ambiguity as to what caste individual migrants belonged. McLeod's New Zealand evidence is in keeping with the broader patterns of migrant identity formation highlighted by Darshan Singh Tatla, who argues that migrants from Punjab before 1947 "defined themselves as Doabias, Malwais, or Majhails."[134]

By the early twentieth century, the economic prospects and physical mobility of Punjabis in Australasia became constrained as they became targets of anti-Asian agitations that vented the anxieties of settler populations and connected white workers, labor leaders, and progressive politicians. Initially at least, Punjabis frequently occupied an ambivalent position in these debates because they were British citizens (unlike migrants from Canton or Guangdong, for example) and because they were renowned for their military prowess and loyalty (unlike Gujaratis).[135] As Australasian states set about constructing exclusionary regimes, other Punjabis sought new opportunities that they had heard of existing in Mitkan (America). A substantial literature has developed around early migration to both Canada and the United States, with a significant cluster of work on the revolutionary Ghadr movement that developed on America's west coast in the early twentieth century and whose rank-and-file support base was largely Sikh.

Here, however, I will limit my discussion to three crucial points about the early Punjabis in North America. First, starting from the beginning of their arrival in North America in the early twentieth century, these

Punjabis began to establish significant institutions, especially newspapers, that forged crucial links between themselves, the Punjabis at home, and other Punjabi migrants. While many of these papers such as *Swadesh Sewak* and the *Free Hindustan* were anticolonial and nationalist in orientation, others such as the *Pradeshi Khalsa* (established in British Columbia in 1910) were concerned specifically with Sikh interests. Publications of both types carried information about North America, the world, and the experience of migration back to Punjab, as well as to Punjabi migrants in Australasia and Southeast Asia.[136] In addition to circulating through gurdwaras and kinship and labor networks, and through international postage, Claude Markovits has also established that Ghadrite literature reached Sikhs through the Sindhi diaspora. A significant number of Sindhis were Nanak-panthis and Sindhi firms often employed Punjabi Sikhs, and thus it appears that the interconnection between these diasporic communities may have facilitated the dissemination of Ghadrite ideology.[137] These various types of networks were crucial in mobilizing support in Punjab itself for Sikh migrants. For example, the Chief Khalsa Diwan and the United India League sent a delegation, armed with up-to-date information disseminated through print, to the governor-general and colonial secretary in 1913 to protest the treatment of Punjabis in North America.[138] These developments bore out the concerns about the rise of an expanded domain of Sikh politics articulated in the secret Criminal Investigation Department (CID) intelligence report prepared by David Petrie in 1911, wherein he suggests that "a spirit of anti-British disaffection is commonly prevalent among Sikhs in Canada," and in which he expresses his worries about the impact of these sentiments "at home." Petrie notes that other anticolonial texts produced outside of India, such as the "seditious" *Gaelic American* were not only circulating in Punjab but were being reproduced in Punjabi periodicals like the English-language *Khalsa Advocate* and the Punjabi-language *Khalsa Samachar*.[139] As N. G. Barrier has shown, these publications created new and powerful communication networks that built connections across vast distances and marked the emergence of the west coast of North America as a crucial hub in early Indian nationalist politics.[140] In many ways the lasting legacies of these texts, which created new mechanisms for information exchange, social debate, and the consolidation of novel forms of political allegiance across national borders as they shaped a greatly extended Punjabi public sphere, and archived the experience of displacement and opportunities of migration for later generations of Sikhs, were of at least equal significance to the Ghadr movement itself, which foundered under close state surveillance in 1915.

Second, the movement of Punjabis into North America (and, for that matter, Australia and New Zealand) was crucial in the production of national identities within an imperial frame. At the same time that Sikhs began to be mobilized around the category "Indian" by Ghadrite leaders and the diasporic nationalist press, they were also inserted into discourses on nationality and citizenship through the restrictive regimes that they encountered, including state practices that both nationalized and racialized them as "Indians." Radhika Mongia has demonstrated that the Canadian demand that migrants from Punjab have Indian passports did not simply reflect understandings of race and nationality but rather was "central to *organizing* and *securing* the modern definition of those categories."[141] In other words, the passport was central in the creation of the "nationalized migrant" as it functioned as the artifact and document that transformed into "Indians" individuals who might have defined themselves through a range of referents (e.g., region, caste, lineage, tribe, or even "religion"). This process of nationalization was not simply the product of one state's innovation but rather was produced out of a sustained debate between state functionaries within the empire (in Canada, India, and Britain) and the implementation of emergent international conventions that were beginning to govern travel across the slowly calcifying borders of nation-states.

Third, the recognition of the importance of state practices needs to be balanced with a sensitivity to the radical strategies of adaptation employed by some Punjabis. In North America many Punjabis found ways of negotiating paths around restrictive legislation; as a result, they quickly became embedded in their new communities. In the United States, a raft of legislation constrained their mobility (notably the Barred Zone Act of 1917); their ability to own agricultural land (e.g., California's "Alien Land Laws" of 1913, which were applied to Punjabis starting in 1923); and, most crucially, their ability to become citizens (notably after the Su-

preme Court's 1923 Thind Decision, which remained in effect until 1946).
Even the basic personal choices of the migrants were restricted: anti-
miscegenation laws (which operated in California until 1948) prevented
these migrants from marrying outside of their race. But, from 1916, over
250 Punjabi men circumvented this restriction by marrying Mexican
women, who could be entered into marriage registers as being the same
race as the Punjabis: usually "brown."[142] As a result of this strategy,
communities of mixed descent grew in Arizona, Texas, the valleys of
Central and Northern California, and especially in the Imperial Valley
along California's border with Mexico.

Thus, as these pioneering Punjabi migrants established small communities around the Pacific rim, they quickly adapted to the local economic
situations, social patterns, state practices (especially those governing migration, citizenship, and property rights), and demographic structures. As
noted above, the variety of different positions that these migrants occupied—as agricultural laborers on the multiethnic California frontier; as
farm workers and farmers among the Maori, Pakeha, and even a few
Gujaratis in New Zealand; and as cane cutters in white-dominated rural
Australia—produced a range of distinctive social formations. Whereas the
indentured laborers who were drawn from a wide range of South Asian
groups to serve on sugar plantations in Surinam, Fiji, and Mauritius were
drawn together as *jahaji bhai* ("ship brothers") and experienced common
work patterns and even food regimes, the diffuse social contexts around
the Pacific in which these early Punjabi migrants found themselves promoted cultural innovation and heterogeneity.[143] In some cases, particularly in California, the rapid and successful adaptation of these early
migrants to their new homes produced new social formations that diverged so radically from their Punjabi Sikh origins that, for example, the
descendants of the migrants are almost totally unaware of their Sikh
heritage, or, in another example, some more recent South Asian migrants
refuse to recognize the pioneer Sikhs within their vision of the history of
South Asian migration and community building in North America.[144] As
Karen Leonard has observed: "The context [of life in late-twentieth-
century America] is so strikingly different from the one in which the
earlier ones lived and worked that the imagination fails, the newcomers

cannot conceive of that earlier world and the choices it forced upon their predecessors."[145]

## Mobility and the Reshaping of Punjab

Although much research needs to be done on the demographic profile of early Punjabi migration, the evidence collected to date suggests some basic patterns. While Malwa supplied the bulk of the Sikhs who served in the military overseas, the primary outflow of independent migrants came from three *tahsils* (subdistrict) that were located within the loop of the Satluj River: Garhshankar tahsil (Hoshiarpur District), and the Nawanshahr and Phillaur tahsils (Jullundur District). The exact beginnings, cause, and pattern of migration out of these districts during the late nineteenth century remains unclear, but several factors can be identified that contributed toward the increased likelihood of people in this region to migrate. The comparatively light recruitment of soldiers from this part of the region almost certainly meant that migration provided a particularly significant option for young men (and the families they belonged to) from these tahsils. McLeod has also suggested that the distinctive social milieu of the *bara pind* (big village) network of this part of Punjab may well have been an important factor in driving out-migration. McLeod further notes that the practice of female infanticide, which was an important element of the particularly high premium these communities placed on *izzat* (face, or honor), resulted in a marked gender imbalance; as a result some young men opted to migrate to seek status in the face of constrained marriage options.[146] More generally, in the 1920s Malcolm Darling argued that the Jat practice of dividing up estates between sons progressively reduced the size of individual holdings in Punjab, and this practice encouraged young Jat men to migrate to earn enough money to allow them to buy larger and more economically viable holdings on their return to Punjab.[147] This assertion is supported by the oral histories and memories nurtured within migrant Punjabi families. Sikhs in Woolgoolga, Australia, for example, stress that their ancestors migrated to "improve our economic position," "to improve our lot," and "to increase our land holdings and position."[148]

Increasing population pressure and the shrinking of common lands attached to villages almost certainly provided key material contexts for the growth of emigration from late-nineteenth-century Punjab. Nawanshahr tahsil, in particular, was subject to the high population pressure that characterized Hoshiarpur District as a whole, and British colonial administrators frequently commented that the region was marked by strong outward migration to other parts of Punjab, to other regions of India, and, in the late nineteenth century, to far-flung parts of the globe. Thus migration from Nawanshahr tahsil to distant lands across the Pacific cannot entirely be separated from the movement of what was described in 1905 as its "surplus population to the fertile plains of Jullundur and to the State of Kapurthala, and to the canals of Amritsar and the river valley of Ferozepore and Ludhiana."[149] Men from the Nawanshahr and Phillaur tahsils in Jullundur District were also highly mobile. By 1904 the *Jullundur District Gazetteer* noted that "it is becoming quite a common thing for men in the District to emigrate to Australia. Some six or seven years ago a few adventurous spirits returned from Australia with a substantial proof of the fact that money could be earned there, and since then it has become quite the thing for one of a large family of brothers to be sent off. The cost of getting there is about Rs. 200. The sugar plantations find work for many of these emigrants: some trade as pedlars, nearly all return after spending five or six years there, with a smattering of English, as 'morning boss,' or 'evening, squire.'"[150] Tom Kessinger's longitudinal study between 1848 and 1968 of "Vilyatpur," a village in Jullundur District, highlights the great importance of mobility and migration in shaping the development of this part of Punjab. Kessinger reminds us that although geographical mobility did not begin with colonialism, migration did increase markedly under British rule.[151] While some individuals continued to move within Jullundur District, in the British period new forms of mobility emerged, thereby reshaping village life.

In the 1890s, two groups of migrants moved out of Kessinger's district. One group of about twenty moved into the newly opened canal colonies in western Punjab, while another group of the same size moved to Australia. The group movement into the Chenab canal colony was encouraged by the colonial state, which targeted experienced agriculturalists and the "well-to-do yeomen" of Jullundur District in the hope that they could, in the words of the Chenab District officer, "constitute healthy agricultural communities of the best Punjab type."[152] Although Kessinger cannot explain the initial impetus for the migration to Australia, he stresses the economic and social significance of this population movement. By 1903, some thirty-five villagers were in Australia, meaning that, remarkably, approximately one-third of the village's men of working age had migrated.[153] Although this flow of men was restricted after the implementation of the "White Australia" policy, the economic influence of this opportunity was long-lasting. Kessinger highlights one "property group" from the village that sent a son (the middle of three sons) and his nephew to Australia in 1896. When the nephew returned in 1908 he was able to acquire eight acres and extend that holding to fourteen acres in 1922, effectively doubling the land base of the property group. The son spent the remainder of his life in Australia, financing further land purchases and the construction of a brick house.[154]

Another significant vector of mobility in Vilyatpur was military service. Although the vicinity of Jalandhar was not seen as a favored recruiting ground, the expansion of recruitment during World War I drew in twelve Julahas in addition to three Jats from the village, suggesting that this source of opportunity was particularly significant for low-caste groups like Julahas who did not normally have the resource base to afford to migrate.[155] Migration, especially abroad, was of great economic significance for families that had several sons and a solid resource base. In effect, the new opportunities opened up by incorporation into the empire allowed the wealthiest groups in the village to become wealthier still through emigration. Families with a history of international migration owned 60 percent of the village's land by 1910 (against a baseline of 50 percent in 1884) and 71 percent of the village's land by 1968.[156]

Thus, by the early 1900s Punjabis were well aware of the economic opportunities that might be pursued in far-off nations, and they were traveling on the railways and steamships that were the crucial sinews of the imperial system. As the case of Kessinger's Vilyatpur shows, it is frequently impossible to trace how this knowledge of opportunity first reached Punjabi villagers, but it seems more than likely that Punjabi military men were almost certainly one vector whereby knowledge of

Telia (Australia) and Mitkan (America) reached Punjab.[157] The importance of transportation and communication networks in informing Punjabis about opportunities in distant lands is also suggested by the relatively
high rate of migration out of Ludhiana District, which had easy access to
the Grand Trunk Road, the great information highway and migratory
route of British India.[158] Information about distant lands, particularly
other colonies and important industrial powers (e.g., the United States),
was disseminated quite widely in Punjab by the 1870s as print culture
flourished in a variety of vernacular languages. Newspapers carried a
wide range of stories from outside of India, making knowledge of the
world accessible to an increasing range of Punjabi social groups.[159] Even
though many villagers might not have been able to read pamphlets, newspapers, periodicals, or textbooks, C. A. Bayly reminds us that low literacy
rates should not obscure the reality that nineteenth-century India was a
"literacy aware society" where the news reports and articles were frequently read aloud and disseminated through commercial exchanges,
familial networks, and bazaar "gossip."[160] "Useful knowledge" about the
world's geography, the wealth of industrialized nations, and the British
Empire was also prominent in the curriculum of schools run by the
colonial state and by a range of British, American, and even New Zealand
missionary societies in Punjab. It seems likely that the information conveyed to Punjabis through these schools created a fuller picture of the
globe and may have contributed to the curiosity and desire for opportunity that drove many migrants.

The elaboration of new communication networks, the rise of colonial
education, and the growing reach of these structures into rural Punjab
thus form a crucial framework for understanding the history of early
Punjabi migration overseas. While many of the migrants' descendants
suggest that their ancestors migrated because they were *garib* (poor),
it seems that colonialism generated this increased mobility not simply
through the imposition of economic constraints, but rather through Punjab's importance for the coercive instruments (army and police) of the
broader imperial system; the region's growing connection to international
labor markets and migration routes; and, eventually, the emergence of

elongated family and community networks that stretched from Punjab to Southeast Asia, Australasia, North America, and East Africa.[161]

By recognizing these dynamics and juxtaposing these stories of mobility, fluidity, and cultural reformulation with the systematizing drives that formed the central concern of the earlier parts of this chapter, I hope to underscore the simultaneity and even the interrelatedness of cultural systematization and hybridization, homogenization and the creation of new forms of difference, and the histories of rootedness and restlessness. When drawn together into the same frame, these frequently contradictory impulses highlight the limitations of Fox's simple view of the colonial state's "making of a culture" or even Oberoi's more nuanced exploration of the creation of the Tat Khalsa episteme: these visions of the encounter of Punjabis with modernity and the fashioning of clear Sikh identities can only stand if we consciously exclude the stories of mobility, cultural loss, creative adaptation, and passionate yet flexible anti-imperial resistance narrated here. These stories are particularly important because the weight of scholarship on the Sikh diaspora is tilted toward the movement of Sikhs into Britain and North America over the past four decades, and thus too frequently the struggles and successes of these early Punjabis on the move are glossed over or are merely treated as a prelude to the recent histories of community formation.

## Conclusion

In this chapter I undercut two sets of analytical assumptions that order the study of Punjabi and Sikh history. First, by highlighting and grappling with the simultaneity of the history of migration and/or diaspora and colonialism I call into question the chronological sequence of tradition-colonialism-nation-diaspora that orders many narratives in Sikh and South Asian history in general. The stories of cultural variation, adaptation, and hybridization that I recount in this chapter must be juxtaposed against the articulation of an increasingly systematized and coherent vision of a distinct Sikh identity within north India and Punjab especially. In so doing, I challenge the tendency to treat as distinct problems the history of the Sikh community within Punjab and the early history of overseas Sikh/Punjabi communities. Second, and following on from this, I attempt to anthropologize both the Tat Khalsa and British commitment to systematizing Sikhism. I suggest that both groups accepted a vision of "religion" that juxtaposed Sikhism against a voracious "popular Hinduism" and that the particular interests of the reformers and the state converged in reproducing this systematized identity through enumeration and military recruitment. I have argued against Fox's rather mechanical interpretation of the Singh (kes-dhari) identity as the product of the hegemonic colonizers "making a culture." Within the dominant interpretative frameworks deployed by the British, the Tat Khalsa was heir to the reforming spirit that was at the heart of the Sikh tradition.

For the British the "Indian Reformation," like the European Reformation, was an ongoing process and not some distant historical fact. The gains that the Khalsa had made needed to be carefully guarded so that they would not be swallowed and destroyed by the relentless pressure of the "boa constrictor" of Hinduism. These were arguments that Sikh reformers supported, as they were anxious to shore up the religious boundaries they had worked to build and they saw the colonial state as a powerful legitimating force for their social vision. Of course, as I have insisted, these points of perceived cultural commensurability and points of contact rested on the rigid dichotomies and hierarchies that were used to highlight the "rationality" and "loyalty" of Sikhs. Contrasting Sikhism's monotheism and the polytheism of popular Hinduism; comparing Sikhism's repudiation of caste with Brahmanical "tyranny"; and juxtaposing the martial qualities of the Khalsa with the supposedly effeminizing tendencies of Hinduism were not empty colonial "discourses" with no material outcome but were in fact key features of the broader political and cultural landscapes of empire. They conferred special status on Sikhs, a status that generated substantial wealth and influence for groups that were prominent in military service, and in turn legitimated this privilege. And, most importantly, these discourses also played a central role in enabling the global service of Sikh soldiers and policemen, thereby opening up distant labor markets as well as exposing generations of Sikh men to the risks of injury and death. In surveying these issues I have offered a reinterpretation of Sikhism in the nineteenth century, and I have established a set of analytical concerns, developed in the remainder of the volume, that demonstrate that cultural and religious boundaries were not simply constructed under colonialism and then calcified but have remained continually under construction as the Sikhs and non-Sikhs discuss the history of the Panth, its current state, and its future.

# 3

# Maharaja Dalip Singh, Memory, and the Negotiation of Sikh Identity

O n 29 July 1999, Prince Charles visited Thetford in Norfolk as part
of a celebration of the eight hundredth anniversary of the town's
mayoralty.[1] During the course of the prince's two-hour visit he discharged
a host of responsibilities, including opening a new footbridge over the
Little Ouse River and attending a reception hosted by the city council.
Further, to the delight of a sizable audience of Sikhs who had traveled
to Thetford from across the United Kingdom, Charles also unveiled
a bronze equestrian statue of Maharaja Dalip Singh, which had been
erected on Butten Island at the junction of the River Thet and the Little
Ouse, close to the center of Thetford.[2] The statue, sculpted by the Staf-
fordshire sculptor Denise Dutton, was the key product of the educational
program and fundraising drive of the Maharajah Duleep Singh Centenary Trust (hereafter MDSCT), which was formed in 1992 to "commemorate the centenary of Maharajah Duleep Singh's death, and to promote a
wider appreciation of Sikh heritage and culture." Set in a series of paths in
the shape of the *khanda* (the insignia of the Khalsa), and framed by a series
of plaques providing an interpretative framework for visitors, the statue
depicts a turbaned kes-dhari warrior on horseback grasping a sword. In
addition to Dalip Singh's coat of arms, the base of the statue features

inscriptions in both Punjabi and English. The English version of the inscription on the base of the statue reads:

> Bringing History and Cultures Together: This plaque commemorates the official unveiling of this monument by H.R.H. The Prince of Wales, K.G.K.T., on 29th July 1999. In 1843 Maharajah Duleep Singh succeeded his father to the throne of the sovereign Sikh kingdom of Punjab. He was destined to be its last ruler. In 1849 following the closely fought Anglo-Sikh wars the British annexed the Punjab. Duleep Singh was compelled to resign his sovereign rights and exiled. It was at this time that the koh-i-noor diamond, later to be incorporated into the crown jewels, passed to the British authorities. Duleep Singh eventually came to Britain and settled at the Elveden estate in Suffolk. He was a close favourite of Queen Victoria and became a prominent local figure in East Anglia. Later in his life he announced his intention to return to his beloved Punjab but was not allowed to do so. He died in Paris on October 22nd 1893 having re-embraced the Sikh faith and whilst still engaged in a struggle to reclaim his throne.

Harbinder Singh, chairman of the MDSCT, affirmed the significance of the occasion: "It restores Duleep Singh to his rightful place in history. He was a key figure in the cementing of Anglo-Sikh relations. Prince Charles' presence today is very fitting because the Maharajah was very close to the Royals and Queen Victoria in particular. We have waited six years for this and today we remove the veil of anonymity that surrounds him."

In presiding over the unveiling and in receiving the sword given to him by the MDSCT, Princes Charles reaffirmed the long relationship between the royal lineages of Britain and Punjab. Just two years previously, in July 1997, Prince Andrew gave a speech to the third annual fundraising event run by the MDSCT, in which he stressed the need to further strengthen Anglo-Sikh relations and hinted at the possibility of extending the role of Sikhs in the British armed forces.[3] In endorsing the program of the MDSCT, Prince Andrew's speech resurrected many of the arguments that I explore in chapter 2 about the distinctiveness of Sikhism and its military tradition. The efforts made by the eldest two sons of Queen

Dalip Singh at Osborne, August 1854.

Elizabeth II to emphasize the unique place of Sikhs in British history and contemporary British life, were not innovations but rather were built on a royal tradition that dates back to Queen Victoria herself.

Queen Victoria's strong and close personal relationship with Maharaja Dalip Singh began not long after his arrival in London in 1854, when the fifteen-year-old Dalip was summoned to meet the queen at Buckingham Palace. In her journal, Queen Victoria reflected: "He is extremely handsome and speaks English perfectly, and has a pretty, graceful and dignified manner. He was beautifully dressed and covered with diamonds. The "Koh-i-noor" belonged to, and was once worn by him."[4] Even though Dalip's beloved Koh-i-noor was recut and subsequently formed a key element of Victoria's crown jewels, there is no doubt that a special bond developed between the deposed maharaja and the ruler of Britain's empire. The queen met all of the members of Dalip Singh's entourage; arranged for him to sit for the portraitist Francis Winterhalter; sketched him playing with her children; and invited him to visit the royal family's Isle of Wight retreat at Osborne. While at Osborne, Dr. Ernst Becker photographed Dalip on 23 August 1854, producing a striking portrait that communicates the displacement of the young maharaja. Whereas the artists attached to his father's court regularly represented Ranjit Singh amidst his retinue and with the trappings of power, Dalip here stands alone on a terrace far from his ancestral seat of power in Lahore. And in contrast to Winterhalter's celebrated portrait of Dalip Singh, which was carefully orchestrated to show Dalip in regal regalia (albeit wearing a cameo of Victoria to suggest his loyalty), Becker's photo presents Dalip as a man between worlds, avoiding the camera's eye and wearing a hybrid mix of European-style trousers, leather shoes, tunic, and three-quarter-length jacket in addition to his turban and jewelry.

Despite his position as a deposed ruler and an exile from his Punjabi estates, Dalip initially embraced his position as a favorite of Victoria, even re-presenting the Koh-i-noor to the queen as a sign of loyalty during his sitting for the Winterhalter portrait.[5] In turn, Victoria delighted in the close relationship that Dalip forged with her family, especially with her children. In addition to playing blindman's bluff, leap-frog, and "bobbing for gingerbread" with the princes and princesses, Dalip was especially

close to Prince Leopold, Victoria's son, who was afflicted by hemophilia.
More generally, Dalip Singh's love of hunting was an important interest
that connected him to the male members of the royal household, and his
large estate at Elveden became a favored retreat for royal hunting parties.
In time, Victoria came to be an important advisor to Dalip Singh, and she
was the godmother of his children. Although their relationship was tested
in the 1870s and 1880s when the maharaja expressed a resurgent interest
in both Punjabi history (especially pertaining to his confiscated estates and
jewels) and Indian politics amid a personal financial crisis, the queen
remained sympathetic to his "plight." Even after Dalip Singh entered into
an international conspiracy against British interests, the queen sent a
representative and a commemorative wreath of immortelles to Dalip
Singh's funeral in Elveden in October 1893.

In this chapter I explore Dalip Singh's exile in the United Kingdom,
his place in the historical consciousness of Punjabis (especially those living
in Britain), and the ways in which he has figured in recent debates over
Britishness and the legacies of empire. At the heart of this chapter is the
estate and village of Elveden itself. Although it is some seven thousand
miles from Punjab, this small settlement has been a crucial site for the
construction of Sikh history and identity over the last 150 years. Because
of its close connection to Maharaja Dalip Singh, the village has become an
important pilgrimage site for British Sikhs. But the prominence of Dalip
Singh in the village's past and the significant position that both Elveden
and nearby Thetford have assumed in the cultural life of the Panth have
opened up acrimonious debates over the position of the British Sikh
community and the very definition of Britishness itself. Over the last
decade, Elveden has intermittently captured the public eye, as metropolitan newspapers have highlighted the village's prominent role in the
life of the British Sikh community and exposed the racial and religious
tensions that have erupted over efforts to commemorate Dalip Singh. The
stakes in these "memory battles" are high, as rural Britons and supporters
of the "countryside movement" proclaim that the countryside embodies
the nation's heritage, a past grounded in tightly knit communities structured around the country house (the source of employment and the site of
key rural rituals such as the hunt) and the church. The efforts of British

Sikhs to celebrate Dalip Singh contest and disrupt such narratives, as they emphasize not only the long history of the British Sikh community but also the maharaja's key role as a patron and benefactor in the supposedly homogenous rural world evoked by the villagers of Elveden.

My chief goal in this chapter is to tease out the political and cultural stakes of these conflicting understandings of Dalip Singh's life and legacy. While in the first section I briefly sketch his career and discuss his place within discourses on Sikh identity within India, my primary focus is on a series of British debates that surrounded him in the 1990s. Dalip Singh returned to prominence in the British public sphere in a major 1990 exhibition at the National Portrait Gallery that aimed to reexamine the world of the Raj. In addition to the exhibit, subsequent debates triggered by the foundation of the MDSCT ensured that the last maharaja of the Punjab occupied an important position in end-of-the-millennium reappraisals of British history and identity.[6] The interweaving of Punjabi and British culture in these discourses necessitates a new approach to modern Sikh history, one that is grounded in a recognition of the mutually constitutive nature of colonial encounters and that is dedicated to delineating the multiple forces and contexts that frame the construction and performance of various Sikh identities, both "at home" in Punjab and "abroad" in North America, Australasia, and especially the United Kingdom.

## Punjab to Elveden via Fatehgarh, Aden, Paris, and Moscow

The details of Dalip Singh's life are well known, thanks to the pioneering work of Ganda Singh, a detailed biography produced by Michael Alexander and Sushil Anand, and a recent short reappraisal by David Jones.[7] Born in September 1838, the young Dalip Singh succeeded Maharaja Sher Singh to the Lahore throne in September 1843, but was stripped of his kingdom with the annexation of the Punjab by the East India Company in March 1849. Fearful of the influence that the deposed maharaja might exercise in Punjab, the East India Company sent Dalip Singh to Fatehgarh in the United Provinces, where he was tutored by his "superintendent," Dr. John Login, a respected East India Company medic and administrator. While in Fatehgarh, Dalip Singh continued to develop the hunting skills that were an important inheritance from the culture of the Lahore court. He also pursued a newfound interest in Christianity through discussions with one of his servants, Bhajan Lal, a Brahman who had converted to Christianity, and through reading the Bible. Dalip's engagement with Christianity caused the East India Company considerable anxiety, and only after a thorough investigation into the circumstances surrounding this interest did Governor-General Dalhousie allow Dalip's baptism on 8 March 1853.[8] Dalip Singh's conversion seemed to encourage his desire to visit Europe, and it helped to convince the East India Company's court of directors to accept Login's plan for Dalip Singh to travel to Britain.[9]

After his arrival in England in 1854, Maharaja Dalip Singh became a well-known public figure both in London and in Suffolk where he acquired the large estate at Elveden in 1863. Dalip's popularity with the royal family and his general renown was such that he led the "foreign princes" at the wedding of Edward, Prince of Wales, and, as noted above, he became a favorite of Queen Victoria herself. His time in Britain was marred, however, by recurring financial worries that were exacerbated by his increasingly fraught relationship with the India Office, and on several occasions he appealed to the queen herself both for advice and to bring her influence to bear on the secretary of state for India.

By 1885, however, the relationship between Victoria and Dalip had become strained as she learned of his plans to return to India in order to foment rebellion against the British Empire—a plan that she initially attributed to his cash-stricken status that was "rendering him desperate."[10] When Dalip learned that the government of India planned on his return to confine him to Ootacamund, a hill station in distant south India, he furiously rejected his plan. Instead, he insisted that he would settle in Delhi with the clear implication that he would use the city as a base to regain his economic status and political influence in Punjab.[11] Dalip's willingness to signal his political aspirations and his threat to cast off Christianity greatly worried the queen, the British government, and the government of India, especially after he issued a proclamation in March

1886 that stated that he was "compelled to quit England" as well as signaled his desire to reembrace Sikhism:

> I now, therefore, beg forgiveness of you Khalsa Jee, or the Pure, for having forsaken the faith of my ancestors for a foreign religion; but I was very young when I embraced Christianity.
>
> It is my fond desire on reaching Bombay to take the Pahul again and I sincerely hope for your prayers to the Sutgooroo on that solemn occasion. But in returning to the faith of my ancestors, you must understand, Khalsa Jee, that I have no intention of conforming to the errors introduced into Sikhism by those who were not true Sikhs—such, for instance, as wretched caste observances or abstinence from meat and drinks, which Sutgooroo has ordained should be received with thankfulness by all mankind—but to worship the pure and beautiful tenets of Baba Nanuk and obey the commands of Gooroo Govind Singh.[12]

Even though the rather idiosyncratic vision of Sikhism embedded within Dalip's proclamation was met with some skepticism in India—with the *Pioneer* observing that the maharaja obviously feared "giving up beefsteak"—it contained no explicit statement of any political designs. Nevertheless, it prompted Queen Victoria to note in her journal that "poor M. D-S . . . is becoming very violent & threatens open defiance, & he's going to India to raise the Sikhs!"[13] As Dalip left England for India on 31 March 1886, his correspondents in India were placed under close surveillance and the Punjab police monitored local opinion closely, concerned by the rumors circulating in the bazaars of Punjab relating to Dalip Singh's political ambitions and his connections with Russia.[14] Indeed, before the text of the maharaja's proclamation reached India, the Viceroy Lord Dufferin ordered that Dalip Singh should be arrested on his arrival in Aden.[15] On 21 April 1886 the British Resident at Aden detained the maharaja, and it was made clear that while the maharaja was welcome to return to Britain, he could not travel on to India. During his detention in Aden, Dalip Singh took the *pahul* (Khalsa initiation rite) and thus formally reembraced Sikhism. He also made desperate last attempts to use his arrest to embarrass the government of India and to lever either financial security or a public investigation into his supposed "disloyalty."[16] When it became clear that he was going to make no progress on either front he decided to relocate to Paris, and as a potent symbol of his severing of ties with Britain he resigned the stipend paid to him under the terms of the Treaty of Lahore that had formalized the annexation of Punjab in 1849.[17]

From Paris, Dalip assumed an aggressive pose in his dealings with Britain and the India Office. In a letter to Sir Robert Montgomery, he expressed his anger at having "been so piously swindled by the Christian British nation" and he affirmed that he had "only one prayer now," which was "to have revenge on the Indian administration and humiliate the Government." He signed the letter "a rebel now in earnest."[18] Despite Britain and Russia's movement toward a mutual agreement about their spheres of influence in Central Asia, Dalip now attempted to court Ernst Kotzebue, the Russian ambassador in Paris, in order to frame a coordinated strike against the British Empire.[19] Dalip drafted a series of proclamations, which renounced the Treaty of Lahore, sought financial aid from potential supporters in India, and rallied Indian troops against Britain. In reality, these proclamations were designed for British audiences, and he sent copies of them to friends and correspondents in Britain, one of whom in turn forwarded the incendiary texts to both the India Office and the queen herself. It seems that Dalip hoped that his proclamations might solicit a generous financial settlement from the British government, but when he received no indication that this would be forthcoming he moved ahead with developing a grand seditious scheme.

The foundation of his plot was a series of coordinated uprisings by the Indian princes and the Indian army that were timed to coincide with an international uprising against British interests initiated by Fenian and Russian strikes against British imperial interests. This plot was formulated with the aid of Patrick and James Casey, Irish exiles in Paris, and Mikhail Katkov, an influential Russian journalist and editor who had close connections to the court in Moscow. In fact, to build Russian support for his plan Dalip traveled to Moscow, where soon after his arrival he drafted a letter to the Tzar Alexander III, confirming his desire to free

"250,000,000 of my people from the British tyrants" with the aid of a Russian military expedition. In his letter Dalip reassured the Tzar by stating: "I guarantee an easy conquest of India." To do so he suggested that he could arrange the support of the "Princes of India," and he reassured the Russians that he was "authorized" to offer three million pounds per annum in tribute from the princes to the tzar.[20]

It appears that Dalip's plan was considered by the Tzar, and in order to facilitate its execution he dispatched to India his loyal servant Aroor Singh who carried a letter explaining the scheme to Dalip's "brother Princes of Hindustan."[21] Aroor Singh, however, proved to be ill suited to the role of secret messenger when he described the plan to a Bengali police inspector who posed as a sympathizer of Dalip Singh. Indeed, Aroor Singh omitted few details as he set out the plan that Indian sepoys were to mutiny on meeting the advancing Russian force, imperial communication networks were to be cut, and the princes were to launch attacks on the raj from the Native States. Most importantly, after the rebellion Dalip Singh would assume authority over India, which he would govern on "liberal principles" while paying a "yearly tribute" to Russia.[22]

The capture of Aroor Singh signaled the collapse of Dalip Singh's plans. Soon after the British authorities in India had exposed the details of Dalip's plot, his chief India-based agent, Sardar Thakur Singh Sandhanwalia, died. Dalip realized that he did not have the £4 million he believed was required to put his own revolutionary army in the field, and despite the positive initial indications that Zobair Pasha in Cairo would support a rebellion against the British, Dalip's attempts to build Egypt into his grand scheme came to nothing.[23] He then returned to Paris, from where he wrote to the queen to request either the return of the Koh-i-noor or direct compensation from her private purse for the prized diamond. In May 1889, Dalip married for the second time (his first wife, Bamba Müller, had died after her return to Britain from Aden) but he continued to be troubled by both money worries and a desire to restore his power in Punjab.[24] His political aspirations were dealt a final blow in January 1890, when in his Paris hotel room he suffered a stroke that left him paralyzed down his left side.

The great sportsman and enthusiastic revolutionary had thus become an object of pity, and his eldest son Victor, who was struggling himself with bankruptcy, encouraged the maharaja to give up his "mad schemes" once and for all.[25] Despite reestablishing a cordial relationship with Queen Victoria (much to her advisors' consternation), Dalip Singh was effectively exiled in Paris. Once he finally realized that his plot against Britain had failed, he once again exhibited a strong interest in Christianity and expressed a wish to "die with his hand upon that Book [the Bible]." In the end a broken man, Dalip died in Paris on 22 October 1893 after an "apoplectic fit."[26] His body was embalmed and returned to England, where he was buried in Elveden on 29 October 1893.

## Dalip Singh in Memory

Dalip Singh's life was a complex drama where displacement mingled with sporting success; social standing was supplanted by disenchantment; and where fantasies of restored wealth and power vanished into nothingness. Yet as the many versions of his life that have circulated over the last century suggest, the meaning of individual lives are not fixed but rather are shaped, contested, and reformed through stories, graphic images, biographies, works of fiction, and various forms of private and public performance. By recounting exemplary lives, acts of heroic martyrdom, or villainous treachery, these representations mold both individual and collective memory. In this sense, memory works both constructively and unevenly: it orders and shapes the complexities of the past, highlighting key points while simultaneously omitting or effacing other qualities, practices, or events, thereby crafting fragments of the past into coherent, if partial, images and narratives. As a result, memory plays a central role in the "invention of tradition," the fashioning of narratives that enable the definition of community and the construction of beliefs and practices that tie individuals together into larger collectives defined by ethnicity, faith, or nationality. These processes have played a central role in the constitution of Sikh traditions, and are an important, if underexplored, problematic in Sikh studies: indeed, questions of community memory run through W. H. McLeod's work on the *janam-sakhis* (traditional narratives of the life of Guru Nanak) and his pioneering volume on bazaar prints.[27]

Dalip Singh is a rich case for a study of the constructive and uneven work of memory, especially given his mobility and shifting fortunes. The complex tangle of his life and the religious and political ambiguities that surround his life inhibit the search for an authoritative vision of him. The multifaceted nature of his character has meant that he has been an extremely useful figure for many—often competing—visions of Sikh history and identity: in fact, there seems to be as many Dalip Singhs as there have been tellers of his tale.

In the most important of the recent studies of Dalip Singh, *The Nation's Tortured Body*, Brian Keith Axel has located the maharaja at the heart of his discussion of the place of the body in Sikh diasporic discourses. But while his work rematerializes the use of Dalip's image by proponents of Khalistan, Axel tends to gloss over the profoundly contested position of Dalip Singh in range of debates within Punjab, India, and the Punjabi diaspora. This is symptomatic of Axel's broader tendency to privilege a "purely" Sikh tradition of political thought—essentially the intellectual underpinnings of the Khalistani movement. Given this concern with the struggle for a Sikh "homeland," Axel not only elides the intricate if precarious webs of political allegiance that Dalip fashioned in the 1880s to 1890s and the complex international context of Dalip's campaign against the crown, but he also represents only a very selective range of the visions of the maharaja articulated by British Sikhs and by other Punjabis residing outside South Asia over the last decade. Most significantly, Axel fails to embed the renewed interest in Dalip Singh in the highly charged debates over Britishness in the 1990s and thus silences the voices of non-Punjabi Britons, especially those from the Elveden-Thetford area. In this chapter I place far greater emphasis on the maharaja's place in this renegotiation of Britishness as well as on charting the different positions that Dalip Singh occupies in texts produced by Sikh authors in India and in Britain. We must appreciate the very different salience of historical figures for communities that occupy different locations and face different demands. Even though the "guestbook" hosted by the MDSCT Web site does record the interest of some Punjabis domiciled in North America, there is no doubt that Dalip Singh means much less to these Sikhs than to their British counterparts. This point was made forcibly to me in early 2002 when one of my Sikh students in Illinois, who had just returned from visiting cousins in Bradford, seemed perplexed by Dalip Singh's popularity in Britain. He told me that "He is no Dip Singh," suggesting that the maharaja did not deserve a place in the lineage of mythologized Sikh heroes and martyrs that many Sikhs in India and throughout the diaspora revere.[28] By mapping these divergent visions of Dalip Singh's life and meaning I stress the complexity and texture of Sikh understandings of their community's history.

Even if this young Sikh student from Chicago feels that Dalip Singh falls short of legendary heroes like Baba Dip Singh, there is no doubt about Dalip Singh's continued prominence in South Asia. Despite Dalip's effective exile in Britain, during the late nineteenth century he occupied an important position in community memory, remaining a potent if contested figure for Punjabis. McLeod, for example, notes that the maharaja was among one of the twelve Sikh heroes reproduced in nineteenth-century woodcuts, and the printers Diwan Butah Singh of Lahore and Partap Singh of Amritsar were reproducing images of Dalip Singh for distribution in Punjab during the 1880s.[29] The tumultuous reception that Dalip received from Sikh soldiers during his visit to Calcutta in 1861 alarmed the British to such an extent that his planned up-country tour was canceled and he was ordered to return to Britain by the governor-general himself.[30] Even though Ram Singh, the "guru" of the Kuka movement, initially rejected Dalip Singh as a "beef-eating alien," later official reports suggest that some Kukas believed "the spirit of Guru Ram Singh has entered him."[31] In 1883, when news reached India that Dalip Singh was planning a permanent return to his homeland, the fledgling nationalist movement seized on Dalip as an icon, circulating pamphlets titled *Maharaja Dalip Singh ki jai* (Victory to Maharaja Dalip Singh).[32] Much of this impetus came not from Punjab but rather Bengal. Bengalis played a central role in the campaign and Sardar Dayal Singh Majithia—who had strong ties with the Brahmo Samaj and an abiding interest in Bengali culture—used his *Tribune* to rally support for Dalip Singh.[33] Indeed, in its obituary for the maharaja, the *Tribune* affirmed Dalip Singh's abiding love of his homeland: "He had forgotten nothing of his life at Lahore. He loved to talk of his old days, and his eyes were filled with tears, as he spoke of his old playmates, his *tahlias,* his favourite horse and the gorgeously uniformed regiment of infants consisting of the cadets coming of the noblest houses in the Punjab."[34] The prospect of the maharaja's return also excited the expectations of those Punjabis whose lineages were connected to the court of Ranjit Singh. In 1887, Lord Dufferin reported to the India Office that "in every village Duleep Singh's affairs are freely and constantly discussed" and that individuals whose families were attached to Lahore court fed this interest as they clamored "to see again the bygone days of their being all powerful."[35]

But Dalip Singh was a contentious figure among Sikh reformers during the 1880s. Baba Nihal Singh's *Kurshid-i-Khalsa* (1885) not only celebrated Ram Singh, the leader of the Kuka movement, as a new guru but also anticipated the imminent restoration of the Lahore throne to Dalip Singh. In response to these claims Gurmukh Singh, an influential and radical figure connected to the Lahore Singh Sabha, declared that *Kurshid-i-Khalsa* was "unauthorized" and excluded Baba Nihal Singh from all Singh Sabhas.[36] British officials were pleased with this swift response: as one officer stated, "it is a gratifying testimony to the loyalty of the leaders of the Sikh community."[37] But even as the Chief Khalsa Diwan attempted to negotiate a path through the growing rift between the Lahore and Amritsar Singh Sabhas, Dalip Singh's aspirations to return to power fed this conflict. While members of the Lahore Singh Sabha rejected Dalip Singh's grand schemes for the reconstruction of his authority, he found active support in Amritsar, particularly from Sardar Thakur Singh Sandhanwalia. As a moving spirit behind the foundation of the Singh Sabha, Thakur Singh Sandhanwalia played a central role as Dalip Singh's "local informant" in the Punjab, remitting a detailed sketch of the property and jagirs that Dalip Singh had claim to in Punjab in November 1883.[38] While this correspondence was crucial in the initial formation of Dalip Singh's plans to return to India, Thakur Singh Sandhanwalia was also instrumental in coordinating operations in 1886 and 1887 that were intended to facilitate Dalip Singh's political resurgence. He dispatched Thakur Singh of Wagha to Aden to perform the pahul rite, thereby formalizing Dalip Singh's readmittance into the Khalsa. In light of these activities, both Thakur Singh Sandhanwalia and Thakur Singh of Wagha were under close British surveillance. In November 1886 Thakur Singh Sandhanwalia arrived in French-controlled Pondicherry in the hope that a new base would allow him to function as an effective agent for the maharaja's interests in India, while avoiding the very real possibility of arrest within British India.[39] Thakur Singh Sandhanwalia's deep commitment to Dalip Singh, however, effectively marginalized him within contemporary Sikh politics: this once-influential figure died far from home in Pondicherry in August 1887, championing an unlikely political cause at a moment when Singh Sabha reformers were locked in crucial exchanges over the very nature of Sikhism and the future of their community.

A more detailed assessment of the responses to Dalip Singh's life and death could be assembled from Ganda Singh's important collection of documents published in 1977 as the third volume in the *History of the Freedom Movement in the Punjab,* a work that rehabilitated Dalip Singh as a key Punjabi figure within the mainstream of Indian nationalism. Ganda Singh's volume was the first in a line of publications produced by South Asians that celebrated Dalip Singh's nationalist credentials.[40] Baldev Singh Baddan's 1998 edited collection embodied this explicitly nationalist approach to the maharaja's life. Frustrated at histories that had emphasized Dalip Singh's acculturation, depicting him as "a thorough English country gentleman of his times" or, even worse, "a pathetic, helpless figure, an object of pity and in British eyes an object of ridicule," Baddan cast Dalip Singh as a precocious nationalist leader.[41] Baddan's volume was an act of nationalist recuperation, as he set about recovering the "rebellious facet" of Dalip Singh's life, especially in the anti-British "avatar" of his later years.[42] In short, Baddan celebrated Dalip Singh as "one of the early and most important freedom fighters of India."[43]

## *Nishaan:* Dalip Singh in the Age of a Global Khalsa

Baddan's conventionally nationalist approach, which erases Dalip's engagement with Christianity and shows no interest in Dalip Singh's significance for British Punjabis or his place in British history more generally, has been challenged by the emergence of explicitly transnational visions of Sikhism, such as those documented in Brian Axel's *The Nation's Tortured*

*Body.*[44] India-based community organizations have constructed increasingly dense and elaborate networks that reach out to North America and Great Britain in the hope of knitting together diasporic and India-based populations. Within this context, Baddan's nationalist vision of Dalip Singh has little purchase with Sikhs. Not only are many Sikhs skeptical of the political effects of such narratives in the wake of Operation Blue Star and the imposition of martial law in Punjab, but Sikh organizations in India are also aware of the importance of Dalip Singh for the British diasporic community and his value as an icon for Sikhs in a "global age." One such group, the Nagaara Trust—an "apolitical organization" whose mission is to propagate "the wonderful message of the Sikh tradition for all mankind"—has committed itself to strengthening Sikhism's international profile and cementing the transnational status of the Khalsa. The Nagaara Trust's preferred mediums indicate its commitment to the globalization of Sikhism: alongside its *Khalsa 300: A Vision Re-visited,* a video targeted at an international audience (available "on both VHS-PAL and NTSC systems"), the Trust runs a Web site and publishes a journal, *Nishaan*, which is available both in print and online.[45] The Trust's dedication to an explicitly global agenda is confirmed by the fact that the journal was launched by Dr. Manmohan Singh, who is the architect of the reforms that liberalized India's economy in the 1990s (as *Nishaan* reminds us, Manmohan Singh "transformed the country's insular economy into a global one") and who is closely associated with the World Bank.

In the premier issue of *Nishaan,* alongside articles on "Gurmat Sangeet," "The Mystic Year 1999," and "Anandpur Sahib: Baisakhi 300," two essays explored Dalip Singh's life and legacy. The first, a brief biographical sketch, emphasized Dalip Singh's role as a modern by highlighting his transformation of Elveden from a "run-down estate into an efficient, modern game preserve" and by noting his commitment to the organization of Sikh political activity and anticolonial struggles late in his life. Despite echoing Baddan's insistence on Dalip Singh's role as a pioneering architect of pancommunal nationalism and his neglect of Dalip Singh's conversion to Christianity, the overwhelming emphasis of *Nishaan* was on Dalip Singh's commitment to the Sikh kingdom of Lahore. The Elveden estate was cast as a material expression of Sikh power and an extension of

the glorious court of Ranjit Singh. By recalling how its halls were "deco-
rated with glass mosaic in the fashion of the shish mahal and dominated
by the huge oil paintings of Ranjit Singh in darbar or at the Golden
Temple and of his brother Sher Singh in regal splendour" and noting its
"sculptures of past glories and cases of jewels," *Nishaan* framed Elveden as
embodying the lost glories of Punjab.

This vision was extended in the second essay, "A Defining Moment of
Posthumous Glory," which described the efforts of the British Sikh community to commemorate Dalip Singh. Again, the emphasis in the essay
was on Dalip Singh as an icon of Sikh faith and political commitment. As
such, his rekindled devotion to Sikhism was highlighted along with the
British government's efforts to stifle his desire to "return to his beloved
Punjab." The concluding sentence—"Even today the Sikh Nation aspires
to regain its Sovereignty"—effectively cast an unbroken chain of Sikh
activism that reaches across time and space from Punjab to Britain, and
from the Nagaara Trust through Dalip Singh back to the very foundation
of the Khalsa itself.

## Dalip Singh as a Postcolonial Icon

*Nishaan*'s attempts to stress Dalip Singh's emblematic status for a global
Sikh community must be read at least in part as the product of the efforts
of British Sikhs to elevate him as an icon of their history. In contrast to
Dalip Singh's marginal position within the cultural memory of North
American Punjabis, his image has been increasingly prominent among
the British Punjabi community and, more generally, within a British
public sphere that has increasingly grappled with questions of religious
difference, race, and Britain's place in Europe and the world beyond.
These debates over ethnicity and national identity have operated at a
variety of levels ranging from an avalanche of academic and popular
works on Britishness to numerous documentaries that have reevaluated
British history and the contribution of migrant groups to British culture;
from debates in the House of Commons to violent clashes on the streets of
northern cities; and from sermons in village churches to football stadium
chants. The work of community activists or think tanks like the Runny-

mede Trust—which has examined the power of Islamophobia, in addition to identifying the pernicious "racial and religious codes" that equate Englishness and Britishness with whiteness at the heart of contemporary discussions of British identity in its *The Future of Multi-Ethnic Britain: The Parekh Report*—have invested political reform and cultural change with new urgency, as well as making persuasive cases for the active reimagining of Britishness. Although these processes predated Labour's landslide victory in 1997, they have proceeded at pace under a Labour government that has opened up sustained debates over race, religion, and ethnicity. Even as Labour has attempted to contain these debates within a neat repackaging of Britishness, Tony Blair's government has struggled to redefine Britain's relationship with Ireland, to find a place for Britain within Europe, and to confront the racial violence and institutional racism embedded in the police and justice system revealed by the Stephen Lawrence and Lakhvinder "Ricky" Reel cases.[46]

The effects and legacies of colonialism have formed a prominent thread in discussions of Britishness since the early 1990s. The landmark exhibition "The Raj: India and the British, 1600–1947," held at the National Portrait Gallery in 1990, undertook a major reassessment of British colonialism under the lingering shadow of the "Raj nostalgia" that was so prominent in British culture in the 1980s.[47] It was within this context that Dalip Singh reentered the British public sphere in a dramatic way as C. A. Bayly—a leading British historian of South Asia and the organizer of the exhibition—selected a portrait of Dalip Singh as its "central image." Axel suggests that Bayly's use of this image functioned as a "classic recuperation of orientalist-cum-colonialist longing," which in effect "separated [the Winterhalter portrait] from a long history of conflicts between Sikhs and the British nation-state."[48]

But this stark analysis is unsettled by Bayly's own reading of the portrait, as well as by reviews of the exhibition and the reaction to the maharaja's image by British Punjabis. In an essay in *History Today,* Bayly argued that the painting by Winterhalter captured the central tensions and ambivalences that characterized the Raj as a whole. While the image depicts Dalip Singh as both confident (in contrast to Francis Hayman's famous image of Mir Jafar's submission to Clive) and exotic (Dalip is

bedecked with jewels and minarets rise in the distant mist), Bayly foregrounded the reality of colonial power relations and the conflict between
the company and the kingdom of Lahore. Bayly noted that in reality
Dalip Singh had been reduced to a "mere pensioner" after his "kingdom,
his religion, and even the famous Koh-i-Nor diamond had been snatched
away from him." In short, although "the image suggests the vigorously
exotic; the reality was defeat and dispossession."[49]

Reviews of the exhibition also highlighted the ambivalence of Dalip
Singh's position in an imperial world and the power relations that underpinned this image. As Michael Ratcliffe, writing in the *Guardian,* observed: "Winterhalter had painted his glittering portrait of Dalip Singh at
Buck House, under the enthralled eye of the Queen herself. This is one of
the most glamorous images, and most deceiving, of the Raj. During the
sittings the converted young Christian Maharaja of the Punjab was actually shown the koh-i-nor diamond, nicked from him on Victoria's behalf
five years before."[50] Ratcliffe's reading undercuts Axel's suggestion that
the Winterhalter portrait was used in the exhibition to project "England's
'noble past.' "[51] In a similar vein, Nina Poovaya-Smith suggested that
"Winterhalter's portrait of the young Maharaja Dalip Singh (1838–1883)
is a studied exercise in presenting or mimicking the veneer of power and
authority, a gloss as superficial as the varnish that overlays the painting. . . .
For by the time this work was produced in 1854, Dalip Singh had already
been dispossessed of his kingdom, his wealth and, for a time, even of his
Sikh religion. He lived in England as something of a pet of Queen Victoria, and it is her portrait he wears round his neck. His later sad attempts
at a new selfhood, when he reverts to Sikhism and dreams of a Sikh state,
confer on him a tragic dignity."[52] Although Bayly, Ratcliffe, and Poovaya-
Smith all allude to Dalip Singh's later anticolonial career, they emphasize
his dispossession and dependency: in short, the Winterhalter portrait was
a potent reminder of the disempowerment and dislocation enacted by
colonialism, a verdict that is supported in a 1996 essay by Simeran Mann
Singh Gell.[53]

In the wake of the exhibition, however, British Punjabis would fashion
a very different reading of Dalip Singh, one that shifted the weight from

his subject status and the power of colonialism to a celebration of him as the founder of a diasporic community. If, for Bayly, Dalip Singh's significance lay in his position as "the heir to the last, great free Indian state," for British Punjabis Dalip Singh's iconic status is not because his image marks the culmination of East India Company colonialism but rather because his travels and his life in Britain laid the very foundations of their community.

These divergent readings reflect the different temporal logics and analytical goals of these historical narratives. Bayly's aim was to organize an exhibition that examined British colonialism in South Asia, and as such he located Dalip Singh within a political narrative that traced the rise of the East India Company as a territorial power and the consolidation of its influence; the shift to Crown Raj after 1857 and the gathering strength of nationalism; and, finally, independence and partition in 1947, the terminal point of the exhibition.[54] British Sikh narratives, however, were organized by a different temporal logic to meet a particular cultural need: the desire to fashion a long and celebratory history that might cement the community's distinctiveness and its contribution to British life. For a community living in a nation deeply concerned with "heritage," and where history is a highly marketable commodity, the construction and dissemination of a "long history" is crucial to claiming legitimacy within the public sphere. Indeed, David Lowenthal has suggested that this pressure to claim distant origins or originary status is an overwhelming feature of the British heritage industry.[55]

The role of "heritage" (and other forms of cultural memory) in the constitution of the nation has been explored in essays by Raphael Samuel and Patrick Wright. But while both of these authors interrogate notions of Englishness, they pay limited attention to the role of the empire in constituting metropolitan culture.[56] Scholars working on the South Asian diaspora have drawn attention to the powerful metropolitan influence of empire, but the significance and contribution of the British Sikh community to national life has received surprisingly little attention from historians. While Rozina Visram's *Ayahs, Lascars and Princes* celebrated the long history of South Asians in the United Kingdom (and was warmly received by notable figures such as Salman Rushdie), its focus on the *collective community* of South Asians did not provide the kind of specific and serviceable history that British Punjabis might have looked for.

Further, leading scholars on the British Sikh community have also failed to provide this type of history. Although Visram devoted four pages to a discussion of Dalip Singh in a chapter on "Indian pioneers in Britain," Roger Ballard entirely effaced the maharaja in his essay on the Sikh community in his influential collection *Desh Pardesh*. Under the heading "Sikhs in Britain—The Early Pioneers," Ballard excised Dalip Singh from the British Sikh community's history as he located their origins in the early twentieth century. He stated: "Although mass migration did not begin until the 1950s, the pioneer founders of Britain's Sikh settlement had arrived much earlier. Details are scanty, but it seems probable that the earliest settlers were Sikh soldiers who had fought in France during the First World War, and stayed on in Britain."[57]

## Dalip Singh as a British Settler

The arguments, narratives, and images produced by the Maharajah Duleep Singh Centenary Trust both countered the identification of Dalip Singh's as the embodiment of colonialism's contradictions and extended the truncated vision of British Sikh history elaborated by Ballard. The MDSCT Web site explains its vision of Dalip Singh and his particular importance for British Punjabis: "As the last Maharajah of the Punjab he remains an important symbol of Sikh sovereignty. The 1993 centenary represented an ideal opportunity to mark a period of great significance in Anglo/Sikh history. The annexation of the Maharajah's Sikh empire marked the commencement of an association between the nations which would eventually see Sikh troops serving with unparalleled gallantry in the World Wars. As we enter a new millennium this association is today represented by a Sikh diaspora which plays an active and responsible part in British society. Through its work Trust seeks to remove the veil of anonymity that has hitherto shrouded the life of its last sovereign and by implication the enormously rich heritage of the Sikh nation."[58]

This statement encapsulates the precise cultural and intellectual moves made by the MDSCT to fashion a very particular understanding of Dalip Singh (and, by extension, of British-Sikh relations). While the MDSCT does emphasize the maharajah's function as an "important symbol of Sikh sovereignty," it downplayed the role of colonialism in extinguishing that sovereignty. Although a gesture was made toward the significance of British colonialism, "annexation" is an impoverished term that fails to encapsulate the profound transformations enacted by the colonizing efforts of the British. In effect, here the MDSCT reconfigures the highly unequal power relations of the colonial past into a potentially positive development. It suggests that colonialism initiated the "commencement of an association between the nations," thereby forging a unique partnership between Britons and Sikhs. The MDSCT emphasized the centrality of military service in cementing this cultural and political relationship by highlighting the "unparalleled gallantry" of Sikh soldiers under imperial service.[59]

Most importantly, however, the MDSCT insisted on Dalip Singh's significance within the local British context of a global Sikh diaspora. His life, it suggested, belonged not simply to a purely Sikh past, but rather to a long and continuing "Anglo/Sikh history," a history of connection and interdependence. In this narrative, the role of Dalip Singh (and his descendants) as grandees of the Suffolk countryside—as patrons of hunting and as generous benefactors to local charities and institutions—foreshadowed the important public role of the contemporary British Sikh community, "which plays an active and responsible part in British society." The insistence by MDSCT on the positive contribution of Sikhs not only served to remind fellow Britons of the willingness of Sikhs to engage with British culture, but (in the wake of Operation Blue Star and the growing strength of the Khalistan movement) also counteracted any fears that Dalip Singh might function as a potential symbol for "radical" political action within Britain, an important move given the efforts of the Khalistan Commando Force to celebrate Dalip Singh as the last raja of the Khalsa Raj.[60]

This emphasis on Dalip Singh as a symbol of cross-cultural cooperation culminated in the construction and unveiling of the Thetford statue. There is no doubt that the MDSCT hoped that the statue would be a unifying force for a British Sikh community that has marked generational divisions and is strongly differentiated along caste lines. The image of the maharaja proclaimed a potent past to British Sikhs who were used to the rhythms and landscapes of city life: it evoked the power of the Sikh kingdom of the Punjab and celebrated the martial values central within Sikh iconography and popular tradition. As a memorial, the statue also attempted to provide what we might term a "memory anchor," a fixed vision of a key element of the collective past, a constant referent for a community whose social fabric is being reshaped by migration, class mobility, intermarriage, doctrinal reformulations and schisms.[61]

At its most basic level, however, the statue is a strong proclamation of an important cultural presence within Britain that could be traced back for almost 150 years. The MDSCT emphasized that "the intention of the memorial itself is to provide a memorial to the Maharajah Duleep Singh, and to illustrate the links symbolized between Indian and English history, and between Sikh and western cultures."[62] As noted earlier, this agenda was made explicit in the statue's inscription, which under the heading "Bringing History and Cultures Together" underscored the interweaving of the British and Sikh crowns and the profound connections that Dalip Singh fashioned between India (or at least Punjab) and Britain. While the inscription reaffirmed that "to this day the Sikh nation aspires to regain its sovereignty," the statue cannot be read as a repudiation of Britishness or as a claim against the Crown. In this formulation, at least, Britishness and a desire for a Sikh homeland are not at all incompatible.

## Race, Religion, and Britishness in Elveden

The MDSCT's identification of Dalip Singh as a symbol of "Anglo-Sikh" relations and its insistence on the "constructive" role played by the Sikh community within Britain are issues that have been contested in Suffolk. Since the 1960s, inhabitants of Thetford and more especially Elveden have expressed discomfort, resentment, and open hostility toward Sikhs who have made the pilgrimage to Elveden from London, the Midlands, and cities of the north. In 1961 the discovery of a Sikh at worship in the church adjoining the cemetery where Dalip Singh was buried outraged villagers, and some demanded the immediate reconsecration of the church.[63] The graveyard resurfaced as a flashpoint in the 1990s, when increasing numbers of Sikhs journeyed to Elveden and the MDSCT publicized plans for its statue and formulated a proposal to formally commemorate Dalip Singh's memory with a cultural festival. In response, locals attempted to limit access to the graveyard and rejected the existence of any abiding bonds between the Sikh community and Elveden. Mabel Schofield, a villager whose close family is buried at Elveden, complained that visiting Sikhs "walk over other graves and leave plastic swords about. They don't think of others. They take too much on themselves, but they probably think I'm prejudiced. It's not worth bothering putting up a plaque [to Dalip Singh], but it's their prerogative . . . If they have celebrations here, I won't go."[64]

Access to the Elveden estate also became a contentious issue in the early 1990s as the Guinness family, which has owned it since the early twentieth century, attempted to limit access to the estate and dismissed proposals for celebrations "involving city dwellers in turbans." The *Guardian* reported that "callers at the estate office are told that the only public place is the churchyard, and once they've had a look at the grave the best thing is to continue along the A11 [road]."[65] In response to these developments, Harbinder Singh of the MDSCT argued that racism underpinned the hostility of both the locals and the Guinness family and suggested that this development was a special concern for Sikhs "because they are such a visible minority with the turban they wear." Again he insisted that the aim of the MDSCT was to celebrate the interweaving of British and Sikh culture: "We want to take away this veil of anonymity about our history and get people to realise that the link between the British and Sikhs is not just as immigrants but as equal partners. We've now found an historical link— all commonwealth immigrants have the link of empire—but we have found a special link. We're trying to strengthen Anglo-Sikhism."[66]

## Memory Battles: History and Identity

Harbinder Singh's arguments, however, were not acceptable to vocal opponents of the MDSCT in Suffolk. Whereas Winterhalter's portrait of Dalip Singh as an exotic prince, which graced billboards and posters in London's Underground (in addition to the cover of the exhibition catalogue), might function as a suggestive signifier of Britain's imperial entanglements to a metropolitan audience, the image of Dalip Singh had a very different cadence in the Suffolk countryside. Elveden is situated in a relatively remote, lightly populated and agriculturally based part of East Anglia, which means that its culture has not been transformed by the large-scale migration of Afro-Caribbean and South Asian Britons that has reshaped many other parts of the United Kingdom. Within this context, villagers rejected the maharaja as an alien, as an irrelevant intrusion on accepted understandings of the region's past, and they dismissed contemporary Sikhs as "foreign" interlopers and "nightmarish" intruders.[67]

These clashes over the rights of Sikhs to gain access to the cemetery and the plans to formally recognize Dalip Singh's contribution to the region can be seen as battles over memory and as disputes over the history of various communities of identification (whether British Sikh, Elveden or Suffolk, or, at the broadest level, Britain itself). If we can understand the project of the MDSCT as fashioning and publicizing a particular form of community memory that would simultaneously unite British Sikhs while drawing the attention of non-Sikhs to the iconic status of Dalip Singh, the local population attempted to excise Dalip Singh from their community memory and protect their vision of Elveden as quintessentially "English."

The Sikh pilgrims who arrived in Elveden in small groups or by the coach-load challenged this vision. The turbans worn by many of the men, the *salwar kameez* of the women, and the sound of spoken Punjabi called into question an unreconstructed white Protestant Englishness. The bodies, dress, and language of the visitors manifested cultural difference in ways that could not easily be absorbed into the vision of England cherished by the villagers. The opening passages of Meera Syal's *Life Isn't All Ha Ha Hee Hee* underscore the unassimilable nature of important facets of Punjabi migrant culture in Britain. The novel opens with an elderly white man collecting the milk bottles from his snow-covered doorstep in Leyton, when he sees a *barat* (a bridegroom's wedding party) approaching a nearby community center:

The horse turned the corner into his road, white enough to shame what fell from the sky, carrying what looked like a Christmas tree on its back. There was a man in the middle of the tinsel, pearls hanging down over his brown skin, suspended from a cartoon-size turban. He held a nervous small boy, similarly attired, on his lap. Behind him, a group of men of assorted heights and stomach sizes, grins as stiff as their new suits, attempted a half-dance half-jog behind the swishing tail, their polished shoes slipping in the slush. A fat man in a pink jacket held a drum around his neck and banged it with huge palms, like a punishment, daring anyone not to join in. "Brrrr-aaaa! Bu-le, bu-le bu-le!" he yelled. . . .

Other neighbours had gathered at windows and doorways, the children giggling behind bunched fingers, their elders, flint-faced, guarding their stone-clad kingdoms warily, in case bhangra-ing in bollock-freezing weather was infectious.

Swamped, thought the old man; someone said that once, we'll be swamped by them. But it isn't like that . . . It's silent and gentle, so gradual that you hardly notice it at all until you look up and see that everything's different.[68]

Although Syal highlights the significant cultural translations required as Punjabis transplanted their culture to a cold and alien environment, she emphasizes that these translations simultaneously reworked the culture of the migrants and transformed British culture itself. The mix of curiosity about and resistance to cultural difference that runs through this passage is also at the heart of Sikh artists Amrit and Rabindra Kaur Singh's *Wedding Jange II,* which depicts the arrival of a bridegroom on horseback at his bride's house. Here the Punjabization of Britain is not only demonstrated through the clusters of Sikhs standing on the road but also in the road itself, which is represented in the highly ornamented pattern of an Indian carpet. At the same time, however, the image is framed by the white neighbors of the bride's family as well as passers-by, who are separated from the main scene by a substantial fence and the profound cultural gap suggested in their clothing and food.

The inhabitants of Elveden tried to insulate themselves from the cultural challenge and change unleashed by Asian migration to Britain. In

Amrit and Rabindra Kaur Singh, *Wedding Jange II*.

1993, racial and religious homogeneity as the foundation of local life were neatly invoked by one villager, who stated: "I have to say the Sikhs are a bit of a nightmare . . . sometimes they look, well, er, rather strange. I suppose we're not used to people like that round here."[69] Implicitly, "the people round here" were white and Christian, not South Asian Sikhs. The willingness of Sikhs to travel to Elveden, and the MDSCT plans to formally celebrate his memory, punctured the "peace," predictability, and homogeneity that villagers treasured. These Sikhs were not only visiting Elveden; they were laying claim to its Britishness. As the *Guardian* observed: "The coach-loads of Sikh children from Wolverhampton who went to Elveden last summer were thrilled. It's the very Englishness of Elveden which makes the story so potent. The wrought iron gates, the empty mansion and the romantic sweep of parklands exert a snobbish fascination. All this once belonged to their co-religionist." The *Guardian* also suggested that it was in cultural encounters such as those playing out in Elveden—"this chocolate-box remnant of 19th century England"—that the future shape of national identity was being defined: "It's a tale for our times—two bits of England representing two nations as disparate as anything Benjamin Disraeli ever considered. Only this time, it's not wealth that divides. A multicultural urban Britain schooled in racial tolerance meets the quintessential rural England—an area on the Norfolk-Suffolk border where landed gentry still hold sway over their estates."[70] These oppositions between city and country, between tradition and the future, and between diversity and homogeneity are striking and run through the debates surrounding the activities of the MDSCT. As we have already seen, the managers of the Elveden estate made it clear in 1993 that they did not welcome "city dwellers in turbans" in the Suffolk countryside. Yet this insistence that Sikhs had no part to play in rural Britain—that the people of Suffolk were "not used to people like that"—was only possible because of the disavowal of Dalip Singh's important contributions to the region's cultural life in the late nineteenth century.

Oral histories produced by the inhabitants of Elveden celebrate rural pastimes and values, identifying them as providing the bonds of community and the basis of daily life. The reminiscences of Reg Trett, for example, are full of accounts of farming, the fruits of the harvest, sports, and hunting.[71] Although the very existence of an Elveden village Web site (a project initiated by the Forest Heath District Council and funded by the National Lottery Board) chafes against the identification of the village as an embodiment of the old rural order, the site nevertheless celebrates the two bastions of rural community, the estate or country house—the "hall"—and the church. Some passing references are made to Dalip Singh (noting, for example, that his generosity enabled the repair of the church in 1869), but his connection with the estate is almost entirely effaced. In effect, this denies his crucial role in the development of the estate as one of the premier sites for hunting in Britain and its popularity with the Victorian elite. In short, the village's Web site excises Dalip Singh from community memory, and this works to delegitimize the claims of British Sikhs about the significance of the hall or the cemetery.[72]

It seems that the people of Suffolk, like Punjabi nationalists, are at great pains to expunge Dalip Singh's brief but prominent role as a bastion of the British rural elite. Although villagers respond to the presence of Sikhs in Elveden by insisting that they are not used to "people like that," a wealth of material establishes Dalip Singh's rapid adoption of the life of a country squire. In many ways, his childhood at the Lahore court, where from a very early age he was schooled in falconry and the use of weapons, and his subsequent exile in Fatehgarh, where he kept elephants and hawks, prepared the maharaja well for an elite life in rural Britain where blood sports were a highly valued cultural tradition.[73] Indeed, Dalip Singh's initial renown as an enthusiast for British rural life and as a skilled hunter was based on his leasing of Castle Menzies in Perthshire, and later he gained national fame as a sportsman after setting a new shooting record at Grandtully in Perthshire (some 440 grouse in a day).[74] It was at Elveden, however, that he became a bulwark of the rural establishment, a reputation he cemented by shooting some 780 partridges with 1,000 cartridges. At the Elveden estate, Dalip Singh hosted famous shooting parties that included the Prince of Wales as an invited guest. As Alexander and Anand note, Dalip Singh welcomed "all the great shots" at Elveden and he hosted "half the grandees in the land."[75] There is also evidence to suggest that for his contemporaries in Suffolk, Dalip Singh embodied the ideals of rural masculinity. T. W. Turner, who eventually

Hunting party at Elveden, 1876. Here Dalip Singh is reclining in the middle of the front row, with the Prince of Wales (holding a walking stick) behind and to the left. Reproduced by permission of the Royal Photographic Collection.

became head gamekeeper at the Elveden estate, noted that it was after watching the maharaja partridge shooting that he decided, "When I get to be a man I will be a gamekeeper if I can."[76]

Thus Dalip Singh's love of horses, hunting, and firearms—passions central to the courtly culture of the Punjab of Ranjit Singh—provided an important entrée into elite British society and formed a common idiom that temporally transcended, or at least mitigated, differences of race and religion (although Dalip was, of course, a Christian while living at Elveden).[77] Such skills were a crucial marker of masculinity and gentility for the British aristocracy, and the *Times of India* celebrated the maharaja's ability to "play the role" of "a fine gentleman." Despite the implication that this was in some sense a performance, the newspaper recognized Dalip Singh's abilities as "landlord, a patron or a host."[78] The statue of Dalip Singh in Thetford suggests these "rural values": the regal maharaja on horseback not only evokes images of great British heroes—such as the famous statue by Carlo Marochetti of Richard the Lion-Hearted outside the Houses of Parliament—but also embodies the rural, masculine ideals so prominent in Sikh iconography and the popular prints produced for the bazaars of Punjab and Southall.

Here we can extend Brian Axel's insights into the iconic status of Dalip Singh, as well as identify another important layer of meaning that attached to what Axel terms "the Maharaja's glorious body."[79] Unlike other South Asian male travelers (especially Bengalis such as Rammohan Roy and Keshub Chandra Sen) who were, as Antoinette Burton has demonstrated, represented within feminized idioms that stressed their "sweetness" and "gentleness," Dalip Singh's masculinity was consistently emphasized within metropolitan discourses.[80] Embodying a military and religious heritage that was juxtaposed against the effeminacy of popular Hinduism, vegetarianism, and the supposed innate femininity of Bengali culture, Victorian reportage hailed Dalip Singh as the antithesis of the effete Bengali *babu*. Of course, these heavily gendered understandings of race and religion had powerful material and cultural effects: the equation of Sikhism with a masculine warrior tradition underpinned the "Punjabization" of the Indian army while simultaneously rendering Sikh women silent and invisible.[81]

Gender continues to be a crucial element in the performance of Sikh identities within contemporary Britain. The statue at Thetford allows the contemporary British Sikh community to maintain an insistence on the distinctive masculinity of the Sikh tradition, a masculinity that is used to set off the Panth from other South Asian communities and to forge a common bond between Britons and Punjabis out of a hypermasculinist discourse. A cultural commensurability between Britons and Sikhs grounded in a shared masculinity—or, at least, a perceived commensurability— remained important even in the late twentieth century, as the feminizing discourse of the *babu* was reworked within the British public sphere to insist on the fundamental otherness of Britons of Bengali/Bangladeshi descent, most notably in the controversial Morrissey song "Bengali in Platforms."[82] In short, Sikhs are frequently identified as the most assimilable of British South Asian communities, in part because of their perceived masculinity and also because of their "loyalty" to empire. But once again, it is important to recognize that the affinities constructed between white Britons and Sikhs are constructed around and reinforced by a series of other oppositions that are used to throw into high relief the supposedly unique features of Sikhism. Most recently, the erosion of the Khalistan movement has again placed Sikhs in a privileged position among South Asian migrant communities, as their faith allows them to distance themselves from South Asian Muslims who, in a climate post-Rushdie and post-9/11, are identified as a threat not only to British secular modernity but to the very nation itself. Within these discourses, British Sikhs are framed as more familiar, more legible, and less threatening than Muslims, a form of positioning that simultaneously hints at the possibility that the difference of Sikhs can be accommodated within the British nation state while using this form of tolerable difference to exaggerate the irreconcilable difference of other migrant groups.

## Conclusion

As Brian Caton has recently demonstrated, the "British rural ideal" has functioned as a crucial influence on the construction of Sikhism from the mid-nineteenth century. British accounts of the court of Ranjit Singh emphasized his attachment to all things military, his love of hunting, and his attachment to horses. Colonial ethnographers and military recruiters celebrated the "sturdy" Jat who was close to the land and deeply attached to traditions of military service.[83] But Dalip Singh's enthusiastic embrace of such values within a metropolitan context disrupted many of the key fictions about heritage, history, and Britishness. Dalip Singh's prominence as an "English squire" along with the Sikh community's celebration of his memory punctured the oppositions drawn by the Guinness family and the *Guardian* between city and country and between urban multiculturalism and rural homogeneity. As the squire of Elveden, Dalip Singh destabilizes any attempts to cast the countryside, rural life, or hunting as refuges for an unreconstructed Englishness that is grounded in the traditions of the past. In essence, Dalip Singh subverts the oppositions between the country and the city that have structured British life from the early modern period, thus challenging the dichotomies that continue to resonate in debates over the role of farming and hunting in the British economy and identity.[84]

It is essential that we recognize the very high cultural stakes attached to these debates over belonging, over the boundaries of community, over what it is to be British. In March 2005 the statue of Dalip Singh in Thetford was defaced. White paint was splashed across the face of the statue and swastikas and the letters "NF" (meaning the National Front) were scrawled across the monument. This attack on the key public expression of the aspirations of British Sikhs to belong to the British nation and to be seen as part of British history reveal that some white Britons continue to nurture deep-seated anxieties over, as well as hatred for, any form of "otherness." While the mayor of Thetford and many residents of the area condemned the defacement of the statue, British Sikhs saw it as an act of desecration and an open attack on their community itself. This reading not only reflected the great significance of the statue to British Sikhs, but also the anxieties that British South Asians felt over the growing prominence of the British National Party and the centrality of race in British politics in the wake of the "War on Terror" and in the time leading up to the 2005 election.[85]

Dalip Singh's life and his afterlife in community memory remind us of the contested connections between British and Punjabi cultures since the nineteenth century, a theme that has received surprisingly limited treatment in the historiography of Sikhism. The dominant tradition within Sikh studies is what I identified in chapter 1 as an "internalist" approach. In this view, Sikh history is to be mainly understood in light of the internal dynamics of the Panth, where the elaboration of Sikh tradition through a genealogy of texts, the competing visions of doctrine and community, and the shifting social composition of the Panth form the key analytical issues. Here I have attempted to balance a sensitivity to the importance of Sikh agency and the power of community organizations with an emphasis on the crucial cultural and political contexts that shape postcolonial Sikh identity, particularly within the British context. In locating the increased prominence of Dalip Singh in the British public sphere within the broader context of the renegotiation of ethnicity and national identity in post-Thatcher Britain, I have not attempted to disavow the claims of British South Asians (particularly those of Punjabi descent) about the significance of Dalip Singh. Rather, I have emphasized that community identity is never simply the product of the dynamics internal to that community. Sikh identity is constantly remade through encounters with other communities (whether of faith, ethnicity, or political allegiance) and access to public institutions and the machinery of government. In other words, Sikh identities are constantly formed and reformed through an uneven polylogic process, whereby understandings of community continue to be formulated, performed, and reformed in response to other groups, whether Punjabi Hindus, Muslims, or *patit* or *mona* Sikhs who are seen to occupy the margins of the community and, within the British context, South Asians of Gujarati or Bangladeshi origin, or Britons of Afro-Caribbean or Anglo-Celtic descent.[86]

It is important to stress that such processes are not confined to the last few decades. Indeed, the mutually constitutive nature of such cross-cultural encounters has been stressed in recent historical work by Rozina Visram, Antoinette Burton, and Michael Fisher on South Asians in Britain from the eighteenth century on.[87] As yet, however, such work on the articulation of Punjabi, and more specifically Sikh, identities within Britain is still fragmentary. In addition to Kathleen Hall's *Lives in Translation,* efforts such as Axel's work on transnational representations of the male Sikh body, Saloni Mathur's essay on the beleaguered Tulsi Ram, and Susan VanKoski's study of Punjabi soldiers in Britain and France during World War I hint at important avenues for future inquiry and reflection.[88]

For over a century and a half the Sikh community, whether at home or abroad, has lived in a world fundamentally reshaped by British colonialism. The transformative power of colonialism not only engendered new social structures and cultural formations in the periphery but also played a central role in the constitution of metropolitan cultures, including understandings of gender, religion, race and national identity. If this essay has warned that internalist approaches to the Sikh past erase important connections with other religions, regions, and nations, it has also demonstrated that the British past can no longer be imagined as an "island story" or a tale of "splendid isolation."

# 4

# Displacement, Diaspora, and Difference
## in the Making of Bhangra

B hangra beats and Punjabi vocals were prominent in the soundscapes of the northern hemisphere in summer 2003. Jay-Z's remix of Panjabi MC's "Mundian To Bach Ke" was not only a club staple but also did well on the charts. Jay-Z's interweaving of the original 1998 version of this underground hit (which combined the vocals of Labh Janjua and the sampled bass line from the theme to the cult 1980's television show *Knightrider*) with his own frenetic rapping about Brooklyn, New York City, and the war in Iraq, was particularly well received in Europe, where it reached number 1 on the charts in Italy and Greece, number 2 in Germany, Austria, and Denmark, and number 5 in the United Kingdom. In the United States it was truly a "cross-over" hit, as it peaked as the eighth-highest selling single and reached as high as 14 on the Rhythm charts and 34 on the Urban charts. In addition, "Mundian" enjoyed regular airplay on both college and mainstream commercial radio, where it was played in excess of 3,200 times a week and reached a radio audience of over thirty-two million listeners, and the song's video was on heavy rotation on MTV2.[1] Even though many American commentators picked "Mundian" as "the song of the summer"—hinting at both its "feel-good" qualities and its perishability as a cultural commodity—during the same period both song and video enjoyed success in the southern hemisphere's winter. In distant Australia, for example, the single peaked at number 12 and the video was featured on New Zealand's primetime free-to-air music video programs *Most Wanted* and *Space*. Most strikingly, the young Maori rapper Scribe, who was at the forefront of the burgeoning New Zealand hip hop scene, reworked "Mundian" on the prerelease version of his triple-platinum *Crusader* album.[2] By the time "Mundian" was cut up by Scribe and his *Pakeha* (white New Zealander) collaborator DJ P. Money, this track had not only reached a massive international market but also had been repeatedly reworked as it was rapidly repackaged, marketed, disseminated, and consumed within the global circuits of popular culture.

While cellular phone companies were quick to cash in on the single's worldwide success among young consumers by providing them with "Mundian" ring tones, leading newspapers and magazines—ranging from the *Guardian* to *USA Today,* the *New York Times* to *Entertainment Weekly,* and the *Houston Chronicle* to the *Village Voice*—excitedly reported on the success of the collaboration between Jay-Z and Panjabi MC and the possibility that subsequent bhangra hits might follow this "breakthrough." Many of these print media reports fell back on a range of hackneyed play-on-word headlines (such as "Jay-Z Remix Spices Interests in Panjabi MC" or "A Passage to India") as Panjabi MC's success was hyped as marking the arrival of bhangra on the global scene. American journalists, in particular, used this exoticizing and orientalist shorthand to frame their "discovery" of bhangra, which was consistently identified as an "ancient," "distant," and "folk" musical tradition. The St. Petersburg *Times* in Florida, for example, suggested that in Jay-Z's remix tradition, in the form of Punjabi MC's "ancient, rhythmic Indian music stylings," met the modernity of "bass-driven rap."[3] This understanding of "Mundian" as the staged encounter between a dichotomized American (post)modernity and Indian tradition not only erases the earlier history of this particular song and Panjabi MC's Britishness, but also effaced two key elements that not only are integral to the particular success of "Mundian" but also to the history of bhangra more generally. The first of these elements is the long transformation of bhangra both within India and beyond—a complex set of changes that sits uneasily with the timelessness that many journalists and critics ascribe to it. Second, and following on from this, is the centrality of migration and cross-cultural engagements (the collaboration of Panjabi MC and Jay-Z is but one example) in the recasting of bhangra over the last three decades.

In charting bhangra's shifting performative traditions, social contexts, and cultural politics, I offer in this chapter a prehistory to the global success of "Mundian To Bach Ke," and I extend my earlier explorations of Sikh memory and identity markers in a postcolonial and diasporic world. Bhangra has played an extremely important role in the articulation of both Punjabi and Sikh identities over the last four decades. It has been a prominent element in the creation of a Punjabi regional identity in the wake of partition; played a central role in the cultural life of diasporic South Asians in the United Kingdom; and functioned as a flexible expressive form that has connected the various Punjabi communities (both within South Asia and outside) into a shared, if highly uneven, cultural space. Equally importantly, bhangra has been a powerful medium in the projection of Punjabi and Sikh culture. Through bhangra lyrics, stage performances, cassettes, CDs and MP3s, music videos, Internet discussion groups, and the press, visions of Punjabi history, Sikh identity, and the values of rural (especially Jat) Punjab have circulated widely in networks of cultural production and consumption since partition.

These cultural products are thus not only widely disseminated within the nation-state of India and among Punjabi diasporic communities, but also have been interwoven into the global cultural markets that integrate, however unevenly, consumers who occupy a wide range of social positions and articulate a bewildering array of ethnic, religious, racial, and gender identities. In this regard, bhangra can be set alongside other cultural forms that have a global reach yet retain a strong imprint of their origin, or what George Lipsitz terms a "poetics of place." Many of the central issues that run through my discussion here of bhangra's place in the global cultural economy are neatly encapsulated by Lipsitz, as follows: "New Orleans jazz and sambas from São Paulo circulate freely throughout the world, but they never completely lose the concerns and cultural qualities that give them determinate shape in their places of origin. Through music we learn about place and displacement. Laments for lost places and narratives of exile and return often inform, inspire, and incite the production of popular music. Songs build engagement among audiences at least in part through references that tap memories and hopes about particular places. Intentionally and unintentionally, musicians use lyrics, musical forms, and specific styles of performance that evoke attachment to or alienation from particular places."[4]

Through an extended discussion of bhangra's place in Punjabi histories and global cultural formations, in this chapter I make three interventions within the field of Sikh studies. First, by exploring bhangra, which cannot be strictly identified as a "Sikh tradition" because it emerged out of a broadly peasant, but more specifically Jat, Punjabi performative tradition that was pancommunal, I suggest that an understanding of contemporary Sikh identity must pay close attention to the broader context of Punjabi culture: both within and outside South Asia.

Second, and more radically, by attempting to delineate the sustained engagement of urban Punjabis with the cultural idioms of the African diaspora I stress that any understandings of the recent development of Punjabi expressive traditions and diasporic identities must recognize the importance of encounters with Afro-Caribbean peoples in Europe and in North America. This is a crucial point, not only for Sikh studies but also for understanding diasporic histories more generally. The vast majority of work on the diaspora either focuses on the relationship between the mobile group and their "homeland" or that group's relationship to their new host state; thus there is limited sociological work and very little historical work that explores the junctures between and interweaving of diasporas. My exploration here of overlapping and intersecting diasporas not only opens up new perspectives on Sikh history, but also is suggestive of an important approach to the cultural history of mobile groups.

Third, in my attempt to analyze popular culture in a serious and sustained manner, this essay marks a fundamental break from the dominant "textualist" approach of Sikh studies. Within the existing scholarship on the Sikhs, the understanding of "popular culture" has largely been connected with the cosmologies and religious observances of the Punjabi peasantry, rather than their expressive traditions, especially those traditions that have only limited connection with religious practice and institutions.[5] Where "popular culture" has been engaged, most notably in W. H. McLeod's pioneering *Popular Sikh Art,* such work has re-instantiated a rigid division between the "popular" and the "high" and has taken considerable pains to justify an interest in expressive forms that cater to "an uneducated taste."[6] Here I suggest that a close examination of forms of popular culture, such as bhangra, can open up questions about the systematization and performance of identities, the circulation of cultural forms, and the relationships between technology, economic structures, and social formations. More specifically, a close consideration of bhangra's histories offers particularly important insights for Sikh/Punjabi studies because it not only raises questions about the relationships between "home" and "away," but also forces us to grapple with both its identity politics and its place in the political economy of global culture. By tacking back and forth between Punjab and Mumbai, South Asia and Southall, and through an extended discussion of the interfaces between Punjabi diasporic communities and the Afro-Caribbean populations of British cities, in this essay I attempt to unravel the complex cultural webs and networks that have molded the development of Punjabi culture and Sikh identities within a global frame. In so doing, I locate both bhangra and Punjabi culture at the cultural "crossroads" identified by Lipsitz as the improvisational, creative, but fraught sites where diverse people meet, engage, and define themselves.

I begin here by paying close attention to the history of bhangra within Punjab itself; by examining bhangra's early history as a localized dance form and the growing equation between bhangra and "Punjabiyat" after partition. These stories, frequently erased in work on bhangra produced by cultural studies scholars and neglected in studies of bhangra's place in the South Asian diaspora, are crucial because they provide a baseline against which the radical transformation of bhangra over the past three decades can be assessed. In the middle sections of the essay I examine the new forms of bhangra that emerged within Britain between the late 1970s and the early 1990s. To do so I explore both the aesthetics and antiracist identity politics of the hybridized form of music that I term "black bhangra," and I trace the erosion of this innovative cultural form by more commercialized forms of bhangra and by "Indipop" in the mid-1990s. In the final section I return to Punjab itself, sketching the ways in which Punjabis "at home" have accessed these new trends and reformulated bhangra yet again in an attempt to shore up "tradition" in the face of what has been termed the "cultural imperialism" of "disco, tango or rock-and-roll."[7]

## Bhangra and the Development of Punjabi Expressive Traditions

Although the literary production, educational system, and print culture of colonial Punjab were dominated by the ascendancy of Urdu—a hegemony initially sponsored by the colonial state and leading orientalists such as G. W. Leitner—rich vernacular traditions flourished despite the limited state support.[8] Most obviously, the reading of Guru Granth Sahib by granthis and the collective performance of *kirtan* (devotional songs) underscore the centrality of both religious observance and oral expression in Punjabi, both spoken and sung, in the cultural world of the Sikh community as a whole. Beyond kirtan and *bani* (the sayings of the gurus), however, we can also identify a rich and diverse array of Punjabi expressive traditions. The folktales narrated by traveling *mirasis* (ballad singers) and village elders that were collected by colonial officials such as Richard Temple and Charles Swynnerton capture the persistence of the "enchanted universe" that Harjot Oberoi has identified as characteristic of precolonial rural Punjabi culture into the colonial period.[9]

Music was a central feature of this cultural world, and an array of folk musical traditions developed around the rhythms of agrarian production and the key points in an individual's life cycle, especially birth, marriage, pregnancy, and death. These celebratory folk songs coexisted with popular narrative ballads that were quickly established as staples of the print culture in the urban centers of Punjab. But even as narrative ballads such as *Hir* (expressed in its most refined form in Waris Shah's *Hir-Ranjha*) or the tragic tale of Sahiban and Mirza were being refined, reworked, and repackaged on Punjabi printing presses, oral versions of these tales remained popular in small villages where they were frequently recited to the accompaniment of music.[10] The profound interdependence of the oral and literate forms within the transformation of Punjabi expressive and musical traditions is in keeping with Stuart Blackburn and A. K. Ramanujan's insistence on the constant "borrowing" backward and forward between oral and written folk narratives within South Asia.[11]

If early-twentieth-century Punjabi music was increasingly influenced by literary expression, from the 1930s it has been increasingly entangled with another form of cultural production: the cinema. Pioneering Punjabi composers such as Ghulam Haider (1910–1953) ensured that Punjabi folk traditions have profoundly influenced Hindi film music. Haider was the first of a string of important Punjabi composers and musical directors who shaped the music of popular Indian film (others include Shyam Sunder, Bhagatram and Husnlal, Feroz Nizami, and Hansraj Behl). Haider played an influential role in shaping early Punjabi films such as *Gul-e-Bakavali* (1939), before revolutionizing Hindi film music with his score for D. M. Pancholi's *Khazaanchi* (1941), a film that established the basic structure of the modern *filmi* song. Haider's influence popularized both the earthy verve of Punjabi folk music and its characteristic percussion instruments, especially the *dholak,* in filmi music.[12] Filmi music, on the other hand, influenced the forms of Punjabi music that were recorded in the post–World War II period and undoubtedly shaped the commercialized Punjabi music that was popularized by Asa Singh Mastana and Surinder Kaur and by more recent performers such as Prakash Kaur, Jamla Jat, and Kuldip Manak.[13]

## Bhangra in Independent Punjab

At the same time that Punjabi music was claiming larger attention within the culture of independent India, one important Punjabi cultural form was undergoing significant change. After partition, new efforts were launched to preserve and to systematize bhangra, a peasant dance particularly associated with the wheat harvest and the festival of Baisakhi. The scant body of source material on Punjabi folk culture before 1947 means that the early history of bhangra remains contentious, and debates over its etymology, origins, and nature are common.[14] What is clear is that by the late nineteenth century, bhangra had emerged as a dance typically performed to the beat of the large *dhol* drum (which was often accompanied by smaller *dholak* or *dholki* drums).[15] The relationship between the vigorous movements of the dancers and the beat was at the center of this performative tradition, rather than the lyrics (which typically celebrated fertility and the joys of harvest) that were sung by the accompanying vocalist or the enthusiastic cries of "braah," "a-ho," "hoi," and "balle shera" of the dancers and/or the gathered crowd. Bhangra rhythms were typically flexible, expressing a wide variety of moods: Iqbal Singh Dhillon suggests that in its ability to express the "festive, virile, romantic and even the mourning," bhangra was and is the "total dance."[16] Traditional Punjabi folk dances like bhangra were always gender specific: women might perform dances like the *giddha*, *luddi*, *sammi*, and *pharuha*, but bhangra itself, like the *jhummir* and *bagha*, was a specifically male dance form.[17] Prior to partition, bhangra was not only gender specific but also, like other forms of rural popular culture, it was a highly localized performative tradition. It was locked into the particular social structures, economic patterns, and cultural forms of a specific space. In bhangra's case, it was principally associated with the Sialkot, Gujrat, Shekhupura, Gujranwala, and Gurdaspur districts of western Punjab, and the bhangra of the villages of Sialkot was widely considered the purest and perhaps even the standard form of bhangra prior to the massive upheavals that transformed the social and cultural landscape of rural Punjab from 1946.[18]

In the wake of partition, bhangra assumed new importance as part of the projection of "Punjabiyat" and the regional government's attempt to construct a coherent state culture that transcended the deep divisions that were laid so bare in the violence of partition. Within this context, bhangra became a ubiquitous feature of the province's culture within independent India. As the Chandigarh *Tribune* observed in 1998: "The *bhangra* dance, today, is no longer associated with the Baisakhi festival alone. On any festive occasion, say *Lohri,* betrothal and marriage ceremonies, the birth of a son, cultural and sports meets, [and] agricultural fairs, including cattle fairs, one can witness this dance."[19]

Bhangra's transformation into an icon of Punjab and "Punjabiness" was carefully cultivated by the regional government. Refugees from the western parts of Punjab that were the cradle of bhangra were the key vector that carried bhangra east into the newly formed Indian Punjab. Refugee camps were a crucial site where a new team-based form of bhangra emerged and where dance was an important shared element of culture within the turbulent context of partition. It allowed displaced people to perform and to reaffirm traditional ties and cultural bonds that transcended the politics of caste and religious community. In April 1948, a bhangra "team" of refugees put together by Chaman Lal Rana entertained Jawaharlal Nehru and Lord Mountbatten at the Kurukshetra refugee camp. Not only was the dance fostered as a way of building community within east Punjab in the wake of partition, but the Punjabi state also began to sponsor bhangra as an emblem of a distinctive Punjabi identity within independent India. Revealingly, the first instance of bhangra as an organized spectacle for a mass public audience was sponsored by the PEPSU (Patiala and East Punjab States Union) government for the Republic Day Parade in Delhi in 1955. Although in 1956 the government of Punjab sponsored a female *giddha* (a dramatic dance based around clapping) team and a male *jhummir* (a dance performed in a circle) team to perform on Republic Day, bhangra enjoyed a special status as iconic of Punjabi culture as a whole and by 1956 had appeared in Hindi films such as *Jagte Raho* and *Naya Daur.* Punjabi educational institutions, particularly Khalsa College and Panjabi University, as well as a range of other schools and colleges began to emphasize the importance of bhangra and organized bhangra teams and competitions. In this new staged form of dance, a wide range of movements associated with other male folk dances were assimilated into tightly synchronized performances that rehearsed a wide range of coordinated movements at considerable speed. New dramatic elements were introduced into bhangra performances and teams were judged on their movement, appearance, and choreography. At the same time, new instruments (the *chimta* and *algoza*) were added to accompany the *dhol*; a new emphasis was placed on the singing of *bolis* (lyrics) by an accompanying singer (whereas the *laakri* [leader] would traditionally have sung prior to the performance of bhangra and during short pauses by the dancers); and "coaches" emerged to drill their teams and to oversee the increasingly complex range of formations and actions used by the dancers.[20]

Through these innovations bhangra, which largely emerged in parts of Punjab that had now passed to Pakistan, had become a way for Indian Punjabis to perform, project, and proclaim a distinctive provincial identity to the newly formed Indian nation. This emblematic role was not confined to South Asia itself but was projected onto an international stage, with a bhangra team from PEPSU representing the province as part of an Indian cultural delegation to China in May 1955.[21] The Punjab state continues to identify bhangra as an integral part of a distinctive regional culture; indeed, bhangra is a prominent element of the Punjab government's Web site, where it is depicted as embodying the "infectious zeal for life" that is identified as both the state's key cultural feature and its chief marketable tourist commodity.[22] The iconic status of bhangra in the projection of Punjabiyat, of course, meant that both the region's culture and Sikhism was imagined through the male body, thereby further reinforcing the hypermasculinist image of Punjabis, both within India and abroad.

But, of course, bhangra has a multiplicity of histories because its development since World War II has taken place within a context of sustained Punjabi mobility both within and beyond South Asia. As an expressive form, it has developed simultaneously within Punjab and in diasporic communities in Asia, Africa, Europe, Australasia, and North America. While the remainder of this chapter attends to this "simultaneity" in bhangra's development within a cultural frame, it is particularly important to examine its development in Britain during the 1980s and early 1990s, when bhangra was profoundly reworked in innovative and challenging ways by two generations of British Punjabis.[23]

## Bhangra in Britain

The new wave of Punjabis who migrated after World War II carried bhangra with them to Britain, and bhangra's subsequent development was closely tied to the changing demographic profile and economic fortunes of these migrants. The sustained growth of the British Punjabi community in the 1960s not only created sizable urban enclaves capable of

fashioning new social institutions and a complex mesh of cultural networks, but also began to equalize the gender ratio of the migrant community. With the resulting consolidation of the migrant Punjabi family and
the foundation of community groups, the building of new gurdwaras and
mandirs, and the proliferation of weddings, British Punjabi social life
increasingly emphasized family activities (as opposed to the hypermasculine culture of the early migrants) and the maintenance of "tradition."
Within this revivified social scene, bhangra emerged as a key marker of
tradition by embodying the transplantation of the rural culture so central
to Punjabi regional identity.

It is hard to underestimate the extent of the temporal and spatial transformations enacted within this transplantation. While bhangra was originally closely associated with Baisakhi, in Britain's fickle spring Baisakhi
was far removed from the warmth and fertility of April in Punjab. Thus
fairly quickly within the British context bhangra was uncoupled from the
rhythms of the seasons and agricultural production that had initially nourished it and instead became a key feature of weddings, birthday parties,
and various family or community celebrations. These transitions were
more abrupt in Britain than in Punjab, and the shift toward increasingly
staged bhangra performances mirrored the transformation of bhangra in
post-independence Punjab itself.[24] Moreover, the very different material,
social, and political underpinnings of diasporic life meant that bhangra
was displaced from its specific locations (and attendant variations) within
the landscape of rural Punjab to the community buildings and rented halls
of Southall, Coventry, Birmingham, and Leeds. While in this community
circuit prominent performers such as Mohinder Kaur Bhamra and Bhu-
jangy adhered closely to many popular bhangra staples, others such as
Deedar Singh Pardesi wove together bhangra and *ghazals* (Urdu poetry
set to music), while many smaller bands combined bhangra with filmi
music, both old and new, in their sets. One key change that followed these
transformations, which is now almost impossible to pinpoint in time, was
the gradual shift in the usage of the term *bhangra* itself, as it came not only
to signify the dance but also to refer to both the dance and the wide range
of popular musical forms produced by Punjabi musicians.

One of the most important of these early groups was Alaap, a group that has been identified as initiating the hybridization of bhangra.[25] Founded in 1977 in Southall, Alaap was prominent in the community circuit, playing at weddings and other celebrations. Their 1979 *Teri Chunni de Sitare* was the first album to be recorded by a British bhangra group, and it is widely recognized as marking the birth of the "Southall scene." In the early 1980s Alaap worked closely with Deepak Khazanchi, who has been described as the "Phil Spector of Bhangra," and the result of this collaboration transformed the aural scapes of the form itself. Khazanchi, an experienced musician and producer who had performed both in East Africa and Britain, introduced into bhangra Western-style instruments, especially bass, guitars, synthesizers, and drum machines, to create a novel sound that nevertheless remained tied to the conventions of bhangra transplanted to Britain.

Writing in 1988, Sabita Banerji described the impact of these recordings: "For perhaps the first time their [British Punjabi] original culture was being served up in a form that was not conservative and old-fashioned, but young, modern and western. It was, above all, their own—neither imitative of the West nor pandering to the tastes of an older generation; neither exclusively Indian, like film music, nor exclusively Western like pop. Thus Bhangra heralded the coming of age of a new generation and gave them a voice with which to tell their white compatriots who they were and what they were; not the shy, insular and conservative creatures they had hitherto been stereotyped as, but ordinary funloving young people."[26] In spite of her easy identification of pop with the West and modernity, Banerji captures the momentous shift that Alaap's new sound initiated. The group's recordings of the early 1980s, beginning with their 1982 album *Dance with Alaap,* marked a series of breakthroughs for bhangra. Alaap produced the first bhangra double album (*With Love from Alaap*), their songs were used both in prominent Punjabi films (*Yari Jatt Di*) and in Hindi films (*Dil, Hatya*), and their *Chunni Ud Ud Jaye* was featured on WOMAD's (World of Music, Arts, and Dance) *Talking Book, Vol. 4: Introduction to Asia,* thereby securing bhangra a firm position within the world-music scene. Alaap's importance in the history of world music and their status as the founders of British bhangra has recently been consolidated with the selection of their "Bhabiye ni Bhabiye" as the first track on the album *The Rough Guide to Bhangra* (2000).

The rapid success of Alaap and other pioneering British groups not only transformed the sound of bhangra but also initiated a radical shift in the ways in which it was performed, consumed, and circulated. Inherited traditions of performance, form, and style were reworked in major urban centers, especially Birmingham, Coventry, and London, and a generation of youths recrafted bhangra as a fundamentally urban music. Just as the systematization of bhangra within Punjab itself after partition relocated the performative tradition from the countryside to the stage, a later generation of British Punjabis moved the genre from the stage of the community center or wedding hall to the streets, as well as to that quintessentially modern urban space, the disco.[27]

The emergence of these new urban forms of bhangra marked an important relocation of bhangra's social context. In the 1970s and early 1980s bhangra enabled British Punjabis to perform "traditional" community rites and rituals of identity, a function it continues to retain in smaller British cities and centers with smaller South Asian populations. Andrew Bennett notes that a young man from Newcastle, which had a small Punjabi population and lacked an energetic music scene, explained to him that bhangra "brings back memories . . . it's like tradition. . . . it gives you a buzz to be doing something a bit traditional."[28] One of Bennett's female informants further underscored the importance of bhangra events in the performance of "traditional" identities, especially for younger British South Asians who feel pressured to wear Western clothes on a daily basis: "Going to a bhangra evening is like the only chance to wear eastern clothes . . . Where I live there's like eleven people who are Asian . . . my mum will go into town with her Indian clothes on, but I wouldn't dare."[29] There is no doubt that for many Punjabis, bhangra, even in its new forms, continued to be seen as evocative of home and elicited nostalgic feelings. But from the early 1980s, in British cities where Punjabis coexisted with substantial Afro-Caribbean populations, radically new visions of bhangra emerged. In short, bhangra became an important performative tradition that allowed Punjabis in Britain to articulate distinctive identities, to contest visions of Britishness, and to craft new cultural alliances across the lines of language, religion, ethnicity, and race.

## The Identity Politics of Bhangra: "Black Bhangra"?

I think it is heuristically useful to term these innovative new forms of bhangra born in Britain's cities in the 1980s and early 1990s as "black bhangra." This term offers some important insights and is more precise than some of the alternative terms that could be deployed to describe these new forms. The term "British bhangra," as is common in Internet chat groups and bhangra Web sites, is misleading because it defines the new traditions primarily through the nation-state, when in fact the new forms reflect the collision, interweaving, and fusion of bhangra and Black musical traditions that reach out beyond the nation of Britain to span what Paul Gilroy terms the "Black Atlantic" in his volume by that name. The name "hybrid bhangra" may offer a more theoretically sophisticated alternative that stresses the cultural interweavings that characterize these innovative forms of bhangra, but it generalizes processes of encounter and exchange between Punjabis and Afro-Caribbean peoples into an abstraction that actually works to obscure the very specific power relationships and cultural borrowings that characterize these relations. Terms that are more precise, such as "Raggamuffin" and "Bhangramuffin," are extremely useful as they demarcate particular forms of expression fashioned out of the repertoires of reggae and bhangra, but these terms cannot capture the broad spectrum of new forms of music woven out of the encounter between bhangra and Afro-Caribbean musical traditions (including, but not restricted to, reggae, soul, R&B, and hip hop).

On the other hand, the term "black bhangra" offers three analytical insights. First, and most generally, it foregrounds the importance of Afro-Caribbean music forms in the reshaping of bhangra from the mid-1980s, a cross-cultural engagement that is frequently elided or masked in popular writings on bhangra, particularly those produced from within South Asia. In designating these forms as the lowercase "black" rather the capitalized "Black," we recognize that although the new aesthetic and lyrical concerns of these artists were the product of the encounter with Afro-

Caribbean peoples, South Asian artists were heirs to a musical heritage and occupied positions in British social formations that were distinct from British Blacks.

Second, by designating these performative traditions as "black bhangra" they become firmly located within the racial politics of the Atlantic world, specifically urban Britain under Thatcher and her immediate successors. Even though, as Tariq Modood has argued, the identification of British Asians with "blackness" was eroded in the later 1990s, it is important to underscore that the reformulation of bhangra coincided with the convergence of South Asian and Black urban struggles against the British National Party and the National Front and, at a more general level, the centrality of race in debates over British identity and its limits in the 1980s and early 1990s.[30] Within this context various South Asian performers, activists, and intellectuals embraced the category of "blackness" as an important statement of their antiracist politics. As one group of feminist antiracist campaigners has stressed, embracing blackness allowed "the unity of action . . . of Asians, Latin Americans and Arabs, Caribbeans and Africans, [and] gives political expression to a common 'colour,' even as the State-created fissures of ethnicity threaten to engulf and overwhelm us in islands of cultural exclusivity."[31] In the early 1990s Tariq Modood further described this position as "political blackness."[32] The alignment of young South Asians with blackness did not preclude or marginalize an individual's South Asian identity, but rather, as Sanjay Sharma has suggested, it marked the articulation of a new "strategic identity politics" that harnessed the particular cultural resonances and political power of Blackness within post-colonial Britain.[33] Thus, following Stuart Hall's reading of diasporic identities, we can view the engagement of these bhangra artists and Punjabi youths with Black culture as an act of positioning, a very conscious act that challenged simplistic biological understandings of cultural difference and claimed a very particular location within the racial and political landscape of 1980s Britain.[34]

Third, the use of "black bhangra" suggests that recent bhangra emerged out of the interstices of two structures central in the formation of modernity in the anglophone world: the "Black Atlantic" and the "imperial social formation" created by British colonialism in South Asia.[35] Although both Black and South Asian diasporas can claim long histories within Britain, the concomitant influx of laborers from the Caribbean and South Asia after World War II meant that Black and South Asian workers rubbed shoulders in Britain's industrial cities. Although the relationships between Blacks and South Asians were frequently uneasy, these encounters initiated important cultural and musical exchanges that would ultimately transform the soundscapes of Britain and beyond.

It is crucial to recognize that the effect of the power and significance of bhangra within British cultural patterns was uneven and was shaped by demographic patterns and local social contexts. The new politically aware and aesthetically innovative forms of bhangra that emerged in the late 1980s and early 1990s typically came from the substantial Punjabi communities that lived alongside or in close proximity to large Afro-Caribbean populations. Southall in west London and Handsworth in Birmingham were two such locations where South Asian youths shared urban space, educational institutions, and class positions with British Blacks. In these very specific sites, young South Asians were active in leftist and antiracist groups that aimed to fashion a new solidarity between Britons of South Asian and Caribbean origin. Even though such multiethnic and multiconfessional neighborhoods were sometimes the sites of tension, conflict, and violence, they were also sites of engagement, exchange, and creativity. The influential artist Apache Indian (a British Punjabi named Steven Kapur),[36] who fashioned a powerful mix of bhangra and reggae in the early 1990s, credits much of his musical style to the particularity of Handsworth's demographic mix: "I had Indian influences because of my background but I loved reggae music. Handsworth had a lot of Jamaican influence."[37]

In a 1987 essay, written less than two years after the "Handsworth riots" of September 1985, Salman Rushdie stressed that the polyglot, multiconfessional, and mixed-race population of Handsworth embodied an emergent new England. Although as Rushdie states, the media coverage of conflict in Handsworth conjured up images of "fire, riot, looted shops, young Rastas and helmeted cops by night," he emphasized instead the productive juxtaposition and complex layers of community within the neighborhood: "What was once a Methodist chapel is now one of many

Sikh gurdwaras. Here is the Good News Asian Church, and there you can see Rasta groundations, a mosque, Pentecostal halls, and Hindu, Jain and Buddhist places of worship. Many of Handsworth's songs are songs of praise. But there's reggae, too; there are toasters at blues dances, there are Punjabi *ghazals* and Two Tone bands."[38]

Thus the emergence of black bhangra ultimately was linked to transformations in the demographic composition, community life, and cultural aspirations of Punjabi communities in Britain. In urban centers, especially London and Birmingham, Punjabi communities clustered together in working-class enclaves, where important elements of Punjabi culture were nurtured but also brought into dialogue with the culture of their working-class, largely Black neighbors. The concentration of Punjabis in Southall nourished the emergence of a vibrant bhangra scene in London during the 1980s. The steady flow of Punjabis (especially from Jalandhar District) into Southall from the early 1950s, initially to work at Woolf's rubber factory, transformed the demographic balance of the Ealing-Southall area and by the mid-1970s Punjabis were the dominant ethnic group in Southall or "*chhota* Punjab" (little Punjab).[39] In centers such as Southall, Punjabi youth in the late 1970s and 1980s began to exercise greater freedoms. While at a broad level this reflected the adjustment to the pressures exerted by British culture as a whole, it also emerged out of specific demographic and economic factors.

Traditional family structures, especially the joint family, were not easily reproduced by diasporic Punjabis in Britain. Because the main surge of Punjabi migration has come relatively recently, Punjabi families in Britain tend to have dense horizontal networks (brothers, sisters, and cousins) rather than the complex intergenerational structures that shape life within Punjab itself.[40] The resulting simplification of kin structures created greater space for some teenagers, as many households lacked the grandparents and the uncles and aunts who might supervise children while parents were working. Punjabi women, frequently identified as the upholders of tradition and rulers of the domestic realm, were in fact extremely active in the formal workforce in Britain (especially in the case of Punjabis who migrated to Britain from East Africa), and their participation rates eclipsed those of other South Asian women and British women as a whole.[41] While this strong engagement with the labor market inevitably devolved some domestic responsibilities onto daughters, it also meant that many Punjabi children were not under the direct motherly supervision that remained common in Punjab.

As a result of these social transformations, some Sikh and Punjabi youths had greater freedoms to associate with non-Punjabi friends, to engage widely with their urban environments, and, in the case of girls and young women, to explore public space without the constraints they would have faced in Punjab. Many second- and third-generation Punjabi Britons felt these inquisitive needs deeply. In 1988 Harwant Singh Bains, a prominent Southall youth worker and antiracist campaigner, observed that "amongst many of my friends, both boys and girls, there is often a yearning to escape from the confines of Southall . . . and to embrace the fugitive freedoms of the 'outside world.' "[42] While Bains hints that these engagements were by their nature hidden and temporary ("fugitive"), novel cultural forms resulted from such opportunities. Marie Gillespie's ethnography of Southall in the late 1980s highlights the productive nature of these encounters with the "outside world": "The cultures of Southall youth bear witness to some remarkable cultural crossovers, "borrowings" and convergences—the fruits of living with cultural difference—and serve as powerful testimony to the essentially dynamic nature of culture, not as a static, determinate and transmittable entity, but as inherently changeable, permeable and responsive to the social world."[43]

The most important of these new social contacts and cultural exchanges occurred between Punjabi youths and their Black counterparts. Young Punjabi men particularly engaged with Black culture, which as Gillespie observed, enjoyed a "very high status" among Southall youth. Afro-Caribbeans were admired for their personal style, musical taste, creative dance moves, the greater personal freedoms they seemed to enjoy, and the cultural self-confidence they exuded. As a result, Black culture became a powerful object of desire for young Punjabis, and they were quick to adopt Afro-Caribbean idioms and vocal mannerisms, fashion, and music. But, as Gillespie reminds us, South Asian girls could not engage as openly with Black culture. When Punjabi girls attended bhangra gigs at the Hammersmith Palais or at the Empire in Leicester Square, they typically wore "traditional" *salwar kameez* while their male kin were able to adopt "hipper" street wear influenced by African American culture and the style of their Black classmates in Southall.[44] Most importantly, community anxieties about Black culture frequently focused on female sexuality, as one of Gillespie's teenage informants makes clear: "I listen to reggae and soul music but my mum hates it if we start enthusing about black singers on *Top of the Pops,* you know saying he's gorgeous and that, so we play our feelings down, we don't show her how much we like black guys cos she worries we'll get mixed up with them . . . The parents think that to marry a black person is worse than marrying a *gore* [white person] and you know some Asians want to be white, I don't know why, but if I had the choice I'd be black."[45]

The work of Bains and Gillespie is a reminder not only that the "outside world" that Punjabi youths were drawn to was often hostile and racist, but also that these engagements often caused concern within the Punjabi communities. The new forms of "black bhangra" were a product of these dilemmas, blending "tradition" with new and exciting elements borrowed from Black British culture and expressive traditions. In effect, "black bhangra" functioned as an empowering way of sampling the exhilaration offered by the "outside world," while retaining important affiliations to inherited identities and cultural forms. This is made clear in Meera Syal's novel *Life Isn't All Ha Ha Hee Hee,* which locates the emergence of new bhangra forms and their appeal within these social shifts. In the novel the character Riz, "the doped-out manager" of a music store in "Little India" introduces local Punjabi teenagers to "the bootleg tapes flooding in from Birmingham and Southall of the British bhangra bands." In extolling the virtues of these new trends, Riz highlights the youthful nature of this new music and its break from filmi-music traditions: "Get a load of this band. British Punjabis, like us, recorded in one of their uncle's garage. Not those fat geezers in the John Travolta suits, swinging their medallions, singing about the bleeding harvest and birds in wet saris. This lot ain't much older than you." The novel's central protagonists are entranced by the new sounds that articulate the frustrations and dilemmas of their own cultural location: "The drums they knew, their parents' heartbeat, folk songs sung in sitting rooms, the pulse of hundreds of

family weddings; but then the guitars, cold steel and concrete, the smell of
the Bullring, the frustration bouncing off walls in terraced houses in
Handsworth, hurried cigarettes out of bathroom windows, secret assigna-
tions in libraries, hurrying home with a mouthful of fear and desire. The
lyrics parodied I Love You Love Me Hindi film crooning, but with subtle
bitter twists, voices coming from the area between what was expected of
kids like them and what they were really up to."[46]

Equally importantly, "black bhangra" grew out of a rejection of the
assimilationist aims that some older economically successful Punjabis articulated. Even if the desire persists until today for "economic assimilation," which was identified by Harwant Singh Bains as a powerful force
among the Punjabis of Southall, the racial violence of the late 1970s—
from the murder of Gurdip Chaggar in 1976 to the Southall "riots" of
1979 and 1981—and the ongoing debates about the elasticity of Britishness
certainly undercut any residual aspirations to "whiteness" that some Punjabis might have nurtured. Even if resistance to the National Front in
Southall during 1981 did not trigger the widespread and long-term politi-
cization of British Punjabis, it did reveal the reluctance of the British state
to rein in British fascists and ultranationalists, groups whose agendas in
the 1980s profoundly threatened the very future of the British Punjabi
community. In light of this, diasporic Punjabis increasingly emphasized
both their distinctive heritage and their British citizenship.[47] Indeed, the
efforts made to highlight their multiple positions in relation to the nation-
state gave these diasporic subjects the ability to critique the British state
from within (or at least from the margins). Within this context, the rapid
embrace of new forms of bhangra by Punjabi youths was part of this
rejection of assimilation, and it must be viewed as part of the contest over
the nature of British South Asian identity and the limits of Britishness
itself. As Gurinder Chadha explains, bhangra "gave back something for
ourselves, it had nothing to do with English people or white society. It
consolidated the debate about whether we are Black, British or Asian."[48]

Many Punjabis responded to these challenges by reasserting the primacy of "tradition," by upholding the unquestioned authority of the cultural forms that they had transplanted to Britain, and by nurturing a
powerful nostalgia for "their Punjab." A strong desire for "traditional"

bhangra over the new styles of bhangra fashioned in Southall or Handsworth was often an important element of this stress on cultural continuity, especially among older Punjabis or in towns with smaller South Asian populations. Within such contexts, hybridized bhangra forms did not develop locally and bhangra remained tightly tied to events that drew on broad involvement from the local South Asian population, regardless of religion, regional origin, or age. Bhangra events in Newcastle, for example, were family occasions where grandparents and grandchildren would participate alongside teenagers and young adults. This active family participation in Newcastle bhangra meant that, despite the efforts of some community activists and DJs to use bhangra as a forum for bringing young British South Asians into contact with Afro-Caribbean culture and politics, bhangra was understood by many young Asian people in Newcastle "primarily as a form of folk music which draws upon and simultaneously promotes particular versions of traditional life."[49] The new sounds and forms of self-presentation that were generated by "black bhangra" were frequently the object of conflict within families, as the explicit borrowings from Afro-Caribbean culture made many Punjabi parents (and some young people) nervous.[50] It is also important to note that while some young Punjabis, such as those encountered by Kathleen Hall in 1991, rejected the most explicitly hybrid forms of "black bhangra," the groups that they upheld as embodying "tradition" (such as Alaap) were in fact central in initiating the radical transformation of bhangra within Britain.[51] This rapid incorporation of what was novel and innovative a decade earlier into the rubric of "tradition" is a reminder of just how elastic and changing this category has been in the Punjabi case.

## Lyrics, Language, and Style

These debates about Britishness identified were carried out through the lyrics, language, and personal style of bhangra artists themselves. In 1990 Gerd Baumann offered a succinct summation of the lyrical concerns of bhangra: "These songs are celebratory in tone, and can focus on the beauties of the harvest season, on natural and human beauty, and on a range of usually male sentiments about attraction, companionship, friendship and love."[52] Virinder Kalra has challenged this characterization, noting that it "does not take into account the diversity that is present in the lyrics of the genre, nor give any credence to the way in which lyrics have been 're-invented' in the modernized form [of bhangra]."[53] There is no doubt that the themes identified by Baumann have remained prominent in both Indian and British-produced bhangra over the last two decades, and that such song texts remain particularly popular in certain contexts, particularly at weddings, parties, and among older Punjabis. But as Kalra insists, new lyrical concerns have emerged and, as a result, have fashioned a greater diversity of thematic concerns in bhangra lyrics.

A central feature of these new lyrical concerns has been an increase in reflections upon migration, the loosening of community bonds in the diaspora, and a longing for the "homeland" (concerns that did, potentially at least, connect with the drive for Khalistan). Nirmal's lyrics to Kalapreet's 1998 song "Us Pradesh Ki Vasna Yaarab" represent one striking example of this new concern. As one verse asks:

> My friend, what is the use of living in that land,
> Where love does not live,
> Where every house looks at you with hate and laughs
> Where souls are cold as ice
> Where the soil is very bad?

This song achieved an iconic status, especially after the use of its powerful dramatization of British Punjabi's angular relationship to the nation and national identities in the opening of Gurinder Chadha's 1988 short film *I'm British . . . But.*

The dangers and difficulties of the diasporic condition are prominent in the bhangra of the 1980s and early 1990s. Johnny Zee's "Why Did I Come to Vilayet?" from his 1994 album *Spirits of Rhythm* offered a humorous but poignant commentary on the conflicted position of the migrant. In the song a Punjabi father worries that his son has been alienated from the very basis of his Punjabi identity ("You've forgotten the taste of saag / and sleeping on a string bed"), and that he has succumbed to the temptations presented by alcohol and Western women.[54] Although

Kalra's emphasis on the importance within the Punjabi lyrics of British bhangra of the diasporic themes of alienation and longing for a distant "homeland" is significant, we must recognize that the use of the vernacular as a vehicle for the evocation of loss coexists with a complex mix of more hybridized linguistic forms and a very broad array of lyrical concerns. Setting aside the long-standing evocations of female beauty, love, and awakening sexuality that remain a powerful stock-in-trade of many bhangra artists, we can identify three other lyrical idioms that have emerged over the last two decades.

The most popular form of lyrical innovation produced within the diaspora came from the interweaving of bhangra and reggae, particularly in the work of Apache Indian. While much has been made of the rhythmic affinities and exchanges between bhangra and reggae, the idioms and vocal style of reggae artists profoundly imprinted British bhangra from the late 1980s. This reflected the close coexistence of Punjabi and Afro-Caribbean communities in Southall and in Birmingham's Handsworth. Indeed, Handsworth is the suburb that produced Apache Indian, who has enjoyed great success in both the Caribbean and India in addition to Britain. The chorus to his single "Arranged Marriage" wove together Punjabi with the Jamaican patois that Apache heard spoken on the streets of Birmingham:

> Me wan gal from Jullundur City
> Me wan gal say a soorni curi
> Me wan gal that say she love me
> Me wan gal sweet like jelebee

And as the third verse concludes:

> Say the gal me like have the right figure
> In she eyes have the surma
> Wear the chunee kurtha pyjama
> And talk the Indian with the patwa[55]

This marriage of West Indian and South Asian elements was central in both the recording and packaging of the music of Apache Indian. During the early 1990s, he recorded in Kingston's famous Tuff Gong studios, drew heavily on the traditions of Jamaican dancehall, and collaborated with reggae great Maxi Priest who sings in Punjabi in the number "Fe Real" on Apache Indian's landmark album *No Reservations* (1991). The cover of *No Reservations* shows Apache Indian in front of a backdrop that melds both the Jamaican and Indian flags, while the collage on its back cover includes Jamaican dollars, Indian rupees, and maps of both Punjab and Jamaica. Apache Indian's music retains reggae's characteristic social concerns, and his musical fusion frequently addresses points of both aesthetic and political convergence between British Blacks and South Asians. As a result, his music has been identified as playing an important role in bridging gaps between South Asian and Afro-Caribbean communities through the creation of a "ragamuffin style, a mixture of reggae and bhangra beat."[56]

A second innovative form also emerged out of the diaspora, but unlike the vernacular longing for the lost homeland highlighted by Kalra, these songs are not the nostalgia evocations of Punjab but rather are angry polemics against the prejudices at the heart of British life. This theme is best typified by Hustlers HC, three kes-dhari Sikhs who married bhangra rhythms not to the creolized stylings of reggae but rather to the gritty and violent urban narratives characteristic of "gangsta rap."[57] By using English as their medium, Hustlers HC carried their message both to young British South Asians and to a wider British community that typically could not access the lyrical content of Hindi or Punjabi songs. Hustlers HC's 1994 single "Big Trouble in Little Asia" foregrounded the rootlessness of the diasporic condition ("Homeless I've grown up, homeless I will roam") produced by British colonialism ("A jewel in the empire made of gold / now it's raped and left out in the cold"), before exhorting the creation of a pancommunal antiracist movement and the rejection of the quietism they saw as weakening the position of British South Asians:

> The Hindu, the Muslim and the Sikh
> United we stand, divided we are weak
> Weakened the most by the coconut
> The sellout to the white, the coward in the fight

The provocative English lyrics of "Big Trouble" end by stressing the need to forcibly protect the community in the face of racist attacks:

> I challenge the BNP [British Nationalist Party] to march on
> Southall Broadway
> Big trouble comes and by any means
> The blood will stain it and it ain't easy to clean[58]

Following on from Hustler HC's merging of English gangsta rap narratives with antiracist politics, the third and most recent reworking of bhangra lyrical forms has been the incorporation of the verbal phrasings of hip hop culture within songs with predominantly Punjabi lyrics. From the mid-1990s, bhangra artists have increasingly invoked the most depoliticized of the hypermasculine traditions of hip hop in the English-language introductions to their songs, choruses, and "shout-outs" where they style themselves as "vocal assassins" who deliver the "fresh flava" or the "bad boy riddim," while remaining loyal to their "crew" or "homies."[59]

This sustained engagement with the musical traditions of the modern "Black Atlantic" that is central to black bhangra was also made manifest in other key areas during the 1980s and early 1990s. One fundamental aspect of the new musical forms fashioned in Southall and the Midlands was the use of new technology and sampling techniques. Bombay Talkie's popular disco-inflected "Chargiye" opened with a twenty-second sample of Clint Eastwood's famous monologue from *Dirty Harry,* while Malkit Singh—who is frequently identified as the best vocal performer in the history of British bhangra—opened his clubland hit "Boliyan" with an elaborate sequence of "space age" effects and a sample from Carl Orff's "O Fortuna," before building the body of the song around the sampled bassline from C & C Music Factory's "Gonna Make You Sweat."

The encounter with hip hop culture has also been an important resource that has allowed new bhangra performers to challenge, reformulate, or entirely dispense with the "traditional" South Asian forms of musical self-presentation. In this new musical world, the inherited South Asian performative traditions, artistic relationships, and cultural styles were radically reworked and, in many cases, deconstructed. The engagement with hip hop culture flattened and subverted the social relationships that traditionally structured the teaching and performance of music in South Asia. "Black bhangra" was not structured by the guru-pupil relationship that shapes the transmission of musical knowledge within the "high" Hindustani musical tradition. These new forms of bhangra not only lacked the *ustads* (master musician) of Hindustani music but also diverged from the rather centralized development of bhangra within Punjab. While the systematization of bhangra in post–World War II Punjab relied heavily on the influence of a few key teachers and institutions, bhangra in Britain was more in keeping with the ethos of hip hop (and punk before it), where many musicians were self-taught and came to music only in their late teens.[60] Within recent bhangra, this turn toward an image targeted at the street and nightclub is most obvious in the case of the many artists who have adopted the monikers common in the work of R&B and hip hop, such as "DJ" or "MC," or styling their group as a "crew" or "squad." This tendency has carried over to the audience for bhangra as well, with some young Punjabis who identify strongly with bhangra adopting the jewelry and clothing of hip hop culture and identifying themselves as "gangstas" or, in a telling vernacularization of this term, as "badmashes."[61]

## Repackaging Bhangra and the End of "Black Bhangra"

While artists continued to cultivate aesthetics and perform identities heavily influenced by hip hop (with names such as Punjabi Hit Squad), the shared political interests between Punjabis and Afro-Caribbean artists and activists took on a less-political orientation in the mid-1990s. In part, this reflected the broader crisis in the strategic alliances between Blacks and South Asians that energized the British leftist and antiracist movements, but it also dramatized a broader shift in the position of South Asians within British culture at large. In the early 1990s, greater attention was directed to the success of South Asian entrepreneurs, and both mainstream and community media placed a renewed emphasis on the pursuit of material wealth and political influence, often at the expense of social justice and the protection of the community's welfare. At the same time,

South Asian cultural forms were increasingly assimilated into the aesthetics of British middle-class life. By 1995, bindis, mehndi, and South Asian food and fashion had become extremely prominent in British youth culture as a whole: "Asian Kool," as it was styled, was a key component of the partial repackaging of Britishness in Tony Blair's "Cool Britannia."

The politics of Hustlers HC or Kalapreet's invocation of Britain as a land where "souls are cold as ice" were out of step with this new context. The political allegiances and sensitivities of "black bhangra" were increasingly overwhelmed by new forms of bhangra where the connection with hip hop and the aesthetics of the Black Atlantic remained but were now stripped of their political teeth and packaged for global consumption.

These transformations are evident in the global success of Birmingham's Bally Sagoo in the mid-1990s. Bally Sagoo's 1995 *Bollywood Flashback* underscores the continued interdependence between bhangra and filmi music along with the reconfiguration of this relationship within the increased desire of Western entertainment multinationals to "penetrate" the markets of South Asia and its various diasporas. Whereas Sagoo's earlier work, particularly the innovative hybridity of his recording of "Mera laung gawacha," unsettled British expectations about musical and ethnic authenticity, by the mid-1990s his career increasingly focused on repackaging Bollywood favorites. As Ashwani Sharma points out, Sagoo's *Bollywood Flashback,* produced by Sony, was a clear attempt "to exploit a huge potential market for Hindi *filmi*-music across the globe." Its use of heavy bass lines and remixing of popular Hindi songs was specifically targeted at a growing middle-class market eager for "modern sounds," both within South Asia and beyond. With these consumers in mind, Sony valorized Sagoo's status as a "migrant," a cultural broker who was able to bring new sounds and technical savvy to Bollywood music.[62] In the wake of *Bollywood Flashback,* Sagoo quickly became identified as a powerful broker in the world of "Indipop," enjoying celebrity status within South Asia because of his role as a presenter on MTV India. These Bollywood remixes, largely devoid of the regional flavor of bhangra or the explicit and raw engagement with Afro-Caribbean musical traditions typical of his earlier work,[63] fashioned him into a global icon of the commodification of cultural mobility and fusion. As a 1997 profile of Sagoo in New

York's *Village Voice* concluded: "Having left India before he was a year old, Sagoo didn't see the ancestral homeland till his late teens. Now, twice a month he fulfills an immigrant's fantasy: flying back to make music and star on TV in the land his parents left in search of a better life. On permanent Air India upgrade."[64] But Sony's venture into the global South Asian market with Bally Sagoo failed to displace the deeply embedded patterns of dissemination and consumption. The power of "cassette culture" in South Asia meant that his Sony albums circulated widely, but the multinational did not recoup the profits it hoped for, because Sagoo's albums were quickly and cheaply copied. No less than forty-three pirated imprints of *Bollywood Flashback* circulated in the music shops, bazaars, and roadside stalls of South Asia.

Sagoo's focus on the remixing of filmi music for global middle-class consumption was short lived. After leaving Sony in 1997, Sagoo moved back toward his Afro-inflected bhangra as well as meeting the demands of a specifically Punjabi audience. In an interview with *Connect* magazine, Sagoo insisted that the resulting album, *Star Crazy 2,* marked an embrace of an authentic and specifically Punjabi tradition, noting that "for 'Star Crazy 2' I went home to the Punjab and recorded with some of the best singers like Hans Raj Hanjs [*sic*] and Surinder Shinda." Although this album marked a return to Punjabi language material and was (in Sagoo's words) "aimed directly at the Punjab," Sagoo, in keeping with his Sony packaging, highlighted his privileged position as a broker of bhangra for the modern world. Echoing Sony's fetishization of his diasporic status, Sagoo noted that after recording these authentic Punjabi vocals in situ, his tapes "were then enhanced with my trademark production back at my studios in Birmingham." Sagoo reminded *Connect* readers that he was not, strictly speaking, a bhangra performer, but rather a producer and packager of music. Given this statement it is not surprising that his model came from the world of African American R&B, as he confessed "I see myself as a sort of Asian answer to the likes of Babyface and other international producers."[65] Although Sagoo's relationship with Sony was far from smooth, his transformation into a carefully packaged and heavily marketed cultural commodity is a long way from the work of early British groups like Alaap or Heera who cut their teeth in the community circuit, distributed their tapes through sari stores, corner shops, and halal butchers, and began the tentative experiments with new sounds and cultural sources almost two decades before.

Perhaps the most striking repackaging of bhangra was not Sagoo's tryst with Sony, but rather the efforts of Sarina Jain to reinvent bhangra as a marketable form of exercise. From her base in Yorba Linda, California, Jain launched her *Masala Bhangra* exercise video in 2000. One commentator lauded this new product as combining "influences from her own Indian heritage with her background in fitness to create a total-body, calorie-burning workout."[66] Peg Jordan, editor of *American Fitness* magazine, attributed the emergence and popularity of such workouts to the rise of a form of multiculturalism based on "the celebration and recognition of the growing ethnicity of our urban areas. Fitness was kind of a white cheerleader domain. Aerobic classes had that look and feel through the '70s and '80s."[67] But rather than providing a critique of the dominant politics of race attached to exercise clubs, for Jordan it seems that *Masala Bhangra* allowed non-Indians to engage in a form of "aerobic orientalism" that gave them access to eternal customs and ancient forms of bodily discipline: "It's a combination of classical Indian dances that move the hips and eyes, and mixes them with some modern dance techniques. It really appeals to the old in all of us. . . . We can trace our ethnic groups back to native, tribal people who danced around fires all night long. It is a beautiful resurgence of this innocent communal dance that is not drill-sergeant oriented."[68] This is a possessive vision (*"We* can trace *our* ethnic groups") that erases cultural difference by stripping any cultural particularity, not to mention historical specificity, attached to bhangra (or even Jain's vision of bhangra). Yet this possessive assimilation rests on a profoundly essentialist vision of Jain herself: "With her flowing black hair and vibrant, sari-inspired outfit, Jain looks nothing like the fitness instructors of yesteryear. As she jumps, spins and flashes her infectious smile, she waves a scarf. It is as much an extension of her body as it is a symbol of the spirit and vitality of her every Indian movement."[69] Jain herself is optimistic about the reception of *Masala Bhangra*, arguing that even though bhangra "is a man's dance," her video would reach a sizable audience, as "hey—times have changed." Jain suggests that these cultural shifts enacted within the diaspora present new opportunities for young women like her: "My goal is to be the Indian Jane Fonda, and that's something I never could have pursued in India. . . . In the U.S., something like this is possible. Everyone's always looking for something new culturally."[70]

## Bhangra and the "Crisis of Tradition"

While Jain's work has had little or no impact within Punjab (where the culture of health clubs and aerobics has yet to take strong root), the work of Bally Sagoo, Apache Indian, and other British bhangra artists was not only crucial in bringing British music into closer connection with Caribbean and American musical traditions, but also played a central role in forging a strong connection between British and South Asian popular culture. This should not come as a surprise, as Lipsitz has stressed that "recorded music travels from place to place, transcending physical and temporal barriers."[71] In the South Asian context, Peter Manuel has demonstrated the importance of "cassette culture" over the past three decades. The sale, duplication, and circulation of cassettes has played a key role in linking new diasporic and Punjabi bhangra traditions: in 1996, for example, it was possible to buy the work of artists such as Alaap as well as Bally Sagoo and Apache Indian in stalls in Simla, Chandigarh, Amritsar, and Delhi.[72]

Although it lacks the affordability and easy circulation of cassette technology, television has also provided an important link between the diasporic communities and their "homelands." While the uneven nature of the global mediascape means that India-based artists have had (and continue to have) limited visibility in Western media, television services in India have been a crucial forum that connect the "homelands" with the production of diasporic artists. The rise of Star TV has been an important vector for transmitting the work of British bhangra artists to South Asian elites, who can consume the music and videos of these acts alongside "Western" pop, R&B, and filmi music. Music is also prominent in state broadcasting and noncable commercial television, particularly within Punjab where music-related programs compose up to two-thirds of airtime.[73] Sacred music, Bollywood songs, Punjabi folk and pop songs, and diasporic bhangra jostle together in this rich sonic and visual world, which stretches out well beyond the political boundaries of Punjab itself. More recently, the rise of the Internet has become an important vehicle for disseminating bhangra and for fashioning new forms of connection between the diaspora and the homeland. Of course, access to the Internet within South Asia remains heavily determined by class position and educational opportunity, but this new technology has allowed certain sectors of India's elite to gain quicker and wider access to the music, art, and style produced by diasporic South Asians and has facilitated their consumption of global popular culture more generally.

These media forms have worked to transform space and subordinate distance, meaning that Punjabis "at home" are familiar with many of the innovative forms of expression produced within the diaspora.[74] And, of course, these innovations have fed into the transformation of bhangra in Punjab itself. A 1998 article in the *Tribune,* for example, noted important transformations in the gendered dynamics of Punjabi folkdances: "It is worth pointing out that in the past in most of the regions of Punjab group dances did not have men and women together, as the latter were confined to the four walls of their homes. They were forced to observe the *purdah* tradition by which they covered their face with *ghund, dupatta* or veil. They were, however, permitted to witness the *bhangra* and other dances of the menfolk but the menfolk were not allowed to watch the *giddha, luddi, jago* etc. But now there has been a sea-change in such traditions. Both men and women come together to perform folk dances in the vicinity of modern villages and on the cultural platforms in the towns and cities of Punjab. It is indeed a healthy trend in a state like Punjab where today men and women join together in all spheres of life to promote culture, education, agro-industrial economy, social welfare scheme etc. for the benefit of society at large."[75]

But such reworkings of bhangra have been subject to fierce debate, especially within Punjab itself. The emergence of night club–based bhangra scenes in the West, in Delhi, and, to a lesser extent, in major Punjab cities, has caused deep concern about the undercutting of "traditional" forms of bhangra. The social frameworks that had molded bhangra within rural Punjab and in the imaginations of many Punjabis have been recast on the dance floors of community centers and nightclubs. Alona Wartofsky's account of "Basement Bhangra" at S.O.B.'s nightclub in Manhattan emphasized the prominence of gender in shaping the dynamics of the dance-floor: "When Rekha [the DJ] opens with sets of hip-hop and reggae dancehall, the floor belongs to young women and couples who dance enthusiastically but demurely. But once she starts spinning the percussive bhangra beats, most women are relegated to the edges of the club, and both the dance floor and the elevated stage become the province of men. Their heads bob from side to side. They lift their shoulders up and down, with one arm raised. A raised hand reaches up and forward, twisting as if screwing in an imaginary overhead light bulb. The other hand may be cupping an ear or clutching one's heart, suggesting that the dancers are hearing and feeling the music."[76]

Rekha Malhotra, the DJ (who was born in Delhi but raised in London), suggested to readers of the *Washington Post* that bhangra was essentially a manifestation of the masculine ethos of Punjabi culture and politics—observing that bhangra " 'definitely has that male vibe,' " before adding that " 'the lyrics can be very nationalistic.' "[77] But while this male-dominated form of expression may superficially appear to embody the maintenance of "traditional" performative traditions in the diaspora, it is clear that in Manhattan these forms are modified and reworked: "As the hour grows later, the dancing becomes more intense. Traditional rural steps meet contemporary urban moves as men take turns clearing the floor to perform intricate combinations. One guy wraps his legs around another man's torso and they spin faster and faster. A minute later they're spinning again, but this time they're break-dancing."[78]

These cultural shifts drew considerable interest. Nine months after the account in the *Washington Post* of "bhangra basement," *Newsday* produced a detailed, almost ethnographic, account of the dance floor: "A group of Sikh men in turbans heeds the record's command, throwing up their arms beneath the DJ booth. Across the dance floor, a young black woman, sporting a sparkling bindi on her forehead, bobs to the percolating beat. A handful of yuppies of all stripes look to both for guidance. For these downtown throngs—as for a generation of Indian Americans—the party has indeed begun."[79] In celebrating the dance floor as space of cultural coexistence and fusion, a site where rhythm and relaxation displace difference and politics, this account veiled the profound cultural transformations being enacted in the "Bhangra basement"—especially the breakdown of the highly structured forms of bhangra performance that characterized the systematized forms of bhangra that emerged after partition and, most importantly, after the free mingling of genders. These were, of course, the very features that the *Tribune* worried about in its 1998 report. Equally importantly, *Newsday*'s optimistic evocation of the "yuppies of all stripes" joining Sikhs and African Americans on the dance floor only hints at the divergent stakes that surround these forms of sociability for individuals from different communities, of different genders, and from divergent class positions.

The emergence of female bhangra DJs like Rekha in New York or Radical Sista in Britain challenged both the gendered norms of Punjabi performative traditions (where women traditionally do not provide the drumbeats central to bhangra) and the social aspirations of Punjabi families. Rekha recognized this herself when she observed: "I'm constantly trying to win the support of my constituency. . . . I had a family friend say, 'Yo, your parents are worried.' . . . There's a concern for, like, settling down. . . . That's the language my mom uses. For her, that probably means marrying."[80] According to *Newsday,* Rekha's mother Satya "no longer entertains hopes that her daughter will follow the stable path of her older sister, Sunita, who works as a paralegal." Satya compares "her daughter's vocation to the flu" as she explains that Satya hoped her daughter's interest in being a DJ "'might go away.'" While *Newsday* highlights these anxieties about social standing and success within the diasporic family, it does not rematerialize the full extent of the transformations that are enacted, at least temporarily, within the nightclub. Even though "yuppies" may take their lead from the presumably authentic moves of Sikh men or boundary-crossing African Americans, there is no doubt that their investment in the "bhangra basement" performative culture is of a different order and has a different cultural weight than for Punjabis or, more specifically, for Punjabi women. This point has been at the heart of Sunaina Maira's recent work on the pervasive gendering of cultural expectations and social limits among members of the South Asian diaspora in the

United States. Maira's ethnographic work has demonstrated that the adoption of the "style" of African American youth culture by young South Asian men elicits limited concern in comparison to the policing of South Asian women's relationship to hip hop culture and African American men.[81]

Iqbal Singh Dhillon has identified these innovations—especially the participation of mixed-gender teams in bhangra competitions and the free mixing of genders in nightclubs—as destabilizing received understandings of music, dance, and gender within Punjab.[82] A recent Chandigarh *Tribune* article highlighted this displacement of tradition in a much more anxious tone than in its 1998 discussion of gender: "The beating of drums, recitation of bolis, clamouring of chimta and kato and the quintessential physical gyrations that formed the basis of Bhangra, the traditional Punjabi dance, seems to have been replaced by a more free-flowing dance form performed to a stereotypical techno music."[83] Against this framework of "tradition in peril," the *Tribune* explored the establishment of the Nachda Punjab Youth Welfare Club "not just for the revival of this traditional art form, but also for its promotion, especially amongst the younger urbanites in the state." Avtaar Singh, the club's president, explained that the club was responding to the "invasion" of "disco, tango or rock-and-roll." One club member, Bhupinder Singh, cast the club as both preserving traditional Punjabi culture and as a missionary organization because he believed that "bringing the dance forms [bhangra, but also the *gidda, jhummar,* and *jandua*] to the forefront is a sacred mission. This is an inherent part of our ethos and committed efforts have to be made for its resurrection." Yet, what is striking is that even if the Nachda Punjab Youth Welfare Club were staging a battle to preserve traditional forms against the cultural imperialism of "disco, tango and rock-and-roll," then it too was fundamentally recasting "tradition" and the gendered dynamics of Punjabi cultural performance. The club had elaborated a new form of the traditionally male Malwai giddha, where male and female performers perform the boli in a call-and-response format while performing the giddha together. But this innovation was not a response to the needs of the "urbanites" that the club was targeting, yet alone the demands of the diaspora: rather, as Avtar Singh explained to the *Tribune*, this new Malwai giddha "is typical of the rustic family life, where there is a lot of verbal duels between a brother-in-law and sister-in-law, husband and wife or between daughter-in-law and mother-in-law." It is this innovation through the incorporation of the norms of "rustic family life" that provides the Nachda club with its defense against the Westernization of bhangra. Lakhwant Singh of the Nachda club stressed that the club was fighting an important battle over the future of Punjabiyat, and that its fortification of tradition was vital to stave off the debasing effects of Western understandings of gender: "Efforts need to be made so that our culture is projected in its true form and not after it has been 'westernised' to suit their need of attracting attention by portraying semi-nude models in Punjabi songs."

Throughout the twentieth century, Sikh community leaders and reformers in particular have exhibited a recurring concern with the morality of dance. As a particularly vibrant and performative expression of popular culture, dance has frequently worried some members of the Panth, and they have expressed anxiety about the effects of dance both on the dancer and, equally important, on the audience. Dance, it seems, has the potential (at least momentarily) to recast gender relationships, express sensuality in unsettling ways, and uncouple the body from the social, cultural, and religious structures that govern it. In the early twentieth century, Singh Sabha reformers were skeptical of the value of bhangra, giddha, and other folk dances, and they were particularly worried over women dancing. In response they were staunchly opposed to public dancing, and they even strove to ban the performance of giddha within households.[84] Although British bhangra groups such as Alaap have performed in gurdwaras, many Sikhs are uneasy about the musical innovations and new forms of sociability that have emerged around bhangra since the 1970s.[85] Given the popularity of new forms of bhangra among diasporic Sikhs and the rise of the nightclub as an important site for Punjabi youths, the most extensive discussions of the relationship between Sikhism and bhangra has been on the Internet. The following is a fairly typical exchange that recently occurred in the "Youth Forum" hosted by the Sikh Network Web site:

I would like to know, is dancing to Bhangra Songs acceptable in Sikhism.

One part says no, as it takes us away from the path of God. A lot of these Bhangra songs talk about caste, and are sexist, or provoke lustful behaviour . . . so is Bhangra a good thing?

[signed] Confused . . . could you help . . . ?

*Reply*:

Bhangra itself is very healthy, it balances the brain hemispheres when done properly.

You are right to be concerned about the content of the lyrics. That is a different topic. You should control your environment whenever you can. Do bhangra in good environments and don't put yourself in bad situations. It takes effort on your part.[86]

The Web site of Nachdi Jawani Bhangra Group, a Toronto-based bhangra group "dedicated to Punjabi culture" (as summarized in the slogan "Punjab, Punjabi, Punjabiat"), explicitly deals with the bhangra issue under a section titled "Sikh Attitude to Bhangra (Dancing)":

Dancing is a mode of entertainment in western countries. Sikhism applies the general test mentioned in the scripture to any entertainment, namely, "Avoid that which causes pain or harm to the body or produces evil thoughts in the mind."

As disco is likely to arouse sexual feelings it is not permitted to the Sikhs. Dances purely for the promotions of physical health or fitness are not taboo. Cultural dances like Bhangra Giddha etc. are not forbidden, but these should not be performed in the presence of guru Granth Sahib. Such dances are meant for social occasions or festivals and have no religious significance.

There are religious dances, which are done by the Hindus (as for example "Ras Lila") and also by Muslims Sufi mystics. Such dances are not permitted in Sikhism. What the Guru permitted was the dance of the mind; and not of the body.[87]

The most significant discussion of bhangra's place within Sikhism is an article titled "Bhangra and Sikhi: Is There a Connection?" This article is widely reproduced on Web sites devoted to Sikh women, the Malaysian Sikh Youth Organisation, gurdwaras, and Sikh student associations.[88] This article distinguishes "traditional bhangra" from "Westernized bhangra," and carefully sets out the relationship between bhangra and Sikhi.

> It was probably even normal for there to be similar dancing and singing on weddings and other joyous occasions. But there is no evidence in Sikh history to suggest that the Gurus had ever promoted it or that it had even ever been performed in their presence. In those days, joyous occasions were marked by Sikhs—by the reading of shabads and singing of shabads and also by the distribution of gifts and food to the poor and needy. In Gurudwaras today, occasions are still celebrated as such today, Bhangra dancing and singing is not acceptable in a Sikh Gurudwara.... Sikhi does not promote Bhangra and therefore it is not correct to believe that Bhangra is a *Sikhi thing.* Yes it is Punjabi—and because the majority of Sikhs are Punjabi—Bhangra seems to have been classed as a Sikh institution over the years. Without entering into the argument as to whether Bhangra should be performed on Sikh weddings and whether a Sikh is a bad Sikh if he or she listens to Bhangra, this page only seeks to suggest that *Bhangra is not a Sikh Institution, But a Punjabi one.*[89]

This argument is in wide currency, with the *Tribune* stating that bhangra is entirely unconnected from religion: "Besides, like other prominent dances of the country *bhangra* has no religious theme as its basis. In fact, Punjab is the only state of the country where its folk dances completely diverge from religion."[90]

But this argument is problematic for two reasons. First, many young Sikhs resist the rigid division between the religious and nonreligious, and they see bhangra as an important part of their "heritage" and an important way in which they might affirm their identity as Sikhs. This tension has been identified by Jacqueline Warwick's work on bhangra in Toronto and in my own discussions with young Sikhs in both Britain and the United States.[91] At a broad level, this situation is reminiscent of the debates over the representation of Sikhs in British textbooks, where the visions of senior members of the community of what constitutes a "proper

Sikh" and what is included in the components of Sikhi diverge from the self-understandings of young Punjabis who define themselves as Sikhs.[92] Second, there is no doubt that many non-Sikhs persist in seeing bhangra as having some connection to Sikhism, even if this is simply the result of the prominence of turbaned kes-dhari Sikhs on album covers, posters, and in bhangra videos. One of my former students, a young Sikh woman from Chicago, has spoken about this issue. The best course of action for Sikh parents and community leaders, she argues, is not to reject new forms of bhangra as irreligious or immoral but rather to embrace the positive aspects of these new forms. The culture around bhangra, this argument suggests, might be supported because it encourages youths in the diaspora to speak Punjabi and because critiques of racism, communalism and caste prejudice that can be found in the work of artists such as Apache Indian might be used to pursue social justice within and beyond Sikh communities. In reality, however, the evidence suggests that many influential Sikhs perceive the new forms of bhangra as a cultural threat, a corrosive force that should be contained, resisted, and rejected wherever possible. This position fashions a rigid division between the religious and the secular, as well as cementing a generation gap between parents fearful of global popular culture and their children's cultural choices.

## Conclusion

The sketch I have drawn here of the history of bhangra reminds us that music and dance have played a key role in the performance of Punjabi identities over the last five decades. These expressive traditions, however, are by their very nature porous and have been constantly remade, redefined, and reworked, as bhangra artists have drawn on cultural idioms from elsewhere in South Asia and, as Punjabis settled abroad, from the musics of Africa, Europe, the Caribbean, and the Americas. The evidence presented here reminds us that the Punjabi diaspora has never been entirely self-contained or hermetically sealed; rather, the networks, institutions, communities, families, and individuals that comprise the diaspora have productively engaged with the various urban environments and cultural landscapes that they have encountered outside India.

In this chapter I have placed particular emphasis on the encounter between the Punjabi diaspora and the Afro-Caribbean diaspora as well as on the very real innovations produced from this cultural "crossroads." Examining this specific encounter—charting its changing shape and delineating its outcomes—will cast new light on an important aspect of the Punjabi/Sikh past that remains understudied. In the broadest sense, this chapter adds weight to a growing body of scholarship—including W. H. McLeod's *Punjabis in New Zealand,* Karen Leonard's *Making Ethnic Choices,* Kathleen Hall's *Lives in Translation,* and Verne Dusenbery and Rashmere Bhatti's innovative history of Punjabis in Woolgoolga— that traces the ways in which Punjabis have negotiated a range of complex encounters with a wide variety of ethnic and religious communities. The effort to understand the processes of engagement, translation, adaptation, accommodation, and innovation that shape these encounters seems to me to be a crucial project for Punjab and Sikh studies to pursue.

# Epilogue

This volume has examined the encounters of Sikhs and Sikhism with the two great agents of modernity: imperialism and migration. These social forces have ensured that the question of identity has been a central concern of Sikhs over the last century and a half. Although the question "Who is a Sikh?" had been posed earlier by Mughal hegemony, and Guru Gobind Singh's foundation of the Khalsa was an early attempt to formulate a definitive answer that set Sikh initiates apart from their fellow Punjabis, the experience of colonialism as well as encounters with state bureaucracies have meant that modern Sikhs have repeatedly faced this question, which modernity poses with great urgency and persistence. In exploring this question of identity, I have set this book against both the dominant "internalist" approach to the Sikh past and recent "externalist" arguments that have suggested that Sikh identities were essentially fabricated by the colonial state. Rather than treating the Panth as being entirely independent and self-contained or, conversely, seeing the kesdhari Sikh as the product of the exigencies of colonialism, I have attempted to balance a sensitivity to the internal dynamics of the Sikh Panth with an insistence on the importance that encounters with non-Sikhs have played in formulating visions of Sikh history and identities. In pursuing this agenda, I have explored a range of locations (Punjab, Australasia, and Britain), cultural sites (graveyards, nightclubs, and Internet sites), archives (such as popular music and Internet discussion groups), and debates (what is the relationship between bhangra and Sikhi?) that have remained largely unexplored within Sikh studies. This approach has revealed both the fluid and contested nature of Sikh identity, as families, social reformers, and community leaders have attempted to reproduce tradition and to make that tradition legible within the very different political and cultural locations that Sikhs have occupied since 1849.

These articulations of a distinctive Sikh identity under modernity have been underpinned by three key components. The first element is geography, as the notion of a Punjabi diaspora, which has become commonplace in recent years, hinges on a discourse of origins. It locates identity in a "homeland," a defined geographical space that is seen as the point of origin for a community that possesses a distinctive history and culture. Of course, it must be noted that this discursive production of a Punjabi homeland fails to recognize the fluid boundaries of the region itself (the Punjab of the Mughals? Ranjit Singh's kingdom? British Punjab? the post-1947 Indian Punjab?). The projection of Punjab as a bounded territorial "homeland" is also problematic for those members of the "diasporic" community who have only thin links to Punjab itself, having been born or raised outside the region. Some of these mobile subjects have had several "homelands" as their families have pursued opportunities across the globe or, as in the notable case of many East African Sikhs, were forcibly displaced from the homes and communities that they had built outside Punjab. Moreover, in its most extreme forms this discourse of origins erases the other forms of geographic identification that have been common among mobile Punjabis: their ties to their ancestral village and district or their very real connections to the city, region, or nation outside Punjab that has become their home. Despite these occlusions, we must recognize that the projection of a Punjabi "homeland" is a powerful cultural act that has been central in shaping the identities of many individuals who have left Punjab by traveling or settling beyond its borders. This regional identity is particularly powerful at sites where multiple South Asian diasporas converge, such as in British cities where migrants who hail from Gujarat, Sylhet, or the Indian Punjab live in close proximity to each other. In these contexts, where many white Britons read these fellow subjects as "South Asian," "Indian," or, more commonly, simply "Asian," the projection and policing of a distinctive regional identity takes on particular importance.

In the Sikh case this spatial element of diasporic identity is closely connected to its spiritual underpinnings—the second element that undergirds the Sikh identity. Although the religious identities of early Punjabis on the move were often fluid and ambiguous, throughout the twentieth century certain distinctively Sikh texts, forms of devotion, social practices, cultural forms and institutions have provided powerful bonds that have connected individuals and communities separated by space. Both sacred texts and popular representations of Sikh history—particularly the bazaar prints of the Sikh gurus and heroes that are seen in shop windows, taxi cabs, and family homes—connect Sikhs across the globe to a Punjabi landscape that is saturated with history. At the same time that these forms of cultural production reaffirm an imaginative link to the very real physical sites where Sikhism emerged, they also consolidate the links between Sikhs. In this volume I have emphasized the divergent cultural and geographical locations that Sikhs have occupied and the very different ways in which Sikh communities have positioned themselves in relation to the political, religious, and racial landscape of their "host" communities. Running through these heterogeneous patterns of community formation, however, are powerful threads of continuity. The reverence of the Guru Granth Sahib, of spoken Punjabi and Punjabi written in the Gurmukhi script, of the role of gurdwaras as both devotional and community centers, and of the commensality of the *langar* (the kitchen and dining area attached to the gurdwara) all reproduce and reaffirm a common Sikh culture, from Singapore to Seattle and Amritsar to Birmingham. Alongside these long-established cultural forms are other forms of cultural production that also work to reaffirm a common Sikh identity that spans the globe. Of particular importance here is the well-established and lively tradition of Sikh periodicals that circulate throughout South Asia and among the diasporic communities and, of course, the more recent emergence of the Internet as a crucial forum for discussions of Sikh religious practice, social practice, and community politics.

The third element that underpins the formation of Sikh identities in the global age is the importance of genealogy and the intergenerational transmission of culture and identity.[1] This is an important issue that is frequently overlooked in readings of the Sikh diaspora that focus narrowly on the Khalistani movement's aspirations for territorial sovereignty. Following in the wake of Verne Dusenbery's emphasis on the role of "ancestra genera" (such as language, ties to ancestral villages, and marriage patterns) in shaping the cultural life of mobile Sikhs, several of my arguments here have emphasized the importance of familial and generational connections, rather than the quest for Sikh sovereignty, in nurturing the development of a global Sikh community.[2] In chapter 2, for example, I stress the ability of early Sikh migrants to Australasia to maintain genealogical connections and to give these relationships a material form through remittances that allowed *pakka* (brick and mortar) family homes to be constructed in ancestral villages as markers of affluence and status. In chapter 3 I also chart the efforts of the MDSCT to fashion and popularize a new community genealogy for British Sikhs. This genealogy used Dalip Singh as a symbol of a close relationship between Sikhs and the British Crown, which was seen to operate alongside connections to ancestral villages in Punjab, thereby allowing British Sikhs to simultaneously affirm their Punjabiness and to make claims on the British public sphere. My discussion of Dalip Singh also was a way to highlight the radical new forms of cultural production that are produced in moments when genealogical connections come under strain. This is particularly clear in the case of bhangra, when this "Punjabi tradition" was profoundly recast within a social context where patterns of intergenerational relationships were reworked and when Sikhs engaged enthusiastically with other communities of descent (whether white or Afro-Caribbean Britons).

My discussion of "black bhangra" framed these forms of dance and music against the backdrop of British colonialism, decolonization, and the place of the empire in molding postwar British life. Throughout this volume I have insisted that the Sikh engagement with modernity occurred within the context of colonialism and migration, and it is this imperial world that has provided the essential context for the shifting visions of Sikh identity discussed here. The deep structures of the modern world—its labor markets, political systems, communication networks, and migration routes—that determine the life experience of many Sikhs were forged in the crucible of empire. It is within these economic relations, demographic movements, and political structures that Sikhs have had to position themselves and to produce visions of their communities, their cultures, and their histories. Colonialism did mark a significant rupture in Sikh history, and, as I argued in chapter 2, British rule not only redefined the economic and political structures that shaped life in Punjab but also posed new questions for Sikhs about their community's identity and its future. In chapter 2, I also demonstrated the ways in which the structures of the British imperial system determined the patterns of Punjabi migration and influenced the development of Sikh networks that spanned the globe by 1900. Chapters 3 and 4 then traced the legacies of empire in post-1945 Britain where large numbers of Sikhs settled and discovered that their social status, religious and racial identities, and economic opportunities were encoded by a powerful set of colonial discourses that framed their economic value and cultural position in very particular ways. In short, the experience of being colonized and living in an imperial world has become a crucial, if largely unacknowledged, foundation of Sikh identities at the start of the twenty-first century.

With these broad understandings in mind it is valuable to reaffirm the key arguments that I have forwarded in this volume. In charting the contestations over and transformations of Sikh identities, the key discursive field that I examined in the early parts of this book is that of "religion," which was central in British attempts to make sense of South Asian cultural traditions and forms of devotion. Religion as a concept had been significantly reworked and refined in the early modern period as the result of fierce doctrinal debates within Europe as well as the unsettling encounters between the Europeans and the non-European peoples that they increasingly traded with and ruled over after 1492. By the late eighteenth century, when the East India Company developed a strong interest in Punjab, Europeans understood "religion" as "a system," that is, as a coherent set of texts, practices, and institutional structures that ordered human relationships with the Divine. As demonstrated in chapter 2, even though Europeans believed that this new understanding of "religion" was universally applicable, it remained colored by the cultural and linguistic freight of Christianity. Early British accounts of Sikhism identified the *Adi Granth* as the "Sikh Bible," described *granthis* as "priests," suggested that Guru Nanak was "India's Luther," and framed the Sikhs themselves as the product of the "Indian Reformation." Very quickly, Sikhism occupied a privileged position within these discourses on Indian religious traditions because East India Company administrators and European travelers saw it as embodying a rational spirit and upheld Guru Gobind Singh's Khalsa as a powerful blow against the perceived inequities of Hinduism and the caste system. In this discussion I stressed that although the dominant British discourse fashioned various "points of recognition" between Britons and Sikhs, the production of cross-cultural affinities also entailed the production of difference, as Sikhism was consistently set against the Brahmanical dominance, irrationality, and social conservatism that the British identified as characteristic of popular Hinduism.

A sequence of texts produced between 1780 and the annexation of Punjab in 1849 established the central features of this discursive field. These precolonial British accounts of Punjab were crucial in the formation of East India Company policy in the newly annexed province in the 1850s, and they guided its attempts to protect the distinctiveness of Sikhism with the hope that as a religious tradition it might be a valuable bulwark to state authority. Within the cultural terrain of colonial Punjab, however, the colonial state's project never enjoyed uncontested hegemony. Many Protestant missionaries and British evangelicals attacked the company's policy toward Sikhism, suggesting that the gurus did not really break free from the "superstitions" of Hinduism and that the company's support of Sikh institutions was a barrier to the Christianization of India. By the 1870s, a range of Punjabi reform movements and voluntary organizations were also attempting to have their visions of Punjabi history and the region's future legitimated by the colonial state. While Arya Samajis were suggesting that Sikhism was not an independent tradition and that Sikhs were really just Hindus, the Tat Khalsa faction of the Singh Sabha worked hard to mark off Sikhs from their Hindu neighbors, constructing a large literature on Sikh identity and a new cycle of life rituals to establish the distinctiveness of Sikhism. I have argued here that while the Tat Khalsa program was innovative in that it accepted the notion of "religion" as a coherent, self-contained system and deployed print culture to new ends, it was also dependent on a preexisting prescriptive tradition (the *rahit-namas*) that was revivified and reformulated within the context of colonialism. In chapter two I suggested, however, that there were very real limits to the success of the Tat Khalsa program. Even though Punjab censuses record a significant growth in the Sikh population between 1881 and 1931 and demonstrate that the Tat Khalsa was very successful in embedding the kes-dhari as the "orthodox" Sikh identity in the mind of both colonial officials and many Punjabi villagers, they also suggest that "religious" identity remained encrusted by caste affiliation and that various "little traditions" and heterodox identities (including the 1,100 Punjabis who defined themselves as "Arya Sikhs" in 1901) continued to exist within the Panth.[3]

Under colonialism, Sikhism was reframed not only by struggles over community boundaries between agents of reform, by the weight attached to "religion" as a distinct social domain, and by the colonial state's enumerative project, but also by its incorporation into the global networks that constituted the British Empire. I conclude chapter 2 by stressing that the increasing systematization of Sikhism as a "religion" and the emergence of new forms of imperial mobility created by the empire were simultaneous developments. As Punjab was absorbed into the "webs of empire," some Sikh men pursued the opportunities presented by overseas service in the Indian army, while others traveled to Southeast Asia where colonial regimes and local rulers hoped to harness the renowned martiality of Sikhs to their armies and police forces. The "webs of empire" were comprised of information networks as well as migratory routes and military markets, and by the 1880s Sikhs in Southeast Asia and in Punjab had heard of other opportunities in Australasia and North America.

Migration across the Pacific to these destinations greatly extended the Punjabi world. Mobile Punjabis did not simply transplant their "cultural baggage" to these distant lands, but rather fashioned a new range of

institutions and cultural patterns, whether through remittance, the foundation of new gurdwaras, the creation of political associations, or the
publication of pamphlets and newspapers. Thus the experience of long-
distance migration, the necessity of making new lives in alien lands, and
encounters with often-hostile bureaucratic regimes produced novel social
formations ranging from those Sikhs who were drawn to the revolutionary Indian nationalism of the Ghadr movement to those who fully im-
mersed themselves in the local cultures among which they lived, such as
those Punjabis in California who married Mexican women and embraced
the Spanish language and key aspects of Mexican culture. These histories
of adaptation and innovation need to be juxtaposed against, and brought
into greater dialogue with, histories of cultural change within Punjab
itself, rather than viewing Sikh history in Punjab and Sikhs abroad as
discrete histories. We also need to examine the ways in which these early
histories of migration reshape our understanding of the "Sikh diaspora"
as an analytical field and, as chapter 3 on Dalip Singh demonstrates,
how they explore the connections between the "old" diaspora of the late
nineteenth and early twentieth centuries and the new post-1945 migrant
communities.

After August 1947 the social and economic lives of Punjabis living east
of the newly constituted border were not monopolized by the newly
independent nation-state of India, nor did the boundaries of the nation-
state confine their imaginations. Even though independence did reposi-
tion India within the global cultural economy, translocal networks and
transnational forces continued to shape the development of all of India's
regions. In the case of Punjab after partition, many of these structures
were either borne out of colonialism (such as the Indian and international
markets for the region's agricultural produce) or were ostensibly new
structures, which in reality drew on or cannibalized older imperial structures.[4] The most important of these were the migration networks that
drew Punjabis, especially young men, to British cities to provide cheap
labor in a depressed postwar economy. If it was the legacies of empire that
opened Britain to these migrants, then they established their new lives
within a metropolitan culture that was itself the product of empire building and its discourses. Given their particular and prominent place within

the representations of Indian religions and regional cultures that circulated within the empire, Sikhs arriving in Britain were expected to
be hard working, dependable, frugal, and loyal—values that were well
suited to the needs of British employers. In other words, although the
Indian empire was over, the constant reiteration of Sikh masculinity and
physical prowess within colonial representations of Sikhism provided a
potent framework for Britons trying to make sense of the new arrivals in
their cities.

By focusing on the incorporation of Sikhs into the global reach of the
British Empire and the transnational cultural formations that have characterized the Panth over the last century and a half, in this volume I have
adopted an explicitly global approach to Sikh history. Following Adam
McKeown's exploration of the global networks that constitute Chinese
diasporas, I have also adopted a global, multisited approach to "provide a
stage from which to understand geographically dispersed activities . . .
which thread through and straddle territorially based units."[5] McKeown
goes on to suggest that the historical study of diasporic cultural formations
effectively undercuts "visions of the world order as a mosaic of discrete
sociopolitical entities that are the primary units from which meaning and
history are created."[6]

By exploring Sikhs on the move I affirm McKeown's argument, but
I place greater emphasis on both religion and popular culture, which
McKeown tends to elide in his focus on economics and state practices. In
this book I have foregrounded the place of religion in diasporic cultural
formations, from Dalip Singh's religious vacillations during his exile to
recent debates over the relationship between bhangra to Sikhi. Despite
the strong focus on the Khalistan movement in research on the post–
World War II diaspora, a reading of a variety of source material suggests
that the cultural life of mobile Sikhs is not primarily attached to either an
existing national "homeland" (India) or an imagined religious "homeland" (Khalistan). Rather, the Sikh diaspora is given shape by a host
of organizations (schools, missionary groups, and charities) and cultural
forums (youth groups and camps, newspapers and periodicals, Web sites
and e-mail lists) that are explicitly concerned with individual spirituality
and community well-being as well as formal institutions that underpin

the Panth itself (including gurdwaras, the Akal Takht, and the SGPC). At the same time, however, Sikhs who are separated by great distances are brought into contact by the production and circulation of various forms of cultural production that chart the common history that unites them as Sikhs; that document the very different social contexts that mold the life of various Sikh communities; and that debate the future of the community. Whether these are Sikh newspapers, polemic historical texts, cassette tapes of sermons and sacred songs, bhangra CDs, or e-mails, these cultural forms help define the boundaries of the community and reaffirm the values that connect Sikhs. At certain points in time and in specific locations, the notion of a Punjab "homeland" has been an important feature of these cultural productions, but we must guard against reducing the diaspora to the Khalistani movement.

Throughout this volume, I have stressed how unevenly these transnational networks and global processes of exchange work, and the ways in which they have very different meanings for Sikhs in various locations. We have seen, for example, the salience of Dalip Singh for British Sikhs eager to claim a position within the British national imaginary, while he is a much less relevant figure for Sikh migrants attempting to cement their position among the middle classes of Chicago or New Jersey. In a similar vein, I have demonstrated the transformation of bhangra from the conjunction of the Punjabi and Afro-Caribbean diasporic communities in British cities in the 1980s, a story of cross-cultural engagement that is radically different from the ethnic strategies adopted by South Asian migrants in the United States, who typically occupy a very different position from African Americans and who work hard to insulate their children from contacts with Black culture.[7] Moreover, particular Sikh communities occupy very different positions in the various economic, religious, cultural, and political threads that constitute the fabric of the diaspora. In the 1980s and early 1990s, for example, Southall youth were proud of the neighborhood's position at the forefront of the global bhangra scene, but they also bemoaned the limited range of "Indian" fashions available to young Punjabi women in London in comparison to Bombay and Delhi and decried Southall as a *"pendu* [peasant or villager] town dominated by village-bred, tradition-bound farmers."[8] On the other hand, professional Sikh families in Chicago might remit substantial amounts of money for house construction, dowries, and education for the families remaining in Punjab, at the same time that they actively consume bhangra cassettes produced in Southall and the latest Indian fashions from Delhi when they shop on Devon Street.

The recording and analyzing texture of these cultural formations is a crucial project for Sikh studies in the coming years. One of my aims in this volume is to suggest some sites of investigation and some alternative archives that provide fresh perspectives on Sikh history and contemporary Sikh culture. In exploring statuary, memory, and music, I break out of the textualist tradition that is at the heart of Sikh studies. Other fertile sites for exploration might be clothing, film, or food; for example, in my research for this volume I came across many references that attached great weight to *saag* (mustard greens) as a marker of Punjabi identity. As I note in chapter 4, for example, in Johnny Zee's "Why Did I Come to Vilayet?" a Punjabi father's concern that his son's migration to Britain has alienated him from his Punjabi roots is expressed through the fatherly admonition "you've forgotten the taste of *saag*." In a similar vein, Pakhar Singh, the protagonist in Tarsem Neelgiri's short story "The Divided Shores," enjoys a homecoming meal of "several *roti*s with *saag*." This meal causes Pakhar Singh to reflect that in Britain "*saag* was not available at all. *Saag* was something only a woman could make, and without Pal Kaur [his wife], *saag* was simply inconceivable."[9] Here Neelgiri locates Punjabiness firmly within a "traditional world" where the women, food, and the ancestral village are potent, and interwoven, anchors of identity.

For both Johnny Zee and Tarsem Neelgiri, saag functions as both a potent signifier of home and a sense of belonging that was unobtainable in Vilayat (Britain). Saag is also prominent in Marie Gillespie's ethnographic work in Southall, which records its weight as a signifier of tradition for Punjabi parents and frequently sets it against the "unhealthy" physical and cultural influence of Western food, especially fast food.[10] Thus food, like the music examined in chapter 4, occupies a central place in anxieties over the reproduction of culture within the diaspora. For Punjabi teenagers in Britain, Marie Gillespie argues, eating "English" or "American" food has been an important way of engaging with both "national" and "global culture."[11] In Meera Syal's *Anita and Me,* ten-year old Meena longs after the fish fingers that are regular fare at the house of her white friend Anita, while her mother disparages British food as being tasteless in contrast to their Punjabi food, which embodies the culture of their "homeland."[12] Gurinder Chadha's *Bend It Like Beckham* (2002) also dramatizes the anxieties of Punjabi parents in Britain over the nexus of food and culture through their worries about the erosion of traditional foodways and gender roles. Jasminder's mother encourages her to learn to make "nice round *chapatis*" and is delighted that Jas is able to make *alu gobhi* (potatoes and cauliflower), which she takes as a sign that her daughter has some of the skills that are integral to being a "good Punjabi girl" and thus may not have rejected her culture.

What I am suggesting here is that aspects of everyday life, which can be explored through ethnography as well as social and cultural history, might be productive sites for the analysis of Sikh and Punjabi history. The study of family relations, patterns of cultural consumption, and cultural anxieties will produce a much richer understanding of the texture of Punjabi/Sikh culture than will a narrow focus on prescriptive texts. Kathleen Hall and Marie Gillespie have begun this project, and their work has opened up important vistas into the development of Punjabi youth culture in Britain. Gillespie's work is particularly striking in that it reveals a range of cultural attachments and discursive fields that have gone beyond the purview of Sikh studies to date. Gillespie demonstrates, for example, that although the geographic location and the ethnic mix of the cast (all white) of popular Australian soap operas such as *Neighbours* and *Home and Away* are far removed from life in Southall, these programs play an important role in the community's life as they stimulate both gossip and earnest cultural conversations. Gillespie persuasively argues that Mrs. Mangle, the dreaded gossip at the heart of the plot of *Neighbours* in the late 1980s and early 1990s, "incarnates for Southall youth the networks of relatives and neighbours, particularly aunts and other female elders, who act as moral guardians of their neighbourhood and whose 'gossip' is feared as a force of constraint of young people's freedom."[13] More broadly, "soap talk" forms a crucial element in Punjabi youth culture in Southall by playing a central role in cementing friendships, defining social expectations, and serving as a vehicle for the indirect critique of familial relations and cultural norms within the Sikh community.[14] In a similar vein, my exploration of bhangra in chapter 4 highlighted the way in which the consumption and production of music has allowed Punjabis to reproduce "tradition," to rework their musical inheritances, and to constructively engage with the music, fashion, and cultural politics of a range of non–South Asian cultures.

The cases that make up this volume remind us that Sikh lives—both at home and in the diaspora—are made up of many disparate elements and are molded by a range of influences from both within and outside the Panth. This point is well made in Amrit Kaur Singh's *All That I Am* (1993). This portrait frames the artist's father with images of people, events, and objects central to his life in India and Britain. Across the top of the painting rest three large panels that frame his life around the large events and connections that have molded his life: the Golden Temple (which confirms his Sikh identity), an image of a khadi-clad Gandhi (suggesting a connection to ethical nonviolent nationalism and social justice), and the ship that carried him to Britain. Underneath these three large panels, however, is an array of smaller images that focus largely on his family (such as a group photograph that includes the artist and her twin sister) and elements of Indian, British, and global culture that have meaning in his life. These include H. G. Well's *War of the Worlds,* movie tickets (one for *Flash Gordon*), an image of King Kong, and an album featuring the renowned "playback" singer Lata Mangeshkar.

To my mind, this painting communicates something of the richness of an individual life—an individual Sikh life. In this regard, I think that the image also offers a challenge for scholars working within Sikh studies, a field of endeavor that has focused largely on the development of the religion's textual tradition and its institutional politics. It suggests that Sikh studies should move beyond its grounding within the Western tradition of religious studies to fully embrace ethnography, art history, social history, and new forms of cultural history. A greater variety of perspectives on the Sikh past will not only enrich our appreciation of Sikhism's multiple histories, but also will help us contextualize the rich vein of scholarship that has been produced over the last four decades. Moreover,

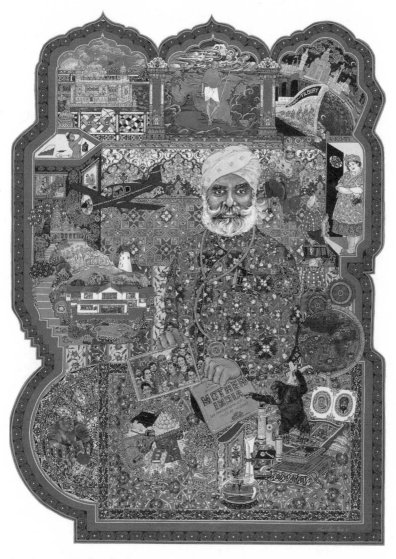

Amrit Kaur Singh, *All That I Am*.

opening up Sikh studies in this way might also allow us to move away from the chief heritage of the colonial period—that is, the notion of "religion" as a self-contained field. *All That I Am* suggests that "religion" exists in a complex, rich, and highly textured world: a world where identity is framed by family as well as faith; a world where meaning is constructed through work, study, and hobbies as well as through sacred texts; and a world where migrants are able to construct rich lives full of meaning and connection even though they are far from their homelands. In its reworking of the Mughal miniature tradition within a postcolonial world of diaspora, this work underscores the permeability of tradition and reminds us of the ability of Sikhs to adapt creatively to the great challenges and hardships that they have faced since 1849. In so doing it neatly encapsulates the multiple contexts within which Sikhs live their lives, the layering of identities within Sikh communities, and the critical engagement of Sikhs with the world—all of which have been at the heart of this volume.

# Notes

## Preface

1 Axel, *The Nation's Tortured Body,* 11.
2 The interfaces between mobility and colonial power have been explored in Ahuja, "Labour Unsettled"; Haynes and Roy, "Conceiving Mobility"; and Singha, "Settle, Mobilize, Verify." On empire and the diaspora, see Harper, "Empire, Diaspora and the Languages of Globalism."
3 On the uses of "diaspora," see Tololyan, "Rethinking Diaspora(s)" and Clifford, *Routes.*
4 Lipsitz, *Dangerous Crossroads.*
5 See, for example, Ballantyne, "Rethinking the Archive."

## 1
## Framing/Reframing Sikh Histories

1 Jeffrey, "Grappling with History," 59–60.
2 See McLeod, *Popular Sikh Art.*
3 See the Web site at www.sikhcybermuseum.org.
4 See, for example, the discussions at the Sikh diaspora Web group site at http://groups.yahoo.com/group/Sikh-Diaspora/.
5 One of the best examples of this is McLeod's role as an "expert witness" in a Canadian court case over the right of Sikhs to wear turbans while

serving for the Royal Canadian Mounted Police. See *Sikh Review* 422 (1994): 74.

6   See, for example, Khurana, *British Historiography on the Sikh Power in the Punjab;* D. Singh, *Western Image of Sikh Religion;* F. Singh, *Historians and Historiography of the Sikhs;* and T. Singh, *Ernest Trumpp and W. H. McLeod.* J. S. Grewal's *Contesting Interpretations of the Sikh Tradition* offers an important overview of the field, while Mandair's "Thinking Differently about Religion and History" offers a critical reading of the secular and historicist underpinnings of Sikh studies.

7   And, of course, we can find scholars who move between these framings or blend them to some extent.

8   Ballantyne, "Resisting the 'Boa Constrictor' of Hinduism."

9   Oberoi, *Construction of Religious Boundaries.*

10  The best guide to these exchanges is Barrier's *The Sikhs and Their Literature.*

11  B. L. Singh, *Autobiography,* 58.

12  Some of these traditions are explored in Fenech, *Martyrdom in the Sikh Tradition.*

13  It is important to note that "Hinduism" itself is a problematic term in the South Asian context. As the product of the orientalist study of South Asian textual traditions and the sociological knowledge produced by the colonial state, there is no equivalent term for "Hinduism" in any pre-colonial South Asian language. Nevertheless, in the nineteenth century the term was adopted by a variety of South Asian leaders, especially those writing in English.

14  See Ballantyne, "Resisting the 'Boa Constrictor' of Hinduism."

15  See G. Singh, *Early European Accounts of the Sikhs.*

16  McLeod, *Guru Nanak and the Sikh Religion,* vii.

17  Ibid., 68–70.

18  Ibid., 146–47.

19  See Fenech, "Contested Nationalisms; Negotiated Terrains."

20  See Deol's "Eighteenth Century Khalsa Identity," "The Minas and Their Literature," "Surdas," and " 'To Hell with War.' "

21  See, for example, Barrier's, "The Formulation and Enactment of the Punjab Alienation of Land Bill" and "Mass Politics and the Punjab Congress."

22  Oberoi, *The Construction of Religious Boundaries,* xii.

23  Mann, Sodhi, and Gill, "Introduction," 1.

24  Sodhi and Mann, "Construction of Religious Boundaries," 167.

25  Sodhi, "Eurocentrism vs. Khalsacentrism," 342.

26  G. Dhillon, "Review of *The Construction of Religious Boundaries,*" 4; S. Singh, "A Work of Scholarly Indulgence," 257.

27  Mann, Sodhi, and Gill, "Introduction," 7–8.

28  See, for example, ibid., 3.

29  Moreover, it is even more ironic that many of the proponents of Khalsa-centrism's critiques of history as a "Western discipline" are themselves trained as engineers, doctors, and scientists.

30  See King's " 'Modernity,' 'Fundamentalism' and Sikhism," 106–11, "The Siege Perilous (Hot Seat) and the Divine Hypothesis," and "*Capax Imperii*—Scripture, Tradition and European Style Critical Method," 3–15.

31  King, "*Capax Imperii*—Scripture, Tradition and European Style Critical Method," 7.

32  On the possibilities of a "post-orientalist" history, see Bose and Jalal, *Modern South Asia*.

33  Sodhi, "Eurocentrism vs. Khalsacentrism," 342–43.

34  M. Sandhu, "Harjot Oberoi—Scholar or Saboteur?" 192–93.

35  This tendency varies between approaches and individual historians: it is much more pronounced in the Tat Khalsa normative tradition than in the political approach of Barrier or the cultural history produced by Oberoi.

36  Banga, *Agrarian System of the Sikhs*; Banga and Grewal, *Maharaja Ranjit Singh and His Times*.

37  Banga, *Five Punjabi Centuries*.

38  Kenneth W. Jones, "Ham Hindu Nahin" (see also his earlier "Communalism in the Punjab").

39  See Sethi, "The Creation of Religious Identities in the Punjab."

40  Oberoi's arguments in *The Construction of Religious Boundaries* can be read as an extended response to Fox's work.

41  Fox, *Lions of the Punjab,* 140.

42  Ibid., 207.

43  Cohn, *Colonialism and Its Forms of Knowledge,* 107; McLeod (ed.), *The Chaupa Singh Rahit-nama*. These images include Imam Bakhsh, "Sikh Soldiers" (Musee national des arts asiatiques—Guimet item 39746); and "Group Portrait of Sikhs from Patiala" (Fraser Album, British Library), which are reproduced in Knight, "The Military Sikhs," 145; and in Goswamy, "Continuing Traditions in the Later Sikh Kingdoms," 174. The changing place of the turban in Sikh identity is explored in McLeod, "The Turban," 57–68.

44  That is, as against a study of Sikh migration or an examination of the development of an overseas Sikh community within a particular nation.

45  Of course, it also underscores the continued importance of print in the definition of Sikh identities and, more generally, in the way in which people imagine their communities.

46  Axel, *The Nation's Tortured Body,* 4.

47  See Dusenbery, "On the Moral Sensitivities of Sikhs in North America" and "The Sikh Person, the Khalsa Panth, and Western Sikh Converts."

48    Mahmood, *Fighting for Faith and Nation;* Mahmood and Brady, *The Guru's Gift.*

49    See Dusenbery, "A Sikh Diaspora?"; McLeod, "The First Forty Years of Sikh Migration"; and Leonard, "Pioneer Voices from California."

50    See McLeod, "A Sikh Theology for Modern Times."

51    Oberoi, *The Construction of Religious Boundaries,* 1–35. See also Thapar, "Syndicated Moksa?"; and Sontheimer and Kulke, *Hinduism Reconsidered.*

52    See, for example, Bhatia and Spencer, *The Sikh Tradition.*

53    Important beginning work on this project can be found in Lee, "John and Henry Lawrence and the Origins of Paternalist Rule in the Punjab"; Lee, *Brothers in the Raj;* and Caton, "Sikh Identity Formation and the British Rural Ideal." More generally, Dewey has offered some important insights in his *Anglo-Indian Attitudes.* The most important works on the subject of land are Barrier, "The Formulation and Enactment of the Punjab Alienation of Land Bill"; and van den Dungen, *The Punjab Tradition.*

54    Jakobsh, in *Relocating Gender in Sikh History,* has also highlighted this dynamic, which she terms the "politics of similarity."

55    The relationship between affinity and difference in the history of colonialism is critically explored in *Journal of Colonialism and Colonial History. Special issue: From Orientalism to Ornamentalism: Empire and Difference in History,* 3.1 (2002); online at http://muse.jhu.edu/journals/journal_of_colonialism_and_colonial_history/toc/cch3.1.htm.

56    Irschick, *Dialogue and History,* 10.

57    Ibid., 8.

58    See my "Race and the Webs of Empire."

59    See my "Rethinking the Archive" and "Empire, Knowledge and Culture," in addition to *Orientalism and Race* and "Race and the Webs of Empire."

60    See Jones, "Ham Hindu Nahin"; and Banerjee, "Bengali Perceptions of the Sikhs" and "Sikh Identity Question."

# 2

# Entangled Pasts

1    For an important study of the politics of diet in colonial Punjab, see Uppal, "Diet, Decay and Desire."

2    See Jones, "Ham Hindu Nahin" and "Communalism in the Punjab"; and Barrier, *The Punjab Alienation of Land Bill of 1900,* and *The Sikhs and Their Literature.*

3    Fox, *Lions of the Punjab,* 140–43 (quote is at 140).

4 Members of the early Khalsa frequently carried, and paid respect to, five weapons: the sword, bow, musket, quoit, and dagger. Guru Hargobind is believed to have worn two swords, one called *piri,* which symbolized his spiritual mission, and the other called *miri,* which designated his struggle against Mughal tyranny. The term *miri-piri* is now taken as the injunction for Sikhs to fight against oppression and injustice.

5 See Marshall, *The British Discovery of Hinduism;* Thapar, "Imagined Religious Communities?"; and Oberoi, *The Construction of Religious Boundaries,* 6–14. These arguments have been extended, with particular regard to British evangelical interpretations of Hinduism, by Geoffrey Oddie's important study: " 'Orientalism' and British Protestant Missionary Constructions of India in the Nineteenth Century."

6 Oberoi, *The Construction of Religious Boundaries,* 419.

7 At least two works by non-British Europeans predated Browne's account, but both can be dismissed as having limited impact on European knowledge of the Sikhs. In September 1606 Father Jerome Xavier, the Portuguese envoy to the court of Jahangir, wrote a short and vague account of Guru Arjan's imprisonment and death at the hands of the Mughals. But this account provided European readers with no substantial information about the Sikhs: Xavier did not use the term "Sikh" and he did not provide the name of the persecuted guru. Colonel Antoine Louis Henri Polier produced a more substantial account of the Sikhs around 1780, which was presented to the Asiatic Society of Bengal in December 1787 as a paper titled "The Siques, or History of the Seeks" (reproduced and discussed in Ganda Singh, "Colonel Polier's Account of the Sikhs," 232–53). Two shorter works by Polier on the Sikhs were published in the *Asiatic Annual* register: "An Extract from a Letter of Major Polier" and "Character of the Sieks."

8 See Browne's letter to John Motteux, dated 17 September 1787, quoted in Fauja Singh, "Early European Writers: Browne, Polier, Forster," 3–4.

9 Buddh Singh Arora collaborated with Lala Ajaib Singh Suraj of Malerkotla to produce his Persian history *Risalah dar Ahwal-i-Nanak Shah Darvesh.* Browne's account was essentially an abridged translation with a brief and rather vague introduction to the Sikh polity together with "a political chart" appended to the end of his account. For a discussion of Browne's work, the textual history of *Risalah dar Ahwal-i-Nanak Shah Darves,* and a reprint of Browne's text, see Ganda Singh, *Early European Accounts of the Sikhs.*

10 Ganda Singh, *Early European Accounts of the Sikhs,* 13–14.

11 Wilkins, "Observations and Inquiries Concerning the Seeks and Their College, at Patna," 292. "College" is Wilkins term for gurdwara. Wilkins traveled to Patna en route from Calcutta to Banaras in 1781; while there,

he briefly visited the birthplace of Guru Gobind Singh, Takhat Sri Harmandir Sahib. He delivered his findings in a paper describing the Sikh presence in Patna and their religion to the Asiatic Society in 1784.

12  See Colley, *Britons*.

13  Malcolm, *Sketch of the Sikhs*.

14  Cunningham, *A History of the Sikhs*, 34.

15  Ibid., 34, 11.

16  See Bayly, *Empire and Information*.

17  See Smith, *Imagining Religion*, xi; and Certeau, *The Practice of Everyday Life*, 50.

18  Asad, *Genealogies of Religion*, 28–29.

19  See Bebbington, *Evangelicalism in Modern Britain*; Porter, *The Creation of the Modern World*; and David, "Sir William Jones, Biblical Orientalism and Indian Scholarship." See also MacMillan, "John Wesley and the Enlightened Historians."

20  Harrison, *"Religion" and the Religions*, 20–25.

21  See Smith, *Imagining Religion*, 49; King, *Orientalism and Religion*, 10–11.

22  See, for example, Hsia, *Social Discipline in the Reformation*.

23  Thomas, *Religion and the Decline of Magic*, 25–77.

24  This phrase is borrowed from Pratt, *Imperial Eyes*.

25  Ballantyne, *Orientalism and Race*, 83–95.

26  See Grewal and Banga, *Early Nineteenth Century Panjab*; and Khan, "Two Historical Works on Punjab."

27  Scrafton, *Reflections on the Government*, 5.

28  Wilkins went on to call Brahma "the Almighty," and, oddly enough, he described Brahmans as "Unitarians" (Wilkins, translator's preface to *The Bhagavat-Geeta*). See also, Marshall, *European Discovery of Hinduism*, 193–94.

29  For a discussion of the Hindu understanding of time, see Basham, *The Wonder That Was India*, 320–21.

30  Stanley, *The Bible and the Flag*, 56.

31  It is important to note the significant divergence between some of the material published in Britain and the material found in the private diaries and personal correspondence of the missionaries themselves. Material printed in England for the English market tended to be more sensational as part of the efforts of Evangelical publicists to raise money, galvanize support, and popularize their religious mission.

32  Trautmann, *Aryans and British India*, 101–3.

33  Grant, "Observations on the State of Society among the *Asiatic* Subjects of *Great Britain*."

34  For evangelical attacks on "popular Hinduism," see Ward, *A View of the History, Literature, and Religion of the Hindoos*; and Davidson, *Evangelicals and Attitudes to India, 1786–1813*, 47.

35  Tumbleston, *Catholicism in the English Protestant Imagination,* 202.

36  Wolffe, *The Protestant Crusade in Great Britain,* 18–20.

37  This battle was often seen in gendered terms: the clash between a vigorous, masculine Protestant tradition and a weak, effeminate Catholicism. This opposition fits well with my argument because the equation of Protestantism and reform with masculinity obviously informed British views of Sikhism in relationship to Hinduism.

38  Charles Grant's polemic against child marriage, polygamy, phallus worship, and temple prostitutes, for example, echoed the tone and content of anti-Catholic pornography that attacked priestly celibacy and fantasized about sexual decadence in monasteries and nunneries. The introductory essay to the 1875 edition of *Foxe's Book of Martyrs* reminded British Protestants that prior to the break with Rome, English "abbots, priors, and monks kept as many women each as any lascivious Mohammedan could desire" (Cobbin, "Essay on Popery," xi).

39  Davidson, *Evangelicals and Attitudes to India,* 47.

40  Cust, *The Life of Baba Nanuk,* 7.

41  For critical responses to Cannadine's *Ornamentalism,* see "From Orientalism to Ornamentalism: Empire and Difference in History," special issue of *Journal of Colonialism and Colonial History* 3 (2002). http://muse.jhu.edu/journals/journal_of_colonialism_and_colonial_history/toc/cch3.1.html.

42  In 1845, Major R. Leech, first assistant agent in the Northwest Provinces, suggested in a memorandum that "the Sikh religion which has long since reached its zenith is now visibly on the decline" (quoted in Barrier, *The Sikhs and Their Literature,* xviii).

43  Lawrence, *Selections from the Records of the Government of India. (Foreign Department) No. VI. General Report on the Administration of the Punjab Territories . . . for the Years 1851–52 and 1852–53* (Calcutta, 1854), 213–44.

44  See Gilmartin, *Empire and Islam.*

45  See Kerr, "Sikhs and State," 154; see also his "British Relationships with the Golden Temple, 1849–90."

46  Lawrence, *Selections from the Records,* 213. See also "Statement of Jagheers . . . ," Government of India, Foreign Department, Political Proceedings, 10 June 1853, number 219.

47  See Griffin, *The Panjab Chiefs.*

48  Kerr, "Sikhs and the State," 160. See also Cohn, "Representing Authority in Victorian India."

49  Lake, *Sir Donald McLeod,* 114.

50  Cox, *Imperial Fault Lines.*

51  Youngson, *Forty Years of the Panjab Mission,* 50.

52  *Church Missionary Intelligencer* 2.7 (July 1851): 156, 148.

53  This manuscript, believed to be the original copy of the *Adi Granth,* was

obtained, after much persuasion, from Sadhu Singh Sodhi, who had previously refused to supply the manuscript to Ranjit Singh. The manuscript was finally shipped to England, under the supervision of John Lawrence, and presented to the India Office Library.

54  Trumpp, *The Adi Granth,* v.

55  Ibid., vi.

56  Ibid., vii–viii.

57  Barrier, "Trumpp and Macauliffe," 169.

58  Trumpp, *Adi Granth*, vii. Trumpp's first task was to construct a vocabulary and grammar for the entire Granth on the basis of his first thorough reading of the text. Although he seems to have gained only limited support from the granthis, he did utilize three existing commentaries on the text. Two of these commentaries "explained in a rough way a number of Hindui and *deshi* (provincial) words," and the third focused on Arabic and Persian loan words (vi).

59  For a discussion of Trumpp's demands for extra fees and the growing hostility toward Trumpp among members of the Punjab government, see the correspondence of Lepel H. Griffin to the Secretary to Government of India, Oriental and India Office Collections, British Library, *Punjab Home Proceedings*, October 1871, A/4; and C. U. Aitchison, Secretary to Government of India, to Punjab Government, *Punjab Home Proceedings*, April 1872, A/15. Trumpp was consistently insensitive in the handling of his responsibilities in the Punjab. He wrote a scathing review of the Pushtu grammar prepared for the government by T. P. Hughes of the C.M.S. mission at Peshawar (*Punjab Home Proceedings*, April 1872, A/27). Hughes, however, recovered from Trumpp's stinging attack to write a sympathetic review of Trumpp's translation (Hughes, "The Religion of the Sikhs").

60  Trumpp, *Adi Granth*, vii.

61  Ibid., cxii.

62  Trumpp provides examples of these "prayers" in ibid., cxii n.4–n.5.

63  Ibid., cxv.

64  Ibid., cxvi.

65  Lepel H. Griffin, Officiating Secretary, Punjab Government, to Secretary to the Government of India, *Punjab Home Proceedings*, April 1872, A/15. Oriental and India Office Collections, British Library.

66  Barrier, "Trumpp and Macauliffe," 171.

67  Macauliffe, "The Fair at Sakhi Sarvar," 78–101. Macauliffe's work on Sakhi Sarvar was extended by Temple in "A Song about Sakhi Sarvar." For more recent analyses of the worship of Sakhi Sarvar in nineteenth-century Punjab, see Oberoi, *The Construction of Religious Boundaries* and "The Worship of Pir Sakhi Sarvar."

68  Macauliffe, *The Sikh Religion*, 1: xxxix.

69   Macauliffe, *A Lecture on How the Sikhs Became a Militant Race*, 27.

70   See Omissi, *The Sepoy and the Raj*; Gell, "The Origins of the Sikh 'Look.'"

71   See especially the works of Gyani Ditt Singh, such as his *Darpoke Singh*, *Durga Prabodh*, and *Nakli Sikh Prabodh*. See also Barrier, *The Sikhs and Their Literature*.

72   See Gyani Ditt Singh, *Mera Ate Sadhu Dayanand Da Sambhand*; and Kahn Singh, *Ham Hindu Nahim*. See also Barrier, *The Sikhs and Their Literature*.

73   Gyani Ditt Singh, *Sultan Poara* (Lahore, 1896) and *Miran Manaut* (Lahore, 1902). See also Barrier, *The Sikhs and Their Literature*.

74   Ibbetson, *Report on the Census of the Punjab*, 137.

75   *Gazetteer of Ambala District, 1883–4* (Lahore, 1884), 37.

76   Clark, "The Decay of Sikhism," 20.

77   Quoted in Macauliffe, *The Sikh Religion*, xi.

78   Macauliffe, *Sikh Religion* I, lvii.

79   Macauliffe, *A Lecture on the Sikh Religion and Its Advantages to the State*, 4.

80   Ibid., 18.

81   On another occasion, Macauliffe argued: "It does not appear rational, much less politic, to allow them to lose their distinctive character, to revert to gross superstition and social deterioration, and to divest themselves of loyalty which in peace as well as in war have made them the mainstay and pride of the British Government in India" (*How the Sikhs Became a Militant Race*, 27).

82   Ibid., 28

83   See Bayly, "From Ritual to Ceremony"; and *Khalsa Akhbar*, 18 September 1886.

84   See Talwar, "The Anand Marriage Act."

85   Note that while this definition stresses the distinctiveness and "systematic" nature of Sikhism (as it itemizes a clearly defined religious identity, a sacred text, religious teachers, and the exclusivity of the "faith"), it makes no mention of the Khalsa or of the bodily regimes advocated by the Tat Khalsa.

86   McLeod, *Sikhs of the Khalsa*, 169–71; see also *The Sikhs*, 68. A brief rahit-nama, *Tanakhah-nama*, is commonly attributed to the poet Nand Lal (1633–1715).

87   These life-cycle rituals were not a feature in earlier rahit namas such as the *Tanakhah-nama* of Nand Lal or the *Chaupa Singh Rahit-Nama*. See McLeod, *The Chaupa Singh Rahit-nama*.

88   McLeod, *Textual Sources*, 79. The Shiromani Gurdwara Parbandhak Committee (SGPC) was the elected body responsible for the principal gurdwaras in Punjab.

89   See, for example, Masson, *Narrative of Various Journeys*, 1: 431–35; Vigne,

*Travels in Kashmir*, 1: 54; and Osborne, *The Court and Camp of Runjeet Sing*, 62, 64, 69, 74. On the Akalis, see Fane, *Five Years in India*, 1: 157.

90 Masson, *Narrative of Various Journeys*, 1: 433.

91 Ali, *The Sikhs and Afghans*, 25.

92 *Lahore Chronicle*, 8 June 1850

93 *Delhi Gazette*, 8 June 1850 (also reprinted in the *Lahore Chronicle*, 15 June 1850).

94 Lawrence, *Selections from the Records*, 39. But see also Lawrence's comments about the lack of discipline in the 3rd Seikh Local Infantry and the Camel Corps (32, 34).

95 Blomfield, *Lahore to Lucknow*, 34, 41–42.

96 Omissi, *Sepoy and the Raj*, 6.

97 *Lahore Chronicle*, 17 November 1858.

98 Omissi, *Sepoy and the Raj*, 10–13.

99 Cited in Omissi, Sepoy and the Raj, 12.

100 Lord Roberts to Stewart, 30 June 1882, quoted in Robson, *Roberts in India*, 257–58.

101 In 1862 Punjab and the North-West Frontier Provinces produced 28 out of the 131 infantry battalions in the Indian army; by 1914 the number had increased to 57 out of 121. By 1904, 57 percent of the troops in the Indian Army came from Punjab and Nepal, and by 1914 these northern recruiting grounds made up 75 percent of the Indian infantry (Omissi, *Sepoy and the Raj*, 11, 19).

102 See, for example, the 1914 *Amritsar District Gazetteer*, which recorded that 6,000 men were serving in the army and 2,000 more were pensioners. As a result some Rs. 25 lakhs per annum came into the district. *Amritsar District Gazetteer* (Lahore, 1914), 162.

103 Falcon, *Handbook on Sikhs for Regimental Officers*, 21.

104 Ibid., 61–22.

105 Ibid., 15.

106 Ibid., 71–73, 98–102.

107 For a firsthand account of these efforts, see Eyre, *The Sikh and European Soldiers of Our Indian Forces*, 7–8. On the kes-dhari/amrit-dhari distinction, see McLeod, *Who Is a Sikh?* 110–15.

108 See Falcon, *Handbook on Sikhs*, especially 6–10; and McLeod, *Sikhs of the Khalsa*, 19, 164, 244.

109 McLeod, *Sikhs of the Khalsa*, 171–73.

110 See, for example, the evidence (especially the quote from H. L. O. Garrett) recorded in Khan, *Census of India 1931*, 305.

111 The census recorded a significant growth in the total Sikh population (a 13.9 percent increase), which was largely driven by a 50 percent increase in those who identified themselves as the "Sikhs of Guru Govind Singh."

112 *Census of India, 1901. Vol. 17: "The Punjab and Its Feudatories and the North-West Frontier Province," Part I: "Report"* (Simla, 1902), 122, 136.

113 Ibid., subsidiary table 5, 173–84.

114 This definition included additional provision that officials were to "enter the religion of the women as stated" (ibid., 124).

115 Ibid., 124, 133.

116 Middleton and Jacobs, *Census of India, 1921, Census of India, 1921. Vol. 15: "Punjabi and Delhi," Part I 'Report.'* 183–86.

117 Markovits, *The Global World of Indian Merchants*, 110.

118 Phillips, *Salem and the Indies*, 330–31, 364, 369. Originally from Marblehead, Massachusetts, Phillips became a significant figure in Salem's trans-Pacific trade by serving on ships that sailed the Indian Ocean between 1788 and 1799.

119 Thomas Metcalf explores the role of the empire in fashioning a set of India-focused networks within the "Indian Ocean Arena" in his recently published *Forging the Raj*, 282–99.

120 *The Proceedings of the Legislative Council of the Straits Settlements*, 1872, 18–33; 1873, paper no. 27, 1–5; 1879, paper no. 32.

121 See Ballantyne, *Orientalism and Race*.

122 For a detailed discussion of the role of military service and political work in shaping Sikh migration to Southeast Asia, see Metcalf, *Forging the Raj*, 250–81.

123 *The Proceedings of the Legislative Council of the Straits Settlements*, 1879, papers 29 and 32.

124 Ibid. See also Endacott, *A History of Hong Kong*, 153.

125 Sandhu, "Sikh Immigration into Malaya," 340 n. 2.

126 See Bird, *The Golden Chersonee and the Way Thither Letter*; Kipling, "Georgie Porgie" (in *Life's Handicap*) and *From Sea to Sea*; Bisland, *A Flying Trip*; and Bland, *Houseboat Days*.

127 Markovits, The *Global World of Indian Merchants*, 48, 255.

128 This phrase is from Darshan Singh Atwal's account of his grandfather's migration to Australia, Bhatti, "From Sojourners to Settlers," 39.

129 Bhatti, "From Sojourners to Settlers," 51.

130 See the reproduction of his diary in ibid., 47.

131 Ibid., 47, 53, 59. See also the photos reproduced on 58–63.

132 McLeod, "The First Forty Years," 248.

133 McLeod, *Punjabis in New Zealand*, 128–31.

134 Tatla, "Imagining Punjab," 163. His assertion that the "shared religious tradition of Sikhism transcended such social categories as caste" is perhaps an over-reading of the evidence.

135 See Ballantyne, *Orientalism and Race*.

136 See, for example, McLeod's discussion in *Punjabis in New Zealand*, 141, of Ghadrites and the reading of Ghadr newspapers in New Zealand.

137   Markovits, *The Global World of Indian Merchants*, 224–25.

138   Grewal, *The Sikhs of the Punjab*, 154.

139   Petrie, *Developments in Sikh politics, 1900–1911.*

140   Barrier, "Sikh Emigrants and Their Homeland."

141   Mongia, "Race, Nationality, Mobility," 196. Mongia's work also demonstrates that debates over Sikhs, and the degree to which they fitted the general category "Indian," were pan-imperial in scope and energized by a complex web of networks and exchanges. The restrictions applied to Sikh migrants to Canada, such as the $200 per capita fee and the requirement that immigrants travel to Canada on a continuous voyage from their nation of citizenship, were questioned by Colonel Swayne, the governor of British Honduras. Swayne not only challenged the climactic and racial arguments that had been mobilized against South Asian migration, but also stressed that these provisions were depriving Canada of a valuable labor resource. He argued that employers such as mill owners preferred to employ Sikhs over whites because they could "be more safely relied upon to give continuous employment." But, at the same time, Swayne worried that the transnational movement of Punjabi workers would disrupt Punjabi society "at home"—as the capital that the workers accumulated would have a markedly destabilizing impact in India (Mongia, "Race, Nationality, Mobility," 203).

142   Leonard, " 'Flawed Transmission?' " 98.

143   Mishra, "The Diasporic Imaginary," 423–24.

144   These issues were brought home for me forcibly in December 2001 when I was traveling in California and sat beside a man named Juan Singh on a Greyhound Bus from San Luis Obispo to San Jose. In conversation, Mr. Singh said that although his ancestors migrated to California at the start of the twentieth century—from "India, north of Delhi"—he was not sure exactly where his ancestors came from. He described his deceased grandfather as a "Hindu," but stressed that he himself was now a Catholic who, like his grandfather and father, had married a Mexican woman. He added further that he and his family (who live in Baja California) spoke Spanish at home.

145   Leonard, " 'Flawed Transmission?' " 97.

146   McLeod, "The First Forty Years," 246–47.

147   See Darling, *The Punjab Peasant in Prosperity and Debt.*

148   Bhatti, "From Sojourners to Settlers," 39–40.

149   *Hoshiarpur District Gazetteer 1904* (Lahore, 1905), 27–28.

150   *Jullundur District and Kapurthala State Gazetteer 1904* (Lahore, 1908), 52–53.

151   Kessinger notes that in 1848 nine men from the village were living elsewhere, including one man who had been away for thirty years. In 1848, there were some 197 males living in the village, so these nine

migrants comprised about 5 percent of the village's adult male population (Kessinger, *Vilyatpur, 1848–1968*, 50, 90).

152 Kessinger, *Vilyatpur,* 90–91 (the quote is from the *Chenab Colony Gazetteer*).

153 Ibid., 92–93.

154 Ibid., 169–70.

155 Ibid., 93.

156 Ibid., 172.

157 McLeod explores this likelihood in "The First Forty Years of Sikh Migration," 250.

158 The classic British description of the Grand Trunk Road comes in chapter 4 of Rudyard Kipling's *Kim*, where Kipling celebrates "the smiling river of life" that conveyed people, goods, and news from all over South Asia and beyond.

159 See also the observation of Reshmore Kaur Toor of Woolgoolga that her grandfather "heard about opportunities in Australia because India was a British colony" (quoted in Bhatti, "From Sojourners to Settlers," 40).

160 Bayly, *Empire and Information*, 36–44.

161 McLeod, "The First Forty years of Sikh Migration," 239.

# 3
# Maharaja Dalip Singh

1 The following paragraph is based on various news reports and Web sites. See, especially, *Daily Telegraph*, 30 July 1999; http://news.bbc.co.uk/hi/ english/uk/newsid_407000/407061.htm; and http://www.mdsct.org.uk/mdsctwebpage/trusthomepage.htm.

2 Throughout this chapter I use "Dalip," the standard modern form of the maharaja's first name, rather than the variations that were commonly used by Victorian Britons: "Duleep," "Dhuleep," "Dulip," and "Dhulip." In quotations, however, I retain the original usage.

3 *Punjab Times International,* 8 October 1997.

4 Cited in Alexander and Anand, *Queen Victoria's Maharajah*, 43.

5 Ibid., 47–48.

6 Axel, *The Nation's Tortured Body*, 39–78.

7 Ganda Singh, *Maharaja Duleep Singh Correspondence*; Alexander and Anand, *Queen Victoria's Maharajah*; Jones, "Maharaja Dalip Singh."

8 See Dalip Singh to Login, 2 December 1850 and 9 December 1850; and Dalhousie to Dalip Singh, 27 July 1852 and 12 March 1853, in L. Login, *Sir John Login and Duleep Singh*.

9 Dalhousie to Login, 4 August 1852, and Dalhousie to Dalip Singh, 31 January 1854, in L. Login, *Sir John Login and Duleep Singh*.

10 Quoted in Alexander and Anand, *The Queen's Maharajah*, 189–90.
11 See, for example, "Memorandum of Conversation between Sir Owen Burne and Maharajah Duleep Singh, 29 Jan. 1886," in Ganda Singh, *Maharaja Duleep Singh Correspondence*, item 216.
12 *Standard,* 25 March 1886.
13 Quoted in Alexander and Anand, *The Queen's Maharajah,* 208–9.
14 See, for example, "Abstracts of Political Intelligence, Punjab Police, 20 March and 4 April 1886," in Ganda Singh, *Maharaja Duleep Singh Correspondence,* item 237.
15 Dufferin to Kimberley, 15 April 1886, in Ganda Singh, *Maharaja Duleep Singh Correspondence*, item 216. The proclamation was printed in the *Pioneer* on 16 April 1886.
16 Res. Aden to Dufferin, 5 May 1886, and Durand to Burne, 28 May 1886, in Ganda Singh, *Maharaja Duleep Singh Correspondence,* items 328, 372.
17 Alexander and Anand, *The Queen's Maharajah,* 225.
18 Duleep Singh to Montgomery, 17 June 1886, in Ganda Singh, *Maharaja Duleep Singh Correspondence,* item 432.
19 Alexander and Anand, *The Queen's Maharajah,* 230–34.
20 Duleep Singh to Tzar Alexander III, 10 May 1887, in Ganda Singh, *Maharaja Duleep Singh Correspondence,* item 428.
21 Duleep Singh to Indian Princes, in Ganda Singh, *Maharaja Duleep Singh Correspondence,* item 450.
22 Edgar to Durand, 11 September 1887, in Ganda Singh, *Maharaja Duleep Singh Correspondence*, item 474.
23 A. S. to Dalip Singh, in Ganda Singh, *Maharaja Duleep Singh Correspondence*, item 543. The *Standard,* 12 November 1888.
24 Alexander and Anand, *The Queen's Maharajah,* 278–79.
25 Ibid., 285.
26 Ibid., 298.
27 McLeod, *Early Sikh Tradition*; *The B40 Janam-sakhi*; and *Popular Sikh Art.*
28 Nevertheless, the public guestbook on the MDSCT Web site suggests that there has been substantial interest on the part of Sikhs both from throughout the diaspora and from India itself. See http://www.mdsct .org.uk/mdsctwebpage/guestbook.htm. Baba Dip Singh (1682–1757) was a celebrated Sikh martyr who was killed as he struggled to reach Amritsar to cleanse Harmandir Sahib after it had been defiled by the Afghans. He remains a tremendously popular figure, and dramatic images of him fighting on against the Afghans after being beheaded are a staple for the calendars, posters, and small prints sold in the bazaars of Punjab and by Punjabi store owners in London, Birmingham, and other British cities.
29 McLeod, *Popular Sikh Art,* 19, and figs. 2, 4, and 5; Ganda Singh, *Maharaja Duleep Singh Correspondence,* items 117, 207.
30 Ahluwalia, "Duleep Singh—The Crusader," 92.

31  Ganda Singh, *Maharaja Duleep Singh Correspondence,* items 100, 299. The
    Kukas, or Namdharis, maintain that the tenth Guru lived on beyond
    1708, his traditional death date, and that he bestowed succession on Balak
    Singh (1799–1862). This movement, which placed great value on cow
    protection and vegetarianism, caused the British considerable anxiety and
    was under close surveillance by the colonial state.

32  Ahluwalia, "Duleep Singh—The Crusader," 95.

33  *Tribune,* August 1883. On Sardar Dayal Singh Majithia and the *Tribune,*
    see Ananda, *A History of the Tribune.*

34  *Tribune,* 25 October 1893.

35  Cited in Chakrabarty, *Duleep Singh,* 177.

36  *Kurshid-i-Khalsa* (Jalandar, 1885). Baba Nihal Singh's invocation of Bhai
    Ram Singh and Dalip Singh was somewhat ironic given that Ram Singh
    had denounced Dalip Singh. For British views of these debates, see "Secy
    of Punjab Govt. to Foreign Department," in B. N. Singh, *Summary of
    Correspondence in the Case of Maharaja Dalip Singh.*

37  See W. M. Young to H. M. Durand (Enclosure C), 24 May 1886, in Ganda
    Singh, *Maharaja Duleep Singh Correspondence,* item 321.

38  Sardar Thakur Singh Sandhanwalia to Maharaja Dalip Singh, 9 Novem-
    ber 1883, in Ganda Singh, *Maharaja Duleep Singh Correspondence,* items
    117–18.

39  British surveillance of Thakur Singh Sandhanwalia and Thakur Singh
    of Wagha is recorded in Ganda Singh, *Maharaja Duleep Singh Correspon-
    dence,* items 321–22, 346, 467–72.

40  See, for example, Chakrabarty, *Duleep Singh*; Chakrabarty and Gulati,
    *The Tragic Tale of Maharaja Duleep Singh*; and Chakrabarty and Kapur,
    *Maharaja Duleep Singh.*

41  Baddan, "Introduction," in *Fighter for Freedom,* 7.

42  Ibid., 11.

43  Ibid., 12.

44  A telling indicator of Baddan's narrowly nationalist vision is the complete
    omission of any reference to the work of Alexander and Anand. Com-
    pare this approach with Axel's important study of the transnational artic-
    ulation of Sikh identities in *The Nation's Tortured Body.*

45  See the Nagaara Trust Web site at http://www.nishaan.com/nagaara
    .htm.

46  Stephen Lawrence, a young British Black, was murdered in April 1993 in
    Eltham in southwest London. The police investigation of this case has
    been subject to sustained scrutiny, including a Police Complaints Author-
    ity inquiry (which defended the investigation) and an official inquiry
    headed by Sir William MacPherson. Lakhvinder "Ricky" Reel was found
    dead in the Thames River in October 1997, a week after he (and a group
    of South Asian friends) were the subject of a racially motivated attack in

Kingston in west London. Despite the widespread belief that Reel was murdered, the police insist that his death was accidental.

47     Bayly, "Exhibiting the Imperial Image," 13.

48     Axel, *The Nation's Tortured Body*, 69.

49     Bayly, "Exhibiting the Imperial Image," 14.

50     *Observer,* 9 December 1990.

51     Axel, *The Nation's Tortured Body*, 69.

52     *Guardian,* 12 November 1990.

53     Gell, "The Origins of the 'Sikh Look,'" 37–83.

54     While the exhibition catalogue puts great emphasis on social and cultural history, the primacy of political events is not only suggested by the chronological sweep of the exhibition (from the foundation of the East India Company through to independence), but also in Bayly's comment directed toward British South Asians that the exhibition tried "to represent Indian nationalism and Muslim movements as fully as it does British conquests, bugles and tiger-shots" (Bayly, "Exhibiting the Imperial Image," 13).

55     David Lowenthal, *The Heritage Crusade and the Spoils of History.* Cambridge, UK, 1998. See also Brewer, *The Marketing of Tradition*; and Fladmark, *Heritage and Museums.*

56     Samuel, *Theatres of Memory;* Wright, *On Living in an Old Country.*

57     Ballard, "Differentiation and Disjunction among the Sikhs," 93.

58     http://www.mdsct.org.uk/mdsctwebpage/background_trust_was_originally_established.htm.

59     This interpretation is also borne out in the mdsct's selection of speakers: in 1997 its annual lecture was delivered by Major Robert Henderson, a former officer in a Sikh regiment.

60     Axel, *The Nation's Tortured Body,* 73.

61     This notion of a "memory anchor" elaborates on Milton's observation that "memorials provide fixed places in a chaotic and shifting landscape, where groups can project shared symbols to consolidate notions of pride, heritage, power, and self" (Milton, "Memorials," 414).

62     http://www.mdsct.org.uk/mdsctwebpage/trusthomepage.htm.

63     *Guardian*, 3 March 1993.

64     Ibid.

65     *Guardian*, 20 January 1993.

66     *Guardian*, 3 March 1993.

67     Ibid.

68     Syal, *Life Isn't All Ha Ha Hee Hee*, 8–9.

69     *Guardian*, 3 March 1993.

70     Ibid.

71     Gillian Turner, interview with Reginald Allen Trett, http://www.elveden

22.freeserve.co.uk/spoken.htm. All of the interviews on this Web site discuss the arrival of American servicemen in Elveden during World War II; it seems that it is only at this point that the "outside world" intruded on life in Suffolk.

72 The history presented of the estate is titled "A Brief Outline of the Development of Elveden Estate during the Ownership of the Guinness Family—1894 to the Present Day," thereby eliding Dalip Singh's ownership of the estate from 1869. See http://www.elveden22.freeserve.co.uk/elveden_estate.htm.

73 The early cultivation of these skills is suggested by a portrait produced in the early 1840s, probably by Imam Bakhsh, which depicts a bejeweled infant grasping a rifle ("Maharaja Dhelip Singh," Musée National des Arts Asiatiques-Guimet, 39750).

74 Alexander and Anand, *Queen Victoria's Maharajah*, 112.

75 Ibid., 111.

76 Turner, *Memoirs of a Gamekeeper*, cited in Alexander and Anand, *Queen Victoria's Maharajah*, 113.

77 On the importance of these in the molding of British self-perceptions and in imperial culture, see MacKenzie, *Empire of Nature*.

78 *Times of India*, 6 May 1873.

79 Axel, *The Nation's Tortured Body*, 39–78.

80 Burton, *At the Heart of Empire*, 36.

81 Elements of the *babu* stereotype and the very different representation of Punjabis (and Sikhs in particular) are explored in my "Resisting the 'Boa Constrictor' of Hinduism," 195–216; Burton, *At the Heart of Empire*, 35–37; and Sinha, *Colonial Masculinity*.

82 This song, from Morrissey's 1988 *Viva Hate* album, proved to be a contentious statement of Englishness with its warning addressed to a young "Bengali in platforms" who "only wants to embrace your culture / And to be your friend forever." The Bengali is told "shelve your Western plans /'Cause life is hard enough when you belong / Life is hard enough when you belong here." For conflicting visions of the significance of these lines, see *Melody Maker*, 19 March 1988 and 3 December 1988; and *Sounds*, 18 June 1988.

83 Caton, "Sikh Identity Formation," 175–94.

84 Williams, *The Country and the City*.

85 See, for example, the *Guardian*, 21 February, 4 March, 12 April, 19 April.

86 On "dialogics," see Irschick, *Dialogue and History*. Of course, it is crucial to underline the deep-seated inequalities that structured such processes, both under colonialism and in this postcolonial age. My use of the phrase "uneven polylogics" is an attempt to draw greater attention to these disparities, which Irschick acknowledges but doesn't emphasise. An im-

portant essay on interregional contexts of identity construction is Banerjee, "Sikh Identity Question," 195–216. See also Vertovec, "Caught in an Ethnic Quandary," 272–90.

87 Burton, *At the Heart of the Empire*; Michael Fisher, *The First Indian Author in English*; Visram, *Ayahs, Lascars and Princes*.

88 Susan VanKoski, "Letters Home, 1915–16," 43–63.

# 4
# Displacement, Diaspora, Difference

1 These figures are given in *New York Trend*, 16 June 2003, and in "Beware! Panjabi MC Set to Takeover Stateside," online at http://www.manhunt.com/news/stories/3057.html.

2 I would like to thank Dan Nicholson for directing me to Scribe's use of this track.

3 *Times* (St. Petersburg), 10 August 2003.

4 Lipsitz, *Dangerous Crossroads*, 4.

5 The best example of this approach is in Oberoi, *The Construction of Religious Boundaries*.

6 McLeod, *Popular Sikh Art*, 1. McLeod's work does begin, however, by criticizing his early "unspoken preconceptions [which] relegated them [the bazaar prints] to a category reserved for the semi-literate and the uncouth" (vii).

7 *Tribune* (Chandigarh), 13 September 1998.

8 See Shackle, "Making Punjabi Literary History," 97–117; and Leitner, *History of Indigenous Education in the Panjab*.

9 Oberoi, *Construction of Religious Boundaries*, 139–203. Steel and Temple, *Tales of the Punjab;* Charles Swynnerton, *Romantic Tales from the Panjab*.

10 See, for example, Swynnerton, *Romantic Tales from the Panjab*, xvii–xix.

11 Blackburn and Ramanujan, *Another Harmony*, 1–40.

12 On the significance of the Punjabi imprint on Bollywood, including that of Ghulam Haider, see "Punjabis in Hindi Films: Omnipresence!" *Screen*, 6–12 September 2002.

13 Of course, Haider was instrumental in giving Lata Mangeshkar her "breakthrough" role in *Majboor* (1948). As yet, there has been no comprehensive history of the relationship between Punjabi and Hindi music in the modern era, but in this paragraph I draw on Manuel, *Cassette Culture*, 177–78, and Pande, *Folk Music and Musical Instruments of the Punjab*.

14 The best discussion of these issues is Dhillon, *Folk Dances of Panjab*. For debates among Punjabis over these issues see www.punjabi.net.

15 Schreffler, "Out of the Dhol Drums."

16    Dhillon, *Folk Dances,* 73–74.
17    Giddha is a dramatic dance based around clapping; luddi is a dance in western Punjab based around circular movements; sammi is a circular dance accompanied by songs and performed under the moonlight; pharuha is a fast form of giddha particularly associated with Malwa. Jhummir is a male dance of western Punjab that is performed in a circle to the accompaniment of jhummir songs, while the bagha is a circular dance of southwest Punjab based around the raising of the arms and thumping feet on the ground.
18    Dhillon, *Folk Dances,* 79.
19    *Tribune* (Chandigarh), 13 September 1998.
20    This paragraph is based on Dhillon, *Folk Dances* 89, 154–55.
21    Ibid., 89.
22    See http://punjabgovt.nic.in/Culture/culture.htm.
23    The simultaneous development of bhangra in Punjab and the diaspora is stressed in Banerji and Baumann, "Bhangra 1984–8," 137–52.
24    On bhangra and community occasions, see Banerji, "Ghazals to Bhangra in Great Britain," 208.
25    Ibid., 208–9.
26    Ibid., 211–13.
27    On the street in bhangra, see Lipsitz, *Dangerous Crossroads,* 130.
28    Bennett, "Bhangra in Newcastle," 110.
29    Ibid.
30    See Modood, "Political Blackness and British Asians" and " 'Black': Racial Equality and Asian Identity," 397–404.
31    Grewal et al., preface to *Charting the Journey,* 1.
32    Modood, "Political Blackness and British Asians."
33    Sharma, "Noisy Asians or 'Asian Noise,' " 43–44.
34    Hall, "Cultural Identity and Diaspora," 222–27.
35    Sinha, *Colonial Masculinity.*
36    Steven Kapur's stage name is an homage to the Jamaican ragamuffin star "Super Cat," who is sometimes known as the "Wild Apache."
37    *Toronto Star,* 16 August 2002.
38    Rushdie, *Imaginary Homelands,* 155–58. See also Gaffney, *Interpretations of Violence.*
39    By 1976 Sidney Bidwell estimated that 30,000 of Southall's 52,000 inhabitants were South Asians, most of whom were Punjabis (*Red, White and Black,* 5).
40    These structures are explored in Baumann, "Managing a Polyethnic Milieu."
41    See Bhachu, "Ethnicity Constructed."
42    Bains, "Southall Youth," 235.
43    Gillespie, *Television, Ethnicity and Cultural Change,* 46–47.

44 Ibid., 46, 181–82.
45 Ibid., 182.
46 Syal, *Life Isn't All Ha Ha Hee Hee*, 41.
47 Kathleen Hall has offered a rich ethnographic study of these processes in *Lives in Translation*.
48 Cited in Sharma, "Noisy Asians or 'Asian Noise,' " 32.
49 Bennett, "Bhangra in Newcastle," 111.
50 See Lipsitz, *Dangerous Crossroads*, 130, for Apache Indian's comments on the conflict in his family over reggae.
51 Hall, *Lives in Translation*, 141.
52 Baumann, "The Re-Invention of Bhangra," 90.
53 Kalra, "*Vilayeti* Rhythms," 85.
54 This song reworked Shaukat Ali's 1974 version of the song "Main Vilayet Kaanon Aiyaa?" in *Memories of Punjab*.
55 Apache Indian, "Arranged Marriage," in *No Reservations* (1991).
56 *Leicester Mercury*, 6 October 2000
57 http://www.nationrecs.demon.co.uk/artistshtm/husler.htm. Their publicity shots disseminated an explicitly Sikh image of the group; for example, the typical images pictured stern kes-dhari Sikhs. Their record label, Nation Records, heralded the Hustlers HC as "the first Sikh rap crew to come out of the UK," and added that "with a strong socio political message they did much to bridge religious divides in the Asian community as well as creating much respect for Sikhs in the Rap fraternity."
58 Hustlers HC, "Big Trouble in Little Asia" (Nation Records, 1994).
59 "Vocal assassin": "Hai hai (Garage)" Punjabi Hit Squad featuring Satwinder Bitti & MC Scandalous; "fresh flava": "Dil chura" (Kavita Sohana remix)—from Punjabi Hit Squad, *The Streets*; "Bad boy riddim" in *Dil karda* by Gibu Sandhu.
60 Nor were the British artists professional in the manner of many Punjabi "folk" musicians—that is, performers who were often members of traditional performing communities (bazigars or natts) or who systematically learned their art from hereditary experts and primarily made their living through their music (Schreffler, "Out of the Dhol Drums," 13, 73–78).
61 Warwick, "Can Anyone Dance to This Music?" 35.
62 Sharma, "Sounds Oriental," 26.
63 It is interesting to note that in a 1997 interview Sagoo insisted that " 'Soul and R&B—that's what I grew up on; that's what I love. . . . By combining bhangra with R&B, I've made something true to me and accessible to others. It's a new chapter in music: Indian soul music' " (*Rolling Stone*, 20 March 1997, 36). What is striking about this description of his music is the elision of his earlier engagement with reggae in favor of the much more polished and, in this context, politically agnostic soul tradition. Contrast this privileging of soul with earlier coverage of "bhangramuffin," which

highlighted the key role of reggae: for example, "What Is This Crazy Bhangra Music, Anyways?" *Eye Weekly* (Toronto), 4 August 1994.

64   "Gimme Indi Pop!" *Village Voice*, 18 February 1997, 69.

65   "Bally Sagoo Returns to His Roots: The British Asian Sound Comes Home," *Connect*, October 1998, online at http://www.connectmagazine .com/OCTOBER1998/Oct98html/OctBally.html. Babyface is a leading African American writer and producer who enjoyed huge international success with his soundtracks to *The Bodyguard* and *Waiting to Exhale* and who played a central part in the careers of Toni Braxton, Boyz II Men, and Bobby Brown.

66   *Newsday*, 1 January 2001, B12. For earlier coverage of Sarina Jain, see the *Times Union* (Albany, N.Y.), 24 October 2000.

67   Quoted in *Newsday*, 1 January 2001.

68   Ibid.

69   Ibid.

70   *Times* (Washington), 13 May 2001.

71   Lipsitz, *Dangerous Crossroads*, 3.

72   See Manuel, *Cassette Culture*.

73   See Schreffler, "Out of the Dhol Drums," 10.

74   Gilroy, *The Black Atlantic*, 194.

75   *Tribune* (Chandigarh), 13 September 1998.

76   *Times* (Washington), 13 May 2001. The reading of bhangra's origins offered by the report's author, Alona Wartofsky, is interesting. In response to some commentators who identify bhangra as an Indian form of hip hop, Wartofsky asserts that "bhangra is not like Indian hip-hop. It's a centuries-old style of Punjabi folk music, characterized by a distinctive drumbeat, that's been updated with drum machines, live percussion and other modern instrumentation." Yet the article's subtitle, "Take Traditional Punjabi Music, Add Drum Machines—and Hip-Hop to It," highlights the hip hop link. It is interesting to note that this article was immediately reworked in the *Hindustan Times*, 13 May 2001, under the headline "Yankees Take to the Floor on Bhangra Beats."

77   *Times* (Washington), 13 May 2001.

78   Ibid.

79   *Newsday*, 28 February 2002.

80   Ibid.

81   See Maira, *Desis in the House.*

82   Dhillon, *Folk Dances*, 152.

83   *Tribune* (Chandigarh), 26 May 2000.

84   Dhillon, *Folk Dances*, 152.

85   Hall, *Lives in Translation*, 141.

86   "Bhangra: Youth Forum," www.sikhnet.com.

87   See http://www.nachdijawani.com/bhangra.html.

88   See, for example, http://www.sikhwomen.com; http://www.snsm.org
     .my; http://www. seattlegurdwara.com; and http://www.sjsu.edu/orgs/
     sikh.
89   See http://www.sikhi.demon.co.uk/bhangra.htm.
90   *Tribune* (Chandigarh), 13 September 1998.
91   See Warwick, "Can Anyone Dance to This Music?"
92   Nesbitt, "Sikhs and Proper Sikhs." See also her "The Presentation of
     Sikhs in Recent Children's Literature in Britain."

# Epilogue

1   The most influential discussion of this generational dynamic comes from
    the Boyarins' discussion, in their essay "Diaspora," of genealogy within
    the Jewish context.
2   See Dusenbery, "On the Moral Sensitivities of Sikhs in North America"
    and "The Sikh Person, the Khalsa Panth, and Western Sikh Converts."
3   *Census of India 1901: Vol. 17: "The Punjab and Its Feudatories and the
    North-West Frontier Province," Part I: "Report"* (Simla, 1902), Subsidiary
    table 5, 173–84.
4   The relationship between layers of globalizing structures and the ways in
    which new forms of globalization "cannibalize" earlier forms is explored
    in Appadurai, *Modernity at Large*, and in Bayly, " 'Archaic' and 'Modern'
    Globalization in the Eurasian and African Arena."
5   McKeown, *Chinese Migrant Network*, 5.
6   Ibid., 6.
7   See Prashad, *The Karma of Brown Folk*; and Maira, *Desis in the House*.
8   Gillespie, *Television, Ethnicity and Cultural Change*, 181.
9   Nilgiri, "The Divided Shores," 92.
10  "My mum's always on about saag and how good it is for you" (Gillespie,
    *Television, Ethnicity and Cultural Change*, 201).
11  Ibid., 199–203.
12  *Anita and Me* (Metin Huseyin dir., 2003).
13  Gillespie, *Television, Ethnicity and Cultural Change*, 142.
14  Ibid., 145.

# Glossary

**Adi Granth**   The principal Sikh sacred text, containing teachings of the first nine gurus

**Akal Takht**   Seat of temporal authority and important shrine in Amritsar

**amrit**   "The nectar of immorality" used in the Khalsa initiation rite

**amrit-dhari**   One who has taken amrit as part of the Khalsa initiation

**ardas**   A formal prayer frequently recited at the end of Sikh rituals

**Arora**   An important Punjabi mercantile caste

**Baisakhi**   The Sikh New Year festival, which marks the onset of a new agricultural cycle

**Bani**   The sayings of the gurus

**Chuhra**   A Dalit Sikh; member of the sweeper caste

**darbar**   Court; ceremonial gathering

**Dasam Granth**   Second sacred text; according to tradition it was produced by Guru Gobind Singh

**dastar**   Turban

**"five Ks"**   Panj kakkar; the five external symbols worn by amrit-dhari Sikhs: kes (uncut hair), kangha (comb), kara (steel bracelet), kirpan (dagger), and kachh (short pants)

**granthi**   Reader of the Granth

**gurdwara**   Sikh place of worship

**Guru Gobind Singh**   Tenth guru (b.1666–d.1708 CE)

**Guru Granth Sahib**   The Adi Granth as guru. The Granth became the embodiment of the eternal guru after the death of Guru Gobind Singh

**Guru Nanak**   First guru and founder of Sikhism (b.1449–d.1538 or 1539 CE)

**izzat**   Face; honor

**jagir**   A rent-free grant of land

**Jat**   An influential rural caste, renowned for cultivating skill and skill as soldiers

**jhatka**   Meat prepared from animals that are killed by a single blow

**Julaha**   Weaver caste

**kachh**   Short pants (one of the "five Ks")

**kangha**   Comb (one of the "five Ks")

**kara**   Steel bracelet (one of the "five Ks")

**kes**   Uncut hair (one of the "five Ks")

**kes-dhari**   Sikh with uncut hair

**khadi**   Homespun cotton

**Khalistan**   A putative Sikh homeland

**Khalsa**   Order established by Guru Gobind Singh on Baisakhi day, 1699

**khanda**   The insignia of the Khalsa

**khilat**   Gifts of incorporation given in recognition of service, frequently in the form of robes

**kirpan**   Dagger (one of the "five Ks")

**kirtan**   Collective singing of devotional songs

**kirtan sohila**   Five hymns recited before retiring at night

**langar**   The kitchen and dining hall attached to a gurdwara

**mahant**   The custodians of gurdwaras

**mandir**   Temple (particularly associated with Hinduism)

**Mazhabi**   A Sikh of sweeper caste

**mirasi**   Traditional genealogists and musicians

**miri-piri**   Dual authority over temporal spiritual domains

**mona**   Term, often pejorative, for Sikhs who cut their hair

**Nai**   Barber caste; traditionally influential as marriage brokers

**Nanak-panthi**   Follower of the "way of Nanak"

**pagri**   Turban

**pahul**   Khande-ki-pahul; Khalsa initiation rite

**Panth**   Lit. "path"; the Sikh community

**patit**   Lit. "fallen"; amrit-dhari who commits a serious violation of rahit

**pir**   Renowned Sufi or Sufi teacher

**prachar**   Preaching

**qaum**   People, Nation

**rahiras**   Hymns recited at sundown

**rahit**   Discipline, conduct

**rahit-nama**   Code of conduct for Khalsa Sikhs

**saag**   Mustard greens

**sahaj-dhari**   A Sikh who does not observe rahit

**sangat**   Assembly; collective gathering of Sikhs

**SGPC**   Shiromani Gurdwara Prabandhak Committee: committee that oversees the management of gurdwaras

**shraddha**   Annual ceremony to mark deceased forbears

**Sikhi**   Sikh culture

**tahsil**   subdistrict

# Bibliography

Ahluwalia, M. L. "Duleep Singh—The Crusader." In *Fighter for Freedom: Maharaja Duleep Singh,* edited by Baldev Singh Baddan. Delhi, 1998.

Ahuja, Ravi. "Labour Unsettled: Mobility and Protest in the Madras Region, 1750–1800." *Indian Economic and Social History Review* 35 (1998): 381–404.

Alexander, Michael, and Sushila Anand. *Queen Victoria's Maharajah: Duleep Singh 1838–93.* London, 1980.

Ali, Shahamat. *The Sikhs and Afghans, in Connexion with India and Persia, Immediately Before and After the Death of Ranjeet Singh.* London, 1847.

*Amritsar District Gazetteer.* Lahore, 1914.

Ananda, Prakash. *A History of the Tribune.* Chandigarh, 1986.

Appadurai, Arjun. *Modernity at Large: Cultural Dimensions of Globalization.* Minneapolis, 1996.

Asad, Talal. *Genealogies of Religion: Discipline and Reasons of Power in Christianity and Islam.* Baltimore, 1993.

Axel, Brian Keith. *The Nation's Tortured Body: Violence, Representation, and the Formation of a Sikh "Diaspora."* Durham, N.C., 2001.

Baddan, Baldev Singh, ed., *Fighter for Freedom: Maharaja Duleep Singh*. Delhi, 1998.

Bains, Harwant S. "Southall Youth: An Old-Fashioned Story." In *Multi-Racist Britain,* edited by Philip Cohen and Harwant S. Bains. Basingstoke, 1988.

Ballantyne, Tony. "Empire, Knowledge and Culture: From Proto-Globalization to Modern Globalization." In *Globalization in World History,* edited by A. G. Hopkins. London, 2001.

——. *Orientalism and Race: Aryanism in the British Empire.* Basingstoke, 2002.

——. "Race and the Webs of Empire: Aryanism from India to the Pacific." *Journal of Colonialism and Colonial History* 2.2 (2001). http://muse.jhu.edu/ journals/journal_of_colonialism_and_colonial_history/v002/2.3 ballantyne.html

——. "Resisting the 'Boa Constrictor' of Hinduism: The Khalsa and the Raj." *International Journal of Punjab Studies* 6.2 (1999): 195–216.

——. "Rethinking the Archive: Opening up the Nation-State in South Asia and Beyond." In *After the Imperial Turn: Critical Approaches to National Histories and Literatures,* edited by Antoinette Burton. Durham, N.C., 2003.

Ballard, Roger. "Differentiation and Disjunction among the Sikhs." In *Desh Pardesh: The South Asian Presence in Britain,* edited by Roger Ballard. London, 1994.

Banerjee, Himadri. "Bengali Perceptions of the Sikhs: The Nineteenth and Twentieth Centuries." In *Sikh History and Religion in the Twentieth Century,* edited by J. T. O'Connell, M. Israel, and W. Oxtoby. Toronto, 1988.

——. "The Sikh Identity Question: A View from Eastern India." In *Sikh Identity: Continuity and Change,* edited by Pashaura Singh and N. Gerald Barrier. Delhi, 1999.

Banerji, Sabita. "Ghazals to Bhangra in Great Britain." *Popular Music* 7.2 (1988): 208.

Banerji, Sabita, and Gerd Baumann. "Bhangra 1984–8: Fusion and Professionalization in a Genre of South Asian Dance Music." In *Black Music in Britain: Essays on the Afro-Asian Contribution to Popular Music,* edited by Paul Oliver. Buckingham, 1990.

Banga, Indu. "Agrarian System in Punjab during Sikh Rule." *History of Agriculture* 2.1 (1980): 35–65.

——. *Agrarian System of the Sikhs: Late Eighteenth and Early Nineteenth Century.* Delhi, 1978.

——, ed. *Five Punjabi Centuries: Policy, Economy, Society, and Culture, c. 1500– 1990: Essays for J. S. Grewal.* New Delhi, 1997.

Banga, Indu, and J. S. Grewal, eds. *Maharaja Ranjit Singh and His Times.* Amritsar, 1980.

Barrier, N. G. "Authority, Politics, and Contemporary Sikhism." In *Sikhism and History,* edited by Pashaura Singh and N. G. Barrier. Delhi, 2004.

——. "The Formulation and Enactment of the Punjab Alienation of Land Bill." *Indian Economic and Social History Review* 2.2 (1965): 145–65.

——. "Mass Politics and the Punjab Congress in the Pre-Gandhian Era." *Journal of Indian History* 50.149 (1972): 459–70.

——. *The Punjab Alienation of Land Bill of 1900.* Durham, N.C., 1966.

——. *The Sikhs and Their Literature: A Guide to Tracts, Books, and Periodicals, 1849–1919.* Delhi, 1970.

———. "Trumpp and Macauliffe." In *Historians and Historiography of the Sikhs,* edited by Fauja Singh. Delhi, 1978.

Basham, A. L. *The Wonder That Was India.* London, 1967.

Baumann, Gerd. "Managing a Polyethnic Milieu: Kinship and Interaction in a London Suburb." *Journal of the Royal Anthropological Institute* 1.4 (1995): 725–41.

———. "The Re-Invention of Bhangra: Social Change and Aesthetic Shifts in a Punjabi Music in Britain." *World of Music* 32 (1990): 81–98.

Bayly, C. A. " 'Archaic' and 'Modern' Globalization in the Eurasian and African Arena, ca. 1750–1850." In *Globalization in World History,* edited by A. G. Hopkins. New York, 2002.

———. *Empire and Information: Intelligence Gathering and Social Communication in India, 1780–1870.* Cambridge, U.K., 1996.

———. "Exhibiting the Imperial Image." *History Today* 40 (1990): 12–18.

———. "From Ritual to Ceremony: Death Ritual and Society in Hindu North India since 1600." In *Origins of Nationality in South Asia: Patriotism and Ethical Government in the Making of Modern India.* Oxford, 1999.

Bebbington, David W. *Evangelicalism in Modern Britain: A History from the 1730s to the 1980s.* London, 1989.

Bennett, Andrew. "Bhangra in Newcastle: Music, Ethnic Identity, and the Role of Local Knowledge." *Innovation* 10 (1997): 107–16.

Bhachu, Parminder. "Ethnicity Constructed and Reconstructed: The Role of Sikh Women in Cultural Elaboration and Educational Decision-Making in Britain." *Gender and Education* 3.1 (1991): 237–48.

Bhatia, Sardar Singh, and Anand Spencer, eds. *The Sikh Tradition: A Continuing Reality: Essays in History and Religion.* Patiala, 1999.

Bhatti, Rashmere. "From Sojourners to Settlers." In *A Punjabi Sikh Community in Australia: From Indian Sojourners to Australian Citizens,* edited by Rashmere Bhatti and Verne A. Dusenbery. Woolgoolga, 2001.

Bidwell, Sidney. *Red, White and Black: Race Relations in Britain.* London, 1976.

Bird, Isabella L. *The Golden Chersonee and the Way Thither Letter.* New York, 1884.

Bisland, Elizabeth. *A Flying Trip around the World.* London, 1891.

Blackburn, Stuart, and A. K. Ramanujan, eds. *Another Harmony: New Essays on the Folklore of India.* Berkeley, 1986.

Bland, J. O. P. *Houseboat Days in China.* London, 1909.

Blomfield, David, ed. *Lahore to Lucknow: The Indian Mutiny Journal of Arthur Moffat Lang.* London, 1992.

Bose, Sugata, and Ayesha Jalal. *Modern South Asia: History, Culture, and Political Economy.* London, 1998.

Boyarin, Daniel, and Jonathan Boyarin. "Diaspora: Generation and the Ground of Jewish Identity." *Critical Inquiry* 19.4 (1993): 693–725.

Brewer, Teri, ed. *The Marketing of Tradition: Perspectives on Folklore, Tourism and the Heritage Industry.* Enfield Lock, U.K., 1994.

Burton, Antoinette, ed. *After the Imperial Turn: Thinking with and through the Nation.* Durham, N.C., 2003.

———. *At the Heart of the Empire: Indians and the Colonial Encounter in Late-Victorian Britain.* Berkeley, 1998.

Cannadine, David. *Ornamentalism: How the British Saw Their Empire.* Oxford, 2002.

Caton, Brian P. "Sikh Identity Formation and the British Rural Ideal, 1880–1930." In *Sikh Identity: Continuity and Change,* edited by Pashaura Singh and N. Gerald Barrier. Delhi, 1999.

Certeau, Michel de. *The Practice of Everyday Life,* translated by S. Rendall. Berkeley, 1984.

Chakrabarty, Rishi Ranjan. *Duleep Singh: The Maharaja of Punjab and the Raj.* Oldbury, 1988.

Chakrabarty, Rishi Ranjan, and Prithipal Singh Kapur, eds. *Maharaja Duleep Singh: The Last Sovereign Ruler of the Punjab.* Amritsar, 1995.

Chakrabarty, Rishi Ranjan, and S. P. Gulati, eds. *The Tragic Tale of Maharaja Duleep Singh.* Delhi, 1998.

Clark, H. M. "The Decay of Sikhism." *Panjab Notes and Queries* 3 (1885): 20.

Clifford, James. *Routes: Travel and Translation in the Late Twentieth Century.* Cambridge, Mass., 1997.

Cobbin, Ingram. "Essay on Popery." In *Foxe's Book of Martyrs,* edited by William Bramley-Moore. Rev. ed. London, 1875.

Cohn, Bernard S. *Colonialism and Its Forms of Knowledge: The British In India.* Princeton, N.J., 1996.

———. "Representing Authority in Victorian India." In *The Invention of Tradition,* edited by Eric Hobsbawm and Terence Ranger. Cambridge, 1992.

Colley, Linda. *Britons: Forging the Nation, 1707–1837.* New Haven, Conn., 1992.

Cox, Jeffrey. *Imperial Fault Lines: Christianity and Colonial Power in India, 1818–1940.* Stanford, 2002.

Cunningham, J. D. *A History of the Sikhs.* Edited by H. L. O. Garret. 2nd ed. Lahore, 1915 [1853].

Cust, R. N. *The Life of Baba Nanuk, the Founder of the Sikh Sect of the Hindu Religion in the Punjab: For the Use of Schools.* Lahore, 1859.

Darling, Malcolm Lyall. *The Punjab Peasant in Prosperity and Debt.* Oxford, 1925.

David, Alun. "Sir William Jones, Biblical Orientalism and Indian Scholarship." *Modern Asian Studies* 30.1 (1996): 173–84.

Davidson, Allan K. *Evangelicals and Attitudes to India, 1786–1813. Missionary Publicity and Claudius Buchanan.* Abingdon, 1990.

Deol, Jeevan. "Eighteenth-Century Khalsa Identity: Discourse, Praxis and Narrative." In *Sikh Religion, Culture and Ethnicity,* edited by Christopher Shackle, Gurharpal Singh, and Arvind-pal Singh Mandair. Richmond, U.K. 2001.

——. "The Minas and Their Literature." *Journal of the American Oriental Society* 118.2 (1998): 172–84.

——. "'To Hell with War': Literature of Political Resistance in Early Nineteenth Century Punjab." *South Asia Research* 17.2 (1997): 178–209.

——. "Surdas: Poet and Text in the Sikh Tradition." *Bulletin of the School of Oriental and African Studies* 63.2 (2000): 169–93.

Dewey, Clive. *Anglo-Indian Attitudes: The Mind of the Indian Civil Service.* London, 1993.

Dhillon, Gurdarshan Singh. "Review of *The Construction of Religious Boundaries.*" *Sikh Press* 4.33 (May 1994): 4.

Dhillon, Iqbal Singh. *Folk Dances of Panjab.* Chandigarh, 1998.

Dusenbery, Verne. "On the Moral Sensitivities of Sikhs in North America." In *Divine Passions: The Social Construction of Emotion in India,* edited by Owen M. Lynch. Berkeley, 1990.

——. "A Sikh Diaspora? Contested Identities and Constructed Realities." In *Nation and Migration: The Politics of Space in the South Asian Diaspora,* edited by Peter van der Veer. Philadelphia, 1995.

——. "The Sikh Person, the Khalsa Panth, and Western Sikh Converts." In *Religious Movements and Social Identity. Volume 4: Of Boeings and Bullock-Carts,* edited by Bardwell L. Smith. Delhi, 1990.

Endacott, G. B. *A History of Hong Kong.* London, 1958.

Eyre, Vincent. *The Sikh and European Soldiers of Our Indian Forces: A Lecture.* London, 1867.

Falcon, R. W. *Handbook on Sikhs for Regimental Officers.* Allahabad, 1896.

Fane, Henry Edward. *Five Years in India.* 2 vols. London, 1842.

Fenech, Louis E. "Contested Nationalisms; Negotiated Terrains: The Way Sikhs Remember Udham Singh 'Shahid,' 1899–1940." *Modern Asian Studies* 36.4 (2002): 827–70.

——. *Martyrdom in the Sikh Tradition: Playing the "Game of Love."* New Delhi, 2000.

Fisher, Michael. *The First Indian Author in English: Dean Mahomed 1759–1851 in India, Ireland and England.* Delhi, 1996.

Fladmark, J. M., ed. *Heritage and Museums: Shaping National Identity.* Shaftesbury, 1999.

Fox, Richard G. *Lions of the Punjab: Culture in the Making.* Delhi, 1990.

Gaffney, John. *Interpretations of Violence: The Handsworth Riots of 1985.* Coventry, 1987.

*Gazetteer of Ambala District, 1883–4.* Lahore, 1884.

Gell, Simeran Mann Singh. "The Origins of the 'Sikh Look' ": From Guru Gobind to Dalip Singh." *History and Anthropology* 10.1 (1996): 37–83.

Gillespie, Marie. *Television, Ethnicity and Cultural Change.* London, 1994.

Gilmartin, David. *Empire and Islam: Punjab and the Making of Pakistan.* London, 1988.

Gilroy, Paul. *The Black Atlantic: Modernity and Double Consciousness.* Cambridge, Mass., 1993.

Goswamy, B. N. "Continuing Traditions in the Later Sikh Kingdoms." *The Arts of the Sikh Kingdoms,* edited by Susan Stronge. London, 1999.

Grant, Charles. "Observations on the State of Society among the *Asiatic* Subjects of *Great Britain,* particularly with respect to Morals; and on the means of improving it.—Written chiefly in the Year 1792." Appendix to the *Report from the Select Committee on the Affairs of the East India Company, with Minutes of Evidence. Volume I: Great Britain Parliamentary Papers,* (1831) 734 VIII. London, 1831.

Grewal, J. S. *Contesting Interpretations of the Sikh Tradition.* Delhi, 1999.

——.*The Sikhs of the Punjab: The New Cambridge History of India.* Vol. 2, part 3. Cambridge, U.K., 1990.

Grewal, J. S., and Indu Banga, eds. *Early Nineteenth Century Panjab: From Ganesh Das's Char Bagh-i-Panjab.* Amritsar, 1975.

Grewal, Shabnam, et al., eds. *Charting the Journey: Writings by Black and Third World Women.* London, 1988.

Griffin, Lepel, *The Panjab Chiefs: Historical and Biographical Notices of the Principal Families in the Territories under the Panjab Government.* Lahore, 1865.

Hall, Kathleen, *Lives in Translation: Sikh Youth as British Citizens.* Philadelphia, 2002.

Hall, Stuart. "Cultural Identity and Diaspora." In *Identity, Community, Culture, Difference,* edited by Jonathan Rutherford. London, 1990.

Harper, T. N. "Empire, Diaspora and the Languages of Globalism, 1850–1914." In *Globalization in World History,* edited by A. G. Hopkins. New York, 2002.

Harrison, Peter. *"Religion" and the Religions in the English Enlightenment.* Cambridge, U.K., 1990.

Haynes, Douglas E., and Tirthankar Roy. "Conceiving Mobility: Weavers' Migrations in Pre-colonial and Colonial India." *Indian Economic and Social History Review* 36.1 (1999): 35–67.

Helweg, Arthur. *Sikhs in England: The Development of a Migrant Community.* Oxford, 1979.

*Hoshiarpur District Gazetteer 1904.* Lahore, 1905.

Hsia, R. Po-Chia. *Social Discipline in the Reformation: Central Europe, 1550–1750.* London, 1989.

Hughes, T. P. "The Religion of the Sikhs." *Indian Christian Intelligencer* 2 (1878): 160–69.

Ibbetson, Denzil Charles Jelf. *Report on the Census of the Punjab Taken on the 17th of February 1881.* Calcutta, 1883.

Irschick, Eugene. *Dialogue and History: Constructing South India, 1795–1895.* Berkeley, 1994.

Jakobsh, Doris R. *Relocating Gender in Sikh History: Transformation, Meaning and Identity.* New Delhi, 2003.

Jeffrey, Robin, "Grappling with History: Sikh Politicians and the Past." *Pacific Affairs* 60.1 (1987): 59–72.

Jones, David. "Maharaja Dalip Singh." In *Arts of the Sikh Kingdom,* edited by Susan Stronge. London, 1999.

Jones, Kenneth W. "Communalism in the Punjab: The Arya Samaj Contribution." *Journal of Asian Studies* 28.1 (1968): 39–54.

———. "Ham Hindu Nahin: Arya-Sikh Relations, 1877–1905." *Journal of Asian Studies* 32.3 (1973): 457–75.

———. *Religious Controversy in British India: Dialogues in South Asian Languages.* Albany, N.Y., 1992.

———. *Socio-Religious Reform Movements in British India.* Cambridge, U.K., 1990.

*Jullundur District and Kapurthala State Gazetteer 1904.* Lahore, 1908.

Kalra, Virinder S. "*Vilayeti* Rhythms: Beyond Bhangra's Emblematic Status to a Translation of Lyrical Texts." *Theory, Culture and Society* 17.3 (2000): 80–102.

Kerr, Ian J. "British Relationships with the Golden Temple, 1849–90." *Indian Economic and Social History Review* 21.2 (1984): 139–51.

———. "Sikhs and State: Troublesome Relationships and a Fundamental Continuity with Particular Reference to the Period 1849–1919." In *Sikh Identity: Continuity and Change,* edited by Pashaura Singh and N. Gerald Barrier. Delhi, 1999.

Kessinger, Tom G. *Vilyatpur, 1848–1968: Social and Economic Change in a North Indian Village.* Berkeley, 1974.

Khan, Javed Ali. "Two Historical Works on Punjab: Gulshan-i-Punjab and Makzhan-i-Punjab." *Journal of the Pakistan Historical Society* 44. 4 (1996): 309–34.

Khan, Khan Ahmad Hasan. *Census of India 1931. Vol. 17: "Punjab." Part 1: "Report."* Lahore, 1933.

Khurana, Gianeshwar. *British Historiography on the Sikh Power in the Punjab.* London, 1985.

King, Noel Q. "*Capax Imperii*—Scripture, Tradition and European-Style Critical Method." In *Advanced Studies in Sikhism,* edited by Jasbir Singh Mann and Harbans Singh Saraon. Irvine, Calif., 1989.

——. " 'Modernity,' 'Fundamentalism' and Sikhism: A *Tertium Quid.*" In *Invasion of Religious Boundaries: A Critique of Harjot Oberoi's Work,* edited by Jasbir Singh Mann, Surinder Singh Sodhi, and Gurbakhsh Singh Gill. Vancouver, B.C., 1995.

——. "The Siege Perilous (Hot Seat) and the Divine Hypothesis." In *Invasion of Religious Boundaries: A Critique of Harjot Oberoi's Work,* edited by Jasbir Singh Mann, Surinder Singh Sodhi, and Gurbakhsh Singh Gill. Vancouver, B.C., 1995.

King, Richard. *Orientalism and Religion: Postcolonial Theory, India and the "Mystic East."* London, 1999.

Kipling, Rudyard. *From Sea to Sea and Other Sketches.* London, 1889.

——. *Life's Handicap: Being Stories of Mine Own People.* London, 1891.

Knight, Ian. "The Military Sikhs." In *The Arts of the Sikh Kingdoms,* edited by Susan Stronge. London, 1999.

Lake, Edward. *Sir Donald McLeod: A Record of Forty-two Years Service in India.* London, 1873.

Lawrence, John. *Selections from the Records of the Government of India. (Foreign Department) No. VI. General Report on the Administration of the Punjab Territories . . . for the Years 1851–52 and 1852–53.* Calcutta, 1854.

——. "Statement of Jagheers . . ." Government of India, Foreign Department, Political Proceedings, 10 June 1853, no. 219.

Lee, Harold. *Brothers in the Raj: The Lives of John and Henry Lawrence.* Karachi, 2002.

——. "John and Henry Lawrence and the Origins of Paternalist Rule in the Punjab, 1846–1858." *International Journal of Punjab Studies* 2.1 (1995): 65–88.

Leitner, G. W. *History of Indigenous Education in the Panjab since Annexation and in 1882.* Calcutta, 1882.

Leonard, Karen. " 'Flawed Transmission?': Punjabi Pioneers in California." In *The Transmission of Sikh Heritage in the Diaspora,* edited by Pashaura Singh and N. Gerald Barrier. New Delhi, 1996.

——. "Pioneer Voices from California: Reflections on Race, Religion and Ethnicity." In *The Sikh Diaspora: Migration and the Experience beyond Punjab,* edited by N. G. Barrier and Verne A. Dusenbery. Columbia, Mo., 1989.

Lipsitz, George. *Dangerous Crossroads: Popular Music, Postmodernism, and the Poetics of Place.* London, 1994.

Login, L. *Sir John Login and Duleep Singh.* London, 1890.

Lowenthal, David. *The Heritage Crusade and the Spoils of History.* Cambridge, U.K., 1998.

Macauliffe, M. A. "The Fair at Sakhi Sarvar." *Calcutta Review* 60 (1875): 78–101.

——. *A Lecture on How the Sikhs Become a Militant Race.* Simla, n.d.

——. *A Lecture on the Sikh Religion and Its Advantages to the State.* Simla, 1903.

———. *The Sikh Religion: Its Gurus, Sacred Writings and Authors.* 6 vols. Oxford, 1909.

MacKenzie, John. *Empire of Nature: Hunting, Conservation and British Imperialism.* Manchester, 1997.

MacMillan, Ken. "John Wesley and the Enlightened Historians." *Methodist History,* 38.2 (2000): 121–32.

Mahmood, Cynthia Keppley. *Fighting for Faith and Nation: Dialogues with Sikh Militants.* Philadelphia, 1997.

Mahmood, Cynthia, and Stacy Brady. *The Guru's Gift: An Ethnography Exploring Gender Equality with North American Sikh Women.* Mountain View, Calif., 2000.

Maira, Sunaina Marr. *Desis in the House: Indian American Youth Culture in New York City.* Philadelphia, 2002.

Malcolm, John. *Sketch of the Sikhs; a Singular Nation Who Inhabit the Provinces of the Punjab.* London, 1812.

Mandair, Arvind-pal Singh. "Thinking Differently about Religion and History: Issues for Sikh Studies." In *Sikh Religion, Culture and Ethnicity,* edited by Christopher Shackle, Gurharpal Singh, and Arvind-pal Singh Mandair. London, 2001.

Mann, Gurinder Singh. *The Making of Sikh Scripture.* New York, 2001.

Mann, Jasbir Singh, and Harbans Singh Saraon, eds. *Advanced Studies in Sikhism.* Irvine, Calif., 1989.

Mann, Jasbir Singh, Surinder Singh Sodhi, and Gurbakhsh Singh Gill. "Introduction." In *The Invasion of Religious Boundaries: A Critique of Harjot Oberoi's Work,* edited by Jasbir Singh Mann, Surinder Singh Sodhi, and Gurbakhsh Singh Gill. Vancouver, B.C., 1995.

Manuel, Peter. *Cassette Culture: Popular Music and Technology in North India.* Chicago, 1993.

Markovits, Claude. *The Global World of Indian Merchants, 1750–1947: Traders of Sind from Bukhara to Panama.* Cambridge, U.K., 2000.

Marshall, P. J. *The British Discovery of Hinduism.* Cambridge, U.K., 1970.

Masson, Charles. *Narrative of Various Journeys in Balochistan, Afghanistan and the Panjab.* 3 vols. London, 1842.

McKeown, Adam. *Chinese Migrant Networks and Cultural Change: Peru, Chicago, Hawaii, 1900–1936.* Chicago, 2001.

McLeod, W. H. *The B40 Janam-sakhi.* Amritsar, 1980.

———, ed. *The Chaupa Singh Rahit-nama.* Dunedin, 1987.

———. *Early Sikh Tradition: A Study of the Janam-sakhis.* Oxford, 1980.

———. *Guru Nanak and the Sikh Religion.* Oxford, 1968.

———. *Popular Sikh Art.* Delhi, 1991.

———. *Punjabis in New Zealand: A History of Punjabi Migration, 1890–1940.* Amritsar, 1986.

———. "The First Forty Years of Sikh Migration: Problems and Possible Solutions." In *The Sikh Diaspora: Migration and the Experience beyond Punjab,* edited by N. G. Barrier and Verne A. Dusenbery. Columbia, Mo., 1989.

——. "A Sikh Theology for Modern Times." In *Sikh History and Religion in the Twentieth Century,* edited by J. T. O'Connell, M. Israel, and W. Oxtoby. Toronto, 1988.

——. *The Sikhs: History, Religion, and Society.* New York, 1989.

——. *Sikhs of the Khalsa: A History of the Khalsa Rahit.* New Delhi, 2003.

——. *Textual Sources for the Study of Sikhism.* Manchester, 1984.

——. "The Turban: Symbol of Sikh Identity." In *Sikh Identity: Continuity and Change,* edited by Pashaura Singh and N. Gerald Barrier. Delhi, 1999.

——. *Who Is a Sikh? The Problem of Sikh Identity.* Oxford, 1989.

Metcalf, Thomas R. *Forging the Raj: Essays on British India in the Heyday of Empire.* Delhi, 2005.

Middleton, L., and S. M. Jacobs. *Census of India, 1921. Vol. 15: "Punjabi and Delhi." Part 1: "Report."* Lahore, 1923.

Milton, Sybil. "Memorials." In *The Holocaust Encyclopedia,* edited by Walter Laqueur. New Haven, Conn., 2001.

Mishra, Vijay. "The Diasporic Imaginary: Theorizing the Indian Diaspora." *Textual Practice* 10.2 (1996): 421–27.

Modood, Tariq, " 'Black': Racial Equality and Asian Identity." *New Community* 14.3 (1988): 397–404.

——. "Political Blackness and British Asians." *Sociology* 28.3 (1994): 859–77.

Mongia, Radhika Viyas. "Race, Nationality, Mobility: A History of the Passport." In *After the Imperial Turn: Thinking with and through the Nation,* edited by Antoinette Burton. Durham, N.C., 2003.

Nesbitt, Eleanor. "The Presentation of Sikhs in Recent Children's Literature in Britain." In *Sikh History and Religion in the Twentieth Century,* edited by J. T. O'Connell, M. Israel and W. Oxtoby. Toronto, 1988.

——. "Sikhs and Proper Sikhs: Young British Sikhs' Perceptions of their Identity." In *Sikh Identity: Continuity and Change,* edited by Pashaura Singh and N. Gerald Barrier. Delhi, 1999.

Nilgiri, Tarsem. "The Divided Shores." *From across the Shores: Punjabi Short Stories by Asians in Britain.* London, 2002.

Oberoi, Harjot. *The Construction of Religious Boundaries: Culture, Identity and Diversity in the Sikh Tradition.* Delhi, 1994.

——. "The Worship of Pir Sakhi Sarvar: Illness, Healing and Popular Culture in the Punjab." *Studies in History* 3.1 (1987): 29–55.

Oddie, Geoffrey A. " 'Orientalism' and British Protestant Missionary Constructions of India in the Nineteenth Century." *South Asia,* 17.2 (1994): 27–42.

Omissi, David. *The Sepoy and the Raj: The Indian Army, 1860–1940.* London, 1994.

Osborne, H. G. *The Court and Camp of Runjeet Sing, with an Introductory Sketch of the Origin and Rise of the Sikh State.* London, 1840.

Pande, Alka. *Folk Music and Musical Instruments of the Punjab: From Mustard Fields to Disco Lights.* London, 2000.

Petrie, D. *Developments in Sikh Politics, 1900–1911: A Report,* edited by Nahar Singh. Amritsar, 1972 [1911].

Phillips, James Duncan. *Salem and the Indies: The Story of the Great Commercial Era of the City.* Boston, 1947.

Polier, Antoine Louis Henri. "Character of the Sieks." *Annual Asiatic Register* 2 (1802): 9–12.

——. "An Extract from a Letter of Major Polier." *Annual Asiatic Register* 1 (1800): 32–35.

——. "The Siques, or History of the Seeks." Paper presented to the Asiatic Society of Bengal, December 1787. Reproduced in Ganda Singh, "Colonel Polier's Account of the Sikhs," *Panjab Past and Present* 4.2 (1972): 232–53.

Porter, Roy. *The Creation of the Modern World: The Untold Story of the British Enlightenment.* New York, 2000.

Prashad, Vijay. *The Karma of Brown Folk.* Minneapolis, 2000.

Pratt, Mary Louise. *Imperial Eyes: Travel Writing and Transculturation.* London, 1992.

Robson, Brian, ed. *Roberts in India: The Military Papers of Field Marshal Lord Roberts, 1876–1893.* Stroud, 1992.

Runnymede Trust. *The Future of Multi-Ethnic Britain: The Parekh Report.* London, 2000.

——. *Islamophobia.* London, 1997.

Rushdie, Salman. *Imaginary Homelands: Essays and Criticism, 1981–1991.* London, 1991.

Samuel, Raphael. *Theatres of Memory.* London, 1994.

Sandhu, Kernial Singh. "Sikh Immigration into Malaya during the Period of British Rule." In *Studies in the Social History of China and Southeast Asia: Essays in Memory of Victor Purcell,* edited by Jerome Ch'en and Nicholas Tarling. Cambridge, U.K., 1970.

Sandhu, Manjeet Singh. "Harjot Oberoi—Scholar or Saboteur?" In *The Invasion of Religious Boundaries: A Critique of Harjot Oberoi's Work,* edited by Jasbir Singh Mann, Surinder Singh Sodhi, and Gurbakhsh Singh Gill. Vancouver, B.C., 1995.

Schreffler, Gibb Stuart. "Out of the Dhol Drums: The Rhythmic 'System' of Punjabi Bhangra." Master's thesis, University of California, Santa Barbara, 2002.

Scrafton, Luke. *Reflections on the Government, & c. of Indostan: And a Short Sketch of the History of Bengal, from the Year 1739 to 1756.* Edinburgh, 1761.

Sethi, Anil. "The Creation of Religious Identities in the Punjab, c.1850–1920." Ph.D. dissertation, University of Cambridge, 1998.

Shackle, Christopher. "Making Punjabi Literary History." In *Sikh Religion,*

*Culture and Ethnicity,* edited by Christopher Shackle, Gurharpal Singh, and Arvind-pal Singh Mandair. Richmond, U.K., 2001.

Sharma, Sanjay. "Noisy Asians or 'Asian Noise.'" In *Dis-Orienting Rhythms: The Politics of the New Asian Dance Music,* edited by Sanjay Sharma, John Hutnyk, and Ashwani Sharma. London, 1996.

Singh, Baba Nihal. *Summary of Correspondence in the Case of Maharaja Dalip Singh.* Shimla, 1887.

Singh, Bhagat Lakshman. *Autobiography.* Edited by Ganda Singh. Calcutta, 1965.

Singh, Darshan. *Western Image of Sikh Religion.* Delhi, 1999.

Singh, Fauja, "Early European Writers: Browne, Polier, Forster." In *Historians and Historiography of the Sikhs,* edited by Fauja Singh. Delhi, 1978.

———, ed. *Historians and Historiography of the Sikhs.* Delhi, 1978.

Singh, Ganda. "Colonel Polier's Account of the Sikhs." *Panjab Past and Present* 4.2 (1972): 232–53.

———, ed. *Early European Accounts of the Sikhs.* Calcutta, 1962.

———, ed. *Maharaja Duleep Singh Correspondence.* Patiala, 1977.

Singh, Gyani Ditt. *Darpoke Singh.* Lahore, 1895.

———. *Durga Prabodh.* Lahore, 1899.

———. *Mera Ate Sadhu Dayanand Da Sambhand.* Lahore, 1900.

———. *Miran Manaut.* Lahore, 1902.

———. *Nakli Sikh Prabodh.* Lahore, 1895.

———. *Sultan Poara.* Lahore, 1896.

Singh, Kahn. *Ham Hindu Nahim.* Lahore, 1898.

Singh, Pashaura. *The Guru Granth Sahib: Canon, Meaning and Authority.* Delhi, 2000.

Singh, Sukhmander. "A Work of Scholarly Indulgence." In *The Invasion of Religious Boundaries: A Critique of Harjot Oberoi's Work,* edited by Jasbir Singh Mann, Surinder Singh Sodhi, and Gurbakhsh Singh Gill. Vancouver, B.C., 1995.

Singh, Trilochan. *Ernest Trumpp and W. H. McLeod as Scholars of Sikh History, Religion and Culture.* Chandigarh, 1994.

Singha, Radhika. "Settle, Mobilize, Verify: Identification Practices in Colonial India." *Studies in History* 16.2 (2000): 153–98.

Sinha, Mrinalini. *Colonial Masculinity: The "Manly Englishman" and the "Effeminate Bengali" in the Late Nineteenth Century.* Manchester, 1995.

Smith, Jonathon Z. *Imagining Religion: From Babylon to Jonestown.* Chicago, 1982.

Sodhi, Surinder Singh. "Eurocentrism vs. Khalsacentrism." In *The Invasion of Religious Boundaries: A Critique of Harjot Oberoi's Work,* edited by Jasbir Singh Mann, Surinder Singh Sodhi, and Gurbakhsh Singh Gill. Vancouver, B.C., 1995.

Sodhi, Surinder Singh, and Jasbir Singh Mann. "Construction of Religious

Boundaries." In *The Invasion of Religious Boundaries: A Critique of Harjot Oberoi's Work,* edited by Jasbir Singh Mann, Surinder Singh Sodhi, and Gurbakhsh Singh Gill. Vancouver, B.C., 1995.

Sontheimer, Gunther, and Herman Kulke, eds. *Hinduism Reconsidered.* New Delhi, 1989.

Stanley, Brian. *The Bible and the Flag: Protestant Missions and British Imperialism in the Nineteenth and Twentieth Centuries.* Leicester, 1990.

Steel, Flora Annie, and R. C. Temple, eds. *Tales of the Punjab Told by the People.* London, 1894.

Swynnerton, Charles. *Romantic Tales from the Panjab.* London, 1903.

Syal, Meera. *Life Isn't All Ha Ha Hee Hee.* New York, 1999.

Talwar, K. S. "The Anand Marriage Act." *Panjab Past and Present* 2.3 (1968): 400–10.

Tatla, Darshan Singh. "Imagining Punjab: Narratives of Nationhood and Homeland among the Sikh Diaspora." In *Sikh Religion, Culture and Ethnicity,* edited by Christopher Shackle, Gurharpal Singh, and Arvind-pal Singh Mandair. Richmond, U.K., 2001.

———. *The Sikh Diaspora: The Search for Statehood.* London, 1998.

Temple, R. C. "A Song about Sakhi Sarvar." *Calcutta Review* 73 (1881): 253–74.

Thapar, Romila. "Imagined Religious Communities? Ancient History and the Modern Search for a Hindu Identity." *Modern Asian Studies* 23 (1989): 209–31.

———. "Syndicated Moksa?" *Seminar* 313 (1985): 14–22.

Thomas, Keith. *Religion and the Decline of Magic.* New York, 1971.

Todorov, Tzvetan, *The Conquest of America: The Question of the Other.* Translated by Richard Howard. New York, 1984.

Tololyan, Khachig. "Rethinking Diasporas: Stateless Power in the Transnational Moment." *Diaspora* 5.1 (1996): 3–36.

Trautmann, Thomas R. *Aryans and British India.* Berkeley, 1997.

Trumpp, Ernest. *The Adi Granth, or the Holy Scriptures of the Sikhs, Translated from the Original Gurmukhi, with Introductory Essays.* London, 1887.

Tumbleston, Raymond. *Catholicism in the English Protestant Imagination: Nationalism, Religion and Literature, 1660–1745.* Cambridge, U.K., 1998.

Uppal, Jyotsna. "Diet, Decay and Desire: The Making of Community in Colonial Punjab." Ph.D. dissertation, Columbia University, 1998.

van den Dungen, P. H. M. *The Punjab Tradition: Influence and Authority in Nineteenth-Century India.* London, 1972.

VanKoski, Susan. "Letters Home, 1915–16: Punjabi Soldiers Reflect on War and Life in Europe and Their Meanings for Home and Self." *International Journal of Punjab Studies* 2.1 (1995): 43–63.

Vertovec, Steven. "Caught in an Ethnic Quandary: Indo-Caribbean Hindus in London." In *Desh Pardesh,* edited by Roger Ballard. London, 1994.

Vigne, G. T. *Travels in Kashmir, Ladak, Iskardo, the Countries Adjoining the Mountain-Course of the Indus, and the Himalaya, North of the Punjab.* 2 vols. London, 1842.

Visram, Rozina. *Ayahs, Lascars and Princes: Indians in Britain 1700–1947.* London, 1986.

Ward, William. *A View of the History, Literature, and Religion of the Hindoos: Including a Minute Description of their Manners and Customs, and Translations from Their Principal Works.* 3rd ed. London, 1817–20.

Warwick, Jacqueline C. "Can Anyone Dance to This Music? Bhangra and South Asian Youth." Master's thesis, York University, 1996.

Wilkins, Charles. "Observations and Inquiries Concerning the Seeks and Their College, at Patna." *Asiatick Researches* 1 (1788).

Williams, Raymond. *The Country and the City.* London, 1973.

Wolffe, John. *The Protestant Crusade in Great Britain, 1829–1860.* Oxford, 1991.

Wright, Patrick. *On Living in an Old Country: The National Past in Contemporary Britain.* London, 1985.

Youngson, John F. W. *Forty Years of the Panjab Mission of the Church of Scotland, 1855–1895.* Edinburgh, 1896.

# Index

Tony Ballantyne is a senior lecturer in history at the University of Otago.
He is the author of *Orientalism and Race: Aryanism in the British Empire*,
the editor of *Science, Empire, and the European Exploration of the Pacific*, and
the co-editor (with Antoinette Burton) of *Bodies in Contact: Rethinking
Colonial Encounters in World History* (Duke University Press, 2005).

Library of Congress Cataloging-in-Publication Data

Ballantyne, Tony, 1972–
Between colonialism and diaspora : Sikh cultural formations
in an imperial world / Tony Ballantyne.
p. cm.
Includes bibliographical references and index.
ISBN-13: 978-0-8223-3809-3 (cloth : alk. paper)
ISBN-10: 0-8223-3809-2 (cloth : alk. paper)
ISBN-13: 978-0-8223-3824-6 (pbk. : alk. paper)
ISBN-10: 0-8223-3824-6 (pbk. : alk. paper)
1. Sikhism—Historiography.
2. India—History—British occupation, 1765–1947—Historiography.
3. Sikhism—Relations.
4. Sikh diaspora. I. Title.
BL2017.6.B33 2006
294.6072'2—dc22
2006007727